*Fearless Wives and Frightened Shrews*

# Fearless Wives and Frightened Shrews

The Construction of the Witch
in Early Modern Germany

*Sigrid Brauner*

*Edited with an Introduction*
*by* Robert H. Brown

*Foreword by* Sara Lennox

UNIVERSITY OF MASSACHUSETTS PRESS
AMHERST

LC 94-39001
ISBN 1-55849-767-5 (cloth : alk. paper)
ISBN 1-55849-297-6 (pbk. : alk. paper)

Designed by Susan Bishop
Set in Adobe Janson type by Keystone Typesetting, Inc.
Printed and bound by Sheridan Books, Inc.

*Library of Congress Cataloging-in-Publication Data*
Brauner, Sigrid, 1950–1992.
Fearless wives and frightened shrews : the construction of the
witch in early modern Germany / Sigrid Brauner ; edited with an
introduction by Robert H. Brown ; foreword by Sara Lennox.
p. cm.
Includes bibliographical references and index.
ISBN 1-55849-767-5 (alk. paper)
1. Witchcraft — Germany —History. 2. Feminism — Germany — History.
3. Trials (Witchcraft) — Germany — History. I. Brown, Robert H., 1952–
II. Title.
BF1583.B73  1995
133.4.´3´0943—dc20                                      94-39001

*British Library Cataloguing in Publication Data are available.*

FRONTISPIECE ILLUSTRATION: Hans Baldung Grien, *Three Witches*, 1514.
Credit: Graphische Sammlung Albertina, Vienna

# Contents

# Foreword

## In Memoriam Sigrid Brauner, 1950–1992

Sigrid Brauner died on December 26, 1992, on the island of Jamaica. Her trip to Jamaica was a reward to herself for an exhausting but highly successful semester, her seventh in the Department of Germanic Languages and Literatures at the University of Massachusetts at Amherst. She had completed several major scholarly essays over the course of the semester, had just submitted an application for a Pembroke Center fellowship that was to address the topic "Witches, Cannibals, and the Gendering of Western Identity," and had turned in grades for the ninety students enrolled in her lecture course, "Witches: Myth and Reality." On her first evening in Jamaica, she left her small guest house in an isolated rural area of the island to walk down to the beach to look at the stars. On her way back, she fell from a bridge without a railing into a stony river bed, dying instantly of a skull fracture.

This book, originally her dissertation and now lovingly edited for publication by her friend Hutch Brown, a fellow graduate student at Berkeley, begins to suggest what was lost when Sigrid Brauner died. As her older colleague and close friend, I would like to use this foreword to set the accomplishment her book represents in the larger context of her life. Sigrid Brauner brought to her scholarship, as to the rest of her life, a vision, born of the sixties, of how people could live differently in the world, more passionately, spontaneously, harmoniously; a social analysis that helped her explain why people continued to be unhappy and hurt one another; and a fierce determination to make the world right. Her work was focused on the early modern period because she thought that the roots of contemporary social problems, of gender, race, and class oppression, could be found in the dramatic economic and social restructuring of Europe during that era and in the new social relationships and personality structures that those dislocations produced. In her view, the witch persecutions of early modern Europe vividly illustrated the violence that was inflicted on ordinary people to bring about those changes, their particular costs for women, and women's resistance to the new forms of social control employed against them. She ended her first lecture in her "Witches" course by explaining to her students: "I want to connect you to a terrible but important part of our history. I want to connect you with the strength and power of those women accused of witchcraft. I want to connect you to people who were innocently killed. And I want you to come away with a sense that we all must continue the struggle against the suppression of women and of all others who have been treated unjustly."

Sigrid Brauner began her work on gender and early modern Europe while a student at the University of Frankfurt, where she became a member of the left-feminist collective that produced the path-breaking Suhrkamp volume *Aus der Zeit der Verzweiflung: Zur Genese und Aktualität des Hexenbildes* (1977) (From the time of despair: On the origin and contemporary relevance of the image of the witch). I first met her at the Women in German conference in 1984, where she presented a paper called "Hexenjagd in Gelehrtenköpfen" (Witch hunts in scholars' heads), an early consideration of some of the ideas that would find fuller examination in her dissertation. After completing her dissertation, she extended her gender analysis of texts on witchcraft in early modern Germany to include the discourse of colonialism. In her proposal to the Pembroke Center, she explained that her next research project would focus on a literary analysis of two concepts that emerged in Europe in the early modern period, the "witch" and the "cannibal," exploring their role in the construction of gendered identities in the literary discourse on marriage, exploration, and witchcraft in early sixteenth-century Germany. By examining texts written between 1490 and 1560, her study would, as she put it, "explore how the textual and illustrative representations of the 'witch' and the 'cannibal' are interrelated and constitute and signify new social relationships, such as colonialism, professionalism, and complementary familial roles." She laid the foundations for her Pembroke project in the last essay she finished before she died, "Cannibals, Witches, and Shrews in the 'Civilizing Process,'" her contribution to the Eighteenth Amherst Colloquium. There she argued: "The 'cannibal' and the 'witch' remain objectified figures in the textualization of the discourse of European 'civlization' and they are images which represent the crucial contrasts needed to construct a superior, elite, (masculine) European identity. This identity was simultaneously created and enforced in texts such as travelogues, demonologies, and marriage manuals and it became institutionalized in slave labor, the witch trials, colonial missions, and the family."* Now others will have to carry on Sigrid Brauner's important investigations into the role that the early modern period's discourses of race and gender played in the production of the new reality of modern Europe.

On our campus, as in our profession, Sigrid Brauner was a vibrant and energetic presence. In our department, her critical intelligence, trained in the Marxism, critical theory, and feminism of Frankfurt while open to the newest impulses of contemporary Anglo-American theory, had already begun to transform our graduate and undergraduate courses. She had become a junior fellow of our Institute for Advanced Study in the Humanities (where in 1991 she conducted a faculty seminar on discourses of witchcraft and colonialism), and in 1992 she received a prestigious Lilly teaching fellowship to develop the "Witches" course. She had been elected to the executive committee of our Women's Studies Program and to the executive board of the Massachusetts Society of Professors, our faculty union. She was present at the tiny meetings of the Faculty and Staff for Human Rights and a Responsible University as that group tried to respond to a racist assault in the UMass dorms. In the weeks before her trip to Jamaica, she organized a Five College faculty seminar for medievalists that was intended to rethink the Middle Ages in the light of multiculturalism. In one of my last conversations with her, we discussed how she could work more effectively in our faculty union and what it would take to make that organization of professors behave as she thought a union should. A fiery redhead often dressed in fluorescent colors and always in motion, she was not prepared to reconcile herself to a world that refused to meet human needs (including her own) and was willing to invest the day-to-day effort to bring reality closer to her vision of how the world should be arranged. At her memorial service, one of her colleagues mused, "I didn't like the picture the papers printed of her. It caught her in motion, but not in color. To see Sigi I think you have to have color. I will always think of her in color, a kaleidoscopic burst of energy and good will, of intelligence and passion — a ruby laser turned on us for too short a time to illuminate and heal." In a tribute to her beloved professor, one of the students in her "Witches" course wrote: "I

*Sigrid Brauner, "Cannibals, Witches, and Shrews in the 'Civilizing Process,'" in *"Neue Welt"/"Dritte Welt": Interkulturelle Beziehungen Deutschlands zu Lateinamerika und der Karibik*, ed. Sigrid Bauschinger and Susan L. Cocalis (Tübingen: Francke Verlag, 1994), 20.

will forever remember her kindness, her distinctive voice, her green
cowboy boots and her matching green paisley leggings, and the true
lesson of German 190A, 'Don't give up the fight!' "

Sometime in the late seventies, after she had moved from Germany
to California, Sigrid Brauner wrote a short autobiographical narrative
called "The Balancing Act," which was found among her papers after she
died. There she portrays herself as "longing for a life of contradictions"
and traces the steps that had brought her from a childhood in a German
refugee family from Czechoslovakia to the study of medieval women at
the University of California at Berkeley. "Coming of age in the sixties
was fortunate," she recalled: "finally I could give my dreams concrete
names and live them out with others by embracing the Student Movement." At twenty-three she took her first trip to the United States and
fell in love with San Francisco and its counterculture: "I experienced for
the first time the curious freedom peculiar to the California under-
ground culture of the sixties and early seventies: letting a person just be."
Returning to Frankfurt, she "fell right into the burgeoning women's
movement. The San Francisco dream could be lived at home." Now she
discovered women's studies and feminist scholarship: "Before I had half-
heartedly studied German literature; now my curiosity about women's
history drove me to the library." Though she dreamed of becoming a
feminist researcher, she recognized that there were few women and
hardly any feminists teaching at the university level in Germany and no
jobs in the humanities in any case. Confident that she could do anything,
she packed her bags again and returned to the United States to join the
counterculture. But after living in a survivalist commune in Northern
California while working in the "local redneck hippie bar," she found she
was "still wondering about the lives of medieval women." As a Ph.D.
candidate in German literature at Berkeley, she was often disheartened
by the alienation and competitiveness of graduate study, but "the support of women, the feminist pockets inside the ivory tower" kept her
going. "I taught my first Women's Studies courses here," she remem-
bered, "and I am hooked on it. There is nothing more exciting than
teaching and simultaneously learning from a class where something in
yourself and others moves. Confronting yourself and other women with
our own history can do that." As her account ends, she speculates about
what is likely to become of her: "Maybe I'll be a Women's Studies
teacher in Japan, maybe a feminist counselor in West Germany, maybe
I'll teach German literature in the U.S., maybe I will have learned to do

radio programs, maybe. . . . But there is one thing I do know," her narrative concludes: "whatever I do, it will be another rather complicated balancing act."

Literally, when Sigrid Brauner fell from that bridge, she lost her balance. But as her mentor, colleague, comrade, sister, and friend, I can say that figuratively, in the terms of her own chosen metaphor, she was succeeding at her balancing act. Never without struggle, often suffused by anger and sadness but also by exuberance and joy, she had found a way of juggling dreams and reality, of remaining true to her visions while living daily life with the greatest possible intensity. In the very middle of the bulletin board in her office she had posted the famous declaration by Emma Goldman: "If I can't dance, I don't want to be part of your revolution!" On her bulletin board at home hung a postcard that read: Du fragst mich, / was soll ich tun? / Und ich sage / Lebe wild und gefährlich. (You ask me / what shall I do / And I say / Live wildly and dangerously.) In a poem he wrote shortly after her death, her colleague Stephen Clingman celebrated that spirit and the legacy Sigrid Brauner left for us:

A falling star
Across our sky
Here, then out of sight
Left visions of her flashing hair
And charged us
With her light.

*Sara Lennox*

# Introduction

Sigrid Brauner died in a tragic accident before she was able to revise this manuscript for publication. She had intended to include her more recent work, especially her reflections on gender and her research on witchlike figures in early modern travel literature.* I have mentioned this work or included aspects of it in her manuscript; but the core of the manuscript remains her Ph.D. dissertation.

Brauner and I met in Berkeley as graduate students of German literature at the University of California. I was deeply impressed by her ebullience and freedom of expression; her ideas, manner, and appearance all indicated someone who refused to bow to convention. In those days, it was quite conventional in Berkeley to appear unconventional, but Brauner was serious about the counterculture, integrating it into all aspects of her life. With a keen critical eye, she ferreted out the prejudices in premises and practices that most took for granted, refusing to accept the subtle power imbalances inherent in our culture and society. Unlike most, Brauner never learned to repress herself; she kept the various sides of her personal and professional lives integrated and open to her own critical self-scrutiny. She tackled every problem — no matter how seemingly small — with equal and unrelenting ferocity until she found an acceptable solution that left her integrity intact. In resisting the pressures on her, Brauner developed a formidable strength of character. Even her ebullience and impulsiveness — salient aspects of her personality — reflected her integrity and inner strength.

As part of her resistance to conformity, Brauner devoted herself to understanding the nature and origins of the pressures and constraints she experienced in her life. She came to see that the pressures on her

---

*See Sigrid Brauner, "Gender and Its Subversion: Reflections on Literary Ideals of Marriage," in *The Graph of Sex and the German Text: Gendered Culture in Early Modern Germany 1500–1700*, ed. Lynne Tatlock and Christiane Bohnert, pp. 179–200 (Amsterdam: Rodopi, 1994); and "Cannibals, Witches, and Shrews in the 'Civilizing Process,'" in *"Neue Welt" / "Dritte Welt": Interkulturelle Beziehungen Deutschlands zu Lateinamerika und der Karibik*, ed. Sigrid Bauschinger and Susan Cocalis (Bern: Francke, 1994). Brauner's other publications (see bibliography) more closely reflect her Ph.D. dissertation, the basis of this manuscript.

xiii

were governed by gender, and that therefore they were different for women than for men. Brauner was fascinated by such gender-based figures as the nun, the witch, the virgin, and the proper housewife. Tracing these figures across the Renaissance and the Middle Ages back to antiquity, Brauner explored how the power imbalances invested in them affected the lives of women in medieval and early modern Germany. But she also found elements of resistance in them — especially in the witch (with her independent claim to power) and in the nun (with her communal independence from male authority). Brauner's own life gives eloquent testimony to the active role that women have always played in resisting their subordination and in finding room for their own self-realization independently of men. For Brauner, women's resistance to the roles engendered for them informs the history of gender relations, provoking new forms of repression and inspiring further resistance.

Brauner was deeply influenced by the work of Lyndal Roper, Merry E. Wiesner, and other social historians who have examined conditions under which women lived, worked, and resisted their domestication in early modern Germany. In her manuscript, Brauner starts from the premise that the role of women changed in early modern Europe from a traditional one of supporting (and even supplanting) men in their public and productive roles to one of complementing male activity with a discrete set of "feminine" household tasks performed in the emerging private sphere. Brauner sees a connection among three central developments in early modern Germany: a shift in gender roles for women; the rise of a new urban ideal of femininity; and the witch hunts that swept across Europe from 1435 to 1750. Asking why women were singled out as witches, Brauner notes that the outspoken, self-assertive behavior common among poor rural women — who were usually the ones accused of witchcraft — clashed with the demure, submissive female behavior prescribed by the new feminine ideal. The sharp tongues and brash defiance of the accused shocked the upper-class urban justices who tried them, confirming the accusations against them and leading to their swift convictions. Brauner maintains that the witch hunts functioned to discipline women who failed to display the docility and subservience expected of the new urban housewife.

Brauner's contribution to this theory is twofold. First, by examining key texts by Martin Luther, Paul Rebhun, and Hans Sachs, Brauner shows how the concept of the modern witch emerged as the counterpart to the new feminine ideal of the urban housewife. By demonstrating —

in complex, often brilliant detail — how the binary concepts of "good" housewife and "bad" wife (or witch) were propagated within the educated urban milieu that provided the justices who presided over witch trials, Brauner establishes the importance of the texts she studies for the history of women and gender relations in early modern Germany. Second, drawing on Norbert Elias's theory of the civilizing process, Brauner places the witch hunts — and the concomitant process of domesticating women — in the context of controlling drives and emotions in both sexes. Under the influence of Theresa de Lauretis, Joan Wallach Scott, and other gender theorists, Brauner argues that terms for women like "witch" and "housewife" are always negative delineations of a positive male "other." The repression of women contained in the binary pair witch-housewife is not an end in itself, Brauner maintains, but rather a means of developing the "civilized" self-control in men demanded in the marketplace and halls of power under incipient court capitalism. For example, Brauner shows how the figure of the witch as a recalcitrant housewife in Hans Sachs's works signifies not only the danger of losing control over women in the household, but also the danger of leaving drives and emotions uncontrolled within men in the workplace. In the process of civilization, the oppression of women contained in the binary pair witch-housewife is inextricably bound up with — and engendered by — the (self-)repression of men.

I had the opportunity to watch these ideas take shape while Brauner was writing her Ph.D. dissertation in Berkeley. I was also writing my dissertation, and we met regularly to read and discuss portions of each other's work. Soon after completing her dissertation, Brauner was appointed assistant professor at the University of Massachusetts; with her new duties and research projects, she found little time to revise her dissertation for publication. I helped her edit some of her other work, and I offered to help her prepare her dissertation for publication. After her death, with the permission of her family, I condensed and revised Brauner's manuscript for publication, with the support of Professor Sara Lennox and the University of Massachusetts Press.

On the basis of the manuscript itself — and of my many discussions with Brauner — I made four kinds of changes to her text. I reorganized parts of the text for the sake of clarity; deleted parts that seemed unclear, repetitive, or extraneous; added occasional sentences to clarify or emphasize certain points; and corrected or reformulated the writing in accordance with the rules of standard American English. My purpose was to preserve intact the intent and substance of Brauner's manuscript while altering its form to make the manuscript more transparent to the reader.

After my first set of revisions, the manuscript was reviewed by Professor Sara Lennox (University of Massachusetts) and by Professor Elaine C. Tennant (Brauner's Ph.D. dissertation adviser at the University of California); Professor Tennant also checked my translations from Early New High German into English. After another set of revisions, the manuscript was reviewed again by professional readers appointed by the University of Massachusetts Press. I wish to thank all of those who participated in the review and revision process for their excellent suggestions, criticisms, and contributions. And I would like to express special thanks to Bruce Wilcox, director of the University of Massachusetts Press, without whose active support on Brauner's behalf this volume would not have been possible.

Sigrid Brauner was my close friend. One of the levels of our friendship was academic, and I looked forward to our close professional collaboration in the future. Revising her manuscript — even without her immediate presence — gave me one last chance to work together with her, and I am grateful to those who made it possible. Through her manuscript, I was able to continue to interact with her after her death, which made it easier for me to finally let her go. I hope that those who treasured her might experience something similar when they read her book.

*Robert H. Brown*

*Fearless Wives and Frightened Shrews*

# Chapter One

# The Modern Witch:
# Concept, History, Context

**A**LL WITCHCRAFT comes from carnal lust, which is in women insatiable."[1] So argue Heinrich Kramer and Jakob Sprenger, papal Inquisitors for southern Germany, in their *Malleus maleficarum* (1487), the first work to describe the specific characteristics of the modern witch. Until the fifteenth century, witchcraft was not considered gender-specific; women were believed no more likely than men to be witches. However, Kramer and Sprenger propagated the notion that the "insatiable womb" led women to "consort with devils" and practice witchcraft, whereas God had "preserved the male sex from so great a crime."[2] In fact, "the evils perpetrated by modern witches [modernis maleficis] exceed all other sin which God has ever permitted."[3] Thus redefined for the modern age, witchcraft became a specifically female practice posing an unprecedented threat to God's holy order.

Such notions led to a series of witch hunts lasting from 1435 to 1750 in which tens of thousands of European women were tried and slaughtered. Why were women specifically targeted as witches? Historians have suggested that changing social roles affected women's legal and economic status, making some women — particularly single women from the lower classes — vulnerable to accusations of witchcraft. What remains unexplained, however, is the rise of a gender-specific imagery that stereotyped women as witches. Although the evolution of the modern concept of the witch has been traced by Norman Cohn and Joseph Hansen, the specifically female character of the modern witch has been largely overlooked.[4]

This study explores the issue of gender in the concept of the modern witch that emerged between 1487 and 1560 in German-speaking regions of Europe other than Switzerland (which demands a separate treatment).[5] Although witch trials temporarily subsided during this period, Kramer, Sprenger, and others were redefining the witch in a way that set the stage for the great wave of witch hunts that followed. Two

ILLUSTRATION: Hans Baldung Grien, *Preparing for Witches' Sabbath*, 1509. Credit: Staatliche Graphische Sammlung München.

3

types of literature on witches emerged. The first includes laws, demonologies, legal treatises on witchcraft, and books on learned magic ("magia naturalis"). Mostly written in Latin, these materials were intended for university-trained specialists such as lawyers, scientists, physicians, theologians, and learned magicians. The second type of literature was often composed by the learned elite, but designed to influence the uneducated majority. The spread of printing and the religious struggles surrounding the Reformation led for the first time to the widespread dissemination of vernacular texts for broad lay audiences. The many plays, poems, sermons, and satirical texts dealing with witches during this period invariably have a didactic purpose. While Latin texts designed for learned audiences developed the concept of the modern witch, works in the vernacular speeded the spread of modern notions of witches and witchcraft among ordinary people in Germany.

My purpose is to examine samples of both types of literature for the social stereotypes of women and witches they contain. The texts I have selected either discuss the witch's gender or use the concept of the female witch in a significant way. Kramer and Sprenger's *Malleus maleficarum*, which belongs to the group of demonologies and legal treatises designed for educated audiences, is the first text to address the issue of a witch's gender and the only technical text to explain at length why "modern witches" ("modernis maleficis," as Kramer and Sprenger call them) are women. The other works I examine are mostly written in the vernacular and designed for broad audiences. Martin Luther's thoughts on modern witches in his sermons and commentaries have gone virtually unnoticed, even though they are surprisingly original. Paul Rebhun's *Wedding Play Based on the Wedding at Cana (Ein Hochzeit Spiel auff die Hochzeit zu Cana*, 1538), the play that perhaps best represents the Protestant family values of its time, depicts the modern witch as a force of female disruption within marriage. Finally, Hans Sachs's Shrovetide play *The Devil with the Old Woman (Der teüffel mit dem alten Weyb*, 1545) uses the modern concept of the witch to teach men and women proper marital roles. This selection of texts includes some of the most important writings on witches and witchcraft during the period in question. Technical treatises on witchcraft after the *Malleus* and before 1560 add little to the subject; and none of the Catholics (like Thomas Murner) who wrote vernacular didactic texts at the time developed new viewpoints on the female witch.

By analyzing these texts, I will trace the development of the concept of

CONCEPT, HISTORY, CONTEXT

the female witch while documenting its literary image on the eve of the great witch hunts. I proceed from the hypothesis that notions about witches were influenced by new ideas about women developing in Germany during the fifteenth and sixteenth centuries as humanist and Protestant thinkers reinterpreted the social role of the family and of women within the family. By relating the incipient concept of the modern witch to the early modern construction of gender, I hope to contribute to a better understanding of the social processes that brought an entire society to accept the persecution of women as witches.

But first I will explore the meaning of the word "witch" and the changing roles of women in the fifteenth and sixteenth centuries. What happened during the witch hunts, and what exactly was a witch? Was the definition of witchcraft linked to changing female roles in early modern Germany?

*The Witch Hunts*

The European witch hunts occurred in three phases. An initial period of scattered witch trials from 1435 to 1500 was followed by a near-cessation in trial activity until 1560, when a great series of witch hunts began that lasted until 1750. The number of victims remains unclear. Although nineteenth-century historians speculated that as many as nine million died, estimates now range from 60,000 to 200,000, with 100,000 the most commonly accepted figure.[6] Between 75 percent and 90 percent of those executed were women.[7] Germany had the largest number of witch trials (about half the European total), with the overwhelming majority occurring in the third period, the so-called witch craze, which featured mass trials of up to 300 women.[8] But some German regions were completely spared, and where witch trials did occur, it was only intermittently, generally in great panic-driven waves, with especially heavy spurts in the 1590s, 1630s, and 1660s. Explanations for the timing of these waves of witch hunts include spiraling inflation, periodic crop failures, the growing involvement of university law faculties in state legislation, and a need to police potentially troublesome populations on the part of the rising absolutist states. However, the total number of witch trials and executions in Germany and the specific mechanisms that triggered each new wave are likely to remain a matter of conjecture until a comprehensive history is researched and written.[9]

The first witch trials took place in the mid-fifteenth century in the French Alps and Switzerland. Papal Inquisitors searching for Waldensian heretics believed to be hiding in the mountains instead found peasants rooted in pre-Christian folk beliefs. Under torture, they not only confessed to the devil's pacts and secret meetings routinely ascribed by the church to heretics, but in their fear added lurid tales of nightflying spirits and ritual folk magic that shocked and appalled their interrogators.[10]

As educated men steeped in scholastic learning, the Inquisitors interpreted these folk beliefs and practices as evidence of diabolical influence. Accordingly, they added charges of harmful sorcery to those of heresy, a combination that was to form the basis for allegations of modern witchcraft. Before the fifteenth century, charges of sorcery had been handled separately from heresy by secular courts, because sorcery was thought to harm people and property, not the soul. But the scholastic view of magic as a diabolical art gained currency in the course of the fifteenth century, and both secular judges and papal Inquisitors now began to see magic as a spiritual transgression. As a result, secular courts began to tack charges of diabolism and witchcraft onto sorcery, while Inquisitorial tribunals now associated sorcery with heresy.[11]

No distinction was made between men and women in the early witch trials or in early writings describing what was initially believed to be a new sect of heretics. The French Dominican Inquisitor Nicolaus Jacquerius (in his *Flagellum haereticorum fascinariorum*, 1458) and even Pope Innocent VIII (in a 1484 papal bull) speak of witches as both men and women.[12] In fact, in Inquisitorial trials that began as heresy proceedings, slightly more men than women were charged as witches. There was no uniform sex-specific designation for the new crime of witchcraft; usually, authorities made do with local terms for sorcerers or magicians. Where new words emerged to describe the sect, such as "Gazari" and "Vaudois" in parts of France and Switzerland, they were not sex-specific (both words are derived from names for heretical sects, "Gazari" from Cathars and "Vaudois" from Waldenses). Early witch trials in Germany followed the same pattern.

In the last two decades of the fifteenth century, the pattern suddenly changed. The majority of those tried as witches in France, Italy, Germany, and Switzerland were now women. Moreover, many trials now involved multiple defendants. In Germany, the earliest trials specifically targeting women involved forty-eight defendants in the area near Constance between 1482 and 1486, and fifty women in Innsbruck in 1485. In both cases, the trials were instigated by the Dominican Heinrich

Kramer, papal Inquisitor for southern Germany and coauthor of the *Malleus*. Kramer claimed to have convicted and burned at the stake half of the accused women, although only eight executions are documented.[13] Records from pretrial proceedings in Ravensburg and Innsbruck show that Kramer specifically interrogated women and tried to bring charges of witchcraft against them.

Other early witch trials involving multiple female defendants were instigated by secular authorities. From 1492 to 1494, thirty women convicted of witchcraft were executed in the archbishopric of Trier, and from 1499 to 1502, nineteen alleged witches were burned at the stake in Jülich-Berg.[14] It remains unclear why women in particular were targeted. However, the early persecution of witches seems to have been much more intense in France, Switzerland, and northern Italy than in Germany, where only about twenty-five witch trials occurred before 1500.[15]

One reason for the relative dearth of witch trials in Germany may have been a reluctance in the communities and among the authorities to accept the new concept of the modern witch. Kramer's efforts to prosecute witches in Innsbruck caused such an uproar in the community that he was asked to leave town by the bishop in charge.[16] In the *Malleus*, Kramer and Sprenger bitterly complain of a general lack of cooperation with their efforts to exterminate witches. Although their book was calculated to cure this unfortunate blindness to the danger of witchcraft, after its publication neither author ever convened another witch trial. But where they failed as witch hunters, they succeeded as authors: the *Malleus* was a phenomenal success, becoming one of the most reprinted works in the early history of printing, with most of its editions published in Germany.[17] Clearly, a growing need was felt in educated circles to learn more about this new creature called the modern witch. Who exactly was she?

*The Modern Witch*

The portrait of the modern witch that emerges from trial records and other writings between 1435 and 1750 differs sharply from traditional notions of sorceresses, wise women, and others endowed with supernatural powers who appear in medieval records and literature.[18] Four characteristics distinguish the modern witch: using magic to harm others, attending secret "Sabbath" meetings, flying through the air at night, and sealing a pact with the devil by copulating with him. Though drawn from traditional Christian demonology, each of these elements is re-defined in a new, nontraditional way, then fused with the others to char-acterize the modern witch.

In medieval tradition, it is usually a male scholar — not a woman — who makes a pact with the devil, and sexual contact with the devil is not limited to women. Demons take not only the form of a man (an "in-cubus") to seduce women, but also the form of a woman (a "succubus") to seduce men. Since antiquity, heretics and other dissidents of both sexes were believed to hold secret meetings, sometimes called "Sab-baths." Now, for the first time, such Sabbath meetings were attributed primarily or exclusively to women. Night flying and harmful magic were rooted in folk belief. Female spirits (called "strigae" in church records) were thought to fly about at night, sometimes joined by earthly women, a belief stemming from customs related to caring for the dead. Orig-inally, the night fliers were thought to include men, and the spirits them-selves were not necessarily thought of as evil. People who practiced harmful magic, called "malefici" in church and legal records, were of both sexes. Only when night flying merged with harmful magic in the person of the modern witch did both characteristics come to be associ-ated primarily with women.

Before the fifteenth century, all four characteristics of the modern witch (night flying, secret meetings, harmful magic, and the devil's pact) were ascribed individually or in limited combinations by the church to its adversaries, including Templars, heretics, learned magicians, and other dissident groups. Clerical literature thus played a primary role in formulating and systematizing these characteristics. Folk beliefs about the supernatural emerged in peasant confessions during witch trials, and were sometimes adapted by the educated elite in defining the modern witch. The most striking difference between popular and learned no-tions of witchcraft lay in the folk belief that the witch had innate super-natural powers not derived from the devil. For learned men, this bor-dered on heresy. Supernatural powers were never human in origin, nor could witches derive their craft from the tradition of learned magic, which required a scholarly training at the university, a masculine pre-serve at the time. A witch's power necessarily came from the pact she made with the devil.

With the spread of vernacular literature in the sixteenth century, the learned concept of modern witchcraft finally prevailed. Because it was still evolving, however, it expressed some of the characteristics of witchcraft in incomplete form. For example, Kramer and Sprenger doubted that witches could really fly, arguing that night flight was an illusion inspired by the devil; and the secret witches' Sabbaths were not described in detail by German writers until the seventeenth century. Moreover, a bewildering array of names was used for the modern witch, including the vernacular terms "Hexe," "Unhulde," and "Zauberin," and the Latin terms "lamia," "malefica," "pythonica," "striga," and "venifica" (see the appendix for a discussion of the origins and evolution of these terms). Originally, these terms referred either to spirits with characteristics resembling those of the modern witch (such as night flying), or to specific practitioners of magic (such as soothsayers, traditional wise women, and sorceresses who worked with poisons). In the sixteenth century, these terms gradually lost their distinctions; all now referred to the modern witch.

The profile of the modern witch that emerges from trial records, legal and theological treatises, and popular literature is hardly appealing. The witch renounces Christianity and enters her pact with the devil in exchange for badly needed items such as shoes or money. Although the devil never keeps his end of the bargain, after the woman enters into the pact, she becomes completely subservient to his will. As Satan's loyal servant, she uses the power of his sorcery to undermine Christian society by hurting people and damaging property. She destroys cattle, spreads mysterious diseases, makes men impotent, kills and eats infants, steals milk and butter, and raises disastrous storms. Such activities, known in the records as "evil deeds" ("maleficia"), are secret and invisible.

The witch's purpose is to recruit others to her craft. At night, she flies out on goats, sticks, brooms, and other devices to attend secret Sabbath meetings, where she reports to the devil on her recruiting success. At these meetings, the witch engages in rituals such as dancing the roundelay backwards to dissonant music, eating foul-tasting or unsalted foods, and paying homage to the devil by kissing his behind. The meeting usually ends with some sort of sexual activity, such as intercourse with the devil, which is unpleasant because his penis and semen are ice-cold.

It was hard to spot a witch, because her activities were invisible and she appeared quite normal. The "devil's mark," a wart or other peculiarity located near her private parts, was usually searched for only during a trial. Although the witch was typically described as an old woman, young women and even men and children could be witches.

Obviously, there was nothing to gain and much to lose from becoming a witch. She forfeited her personal freedom and eternal soul (and was cheated in the bargain) in exchange for a terrible lover and social ostracism or worse if discovered. Nevertheless, witches were believed to be quite common.[19] In order to explain this discrepancy, some theologians speculated that God permitted the plague of witches in order to teach moral behavior by negative example. Human nature was so weak and sinful, they argued, that women blatantly ignored their own self-interest to become witches. Gaining nothing from the bargain was logical punishment for their folly.

Sixteenth-century scholars of demonology saw the witch as both victim and culprit. She entered the pact with the devil of her own free will and used his power to hurt others through harmful sorcery. Once she was under the devil's spell, however, she was powerless to resist and required protection from him. If she confessed, her soul could be saved, but the personal and material damage to which she admitted (a mandatory part of a witch's confession) was punishable under secular law by death. The confessed witch was left in the unpleasant position of saving her soul but usually forfeiting her life.

Although witches were genuinely feared in early modern Germany, many people routinely consulted sorcerers and sorceresses for healing and for help in personal affairs involving love or money. Women who practiced folk magic were often accused of witchcraft, even though they did not consider their powers linked to the devil. Alleged witches left no records other than their trial confessions, which were often extorted by means of Inquisitorial procedures ranging from leading questions to torture. Historians therefore agree that witches with the diabolical powers described in the trial records did not exist.[20] Instead, they were created in a complex social process as those on trial were forced under interrogation and torture to assume the very identities of which they were accused.[21] Initially, most suspected witches rejected accusations of witchcraft, only to undergo a psychological transformation as the trial wore on: because God does not punish the innocent, accused women desperately searched their souls and pasts for incriminating thoughts or behavior that would justify their brutal treatment at the hands of the authorities. Many finally gave intimate, detailed confessions. Only after her confession did a woman truly become a witch who could publicly be sentenced and executed.

The process of creating a witch had three key elements: a special form of trial (influenced by Roman and Inquisitorial law) that used forced confession to prove guilt; a concept of the witch created by theologians and other intellectuals from scholastic demonology, traces of folklore, elements of classical mythology, and the late medieval Inquisition of heretics; and a social consensus on the existence of witches and their diabolical powers. These three elements fused between 1435 and 1750 into a historically unique basis for the persecution of witches, one that was closely tied to the social and cultural characteristics of the early modern period in Europe and North America.

Although the profile of the modern witch was well established in some learned circles by the end of the fifteenth century, it took decades for the concept of modern witchcraft to gain general acceptance. From 1500 to 1560, records suggest a hiatus in Inquisitorial witch trials in Germany.[22] Although the secular courts continued to initiate sporadic, isolated proceedings against witches, there is a noticeable gap in witch trials between 1520 and 1550, usually attributed to the turmoil surrounding the Reformation and peasant uprisings, which kept authorities busy. Moreover, after ten printings in its first thirty years, there was not a single reprint of the *Malleus* from 1520 to 1563, and the number of other treatises on witchcraft sharply declined.[23]

It would be wrong to conclude, however, that there was little interest in the modern witch during this period. In the early sixteenth century, new technologies and developments were revolutionizing society, breaking down many barriers between "high" and "low" culture. Among them were the invention of printing and the woodcut, the rising use of the vernacular by writers, the emergence of a literate, educated urban artisan class, and the social, religious, and political changes precipitated by the Reformation. These developments paved the way for a flood of popular witch renditions that more than made up for the declining number of learned treatises on the subject. E. William Monter speaks of "multimedia descriptions of witches" produced by artists, writers, and preachers on the eve of the Reformation.[24] Sigrid Schade points to the many texts about witches that were illustrated by woodcuts showing ordinary women embracing the devil or feasting with him, and to Hans Baldung Grien's paintings of witches as powerful erotic beings. According to Peter Burke, "one of the most striking instances of interaction between the learned and popular traditions is that of the witch."[25] The authors of the Reformation used the new, profitable printing industry to continue a development in vernacular and popular literature that had already been set in motion by the clerical writers of learned texts.

Authors of rank and renown contributed to this discourse. Dukes and emperors asked scholars such as the lawyer Ulrich Molitor (*De laniis et phitonicis mulieribus*, 1489) and the abbot Johann Trithemius (*Antipalus maleficiorum, Liber octo quaestionum*, 1508) to explain the new phenomenon of witches. After witnessing an early witch trial, the liberal theologian Martin Plantsch questioned whether witches really caused any harm (*Opusculum de sagis maleficis*, 1505), while the Benedictine monk Johann Butzbach put his very orthodox thoughts on witches into a poem (*De sex maleficis*, 1514), and the physician Hieronymus Braunschweig questioned whether those who seemed possessed were really under the devil's spell (*Liber de arte destillandi*, 1500). In their literary satires and farces, Sebastian Brant (*Narrenschiff*, 1494), Thomas Murner (*Narrenbeschwörung*, 1512), Johann Neuber von Schwartzenberg (*Teütsch Cicero*, 1531), and Johannes Pauli (*Schimpf und Ernst*, 1533) all lamented the increase of witchcraft, sorcery, and the magic arts. In biting satires like the anonymous *Epistolae obscurum virorum* (1510) and *Eccius dedolatus* (1520), the witch image was used to ridicule scholastic theory. The experimental thinker Agrippa von Nettesheim criticized Inquisitorial procedures in witch trials in his *De incertitudine et vanitate scientiarium* (1527).

Protestant authors — hitherto neglected in research on early modern witches — were keenly interested in the subjects of magic and witchcraft. Martin Luther discussed both topics in various sermons and commentaries, and Philipp Melanchthon, who took an interest in learned magic, wrote on the magic of dreams in his *Liber de anima* (1504) and included the punishment of witches in his Wittenberg church ordinances (1552). The most popular preacher of the Reformation, Geiler von Kaisersberg, devoted a series of sermons to the evil of witchcraft (*Emeis*, 1508). The Strasbourg Protestants Wolfgang Fabricius Capito, Martin Bucer, and Kaspar Hedio set forth their views on witches in an extensive letter to Johann Schwebel on 6 April 1538, and the Wuerttemberg preachers Johannes Brenz (*Homilia de grandine*, 1539) and Johann Spreter (*Hexenbüchlein*, 1540) publicized their views on the topic. Last but not least, the Protestant playwrights Paul Rebhun (*Hochzeit zu Cana*, 1538) and Hans Sachs (*Der teüffel mit dem alten Weyb*, 1545) used the modern witch as a character in plays.

Although views on magic and witchcraft varied widely, many writers — both Protestant and Catholic — adopted one of two main viewpoints. Writers like Spreter (in his early works) or Trithemius supported the *Malleus*'s contention that witchcraft posed a diabolical threat that must be exposed and eliminated through the systematic persecution of witches. Others, like Plantsch and Brenz, appealed to the tradition of the *Canon episcopi* (recorded by Regino of Prüm in 906) in arguing that practitioners of magic such as witches were guilty of no more than idolatry, not diabolical dealings.[26] Accordingly, they took the relatively tolerant view that witches were a divine punishment to be patiently endured rather than systematically extirpated. Occasionally, writers such as Thomas Murner in his *De pythonica contractu* (1499) reverted to equating witchcraft with traditional sorcery, or, like Agrippa de Nettesheim, classified it as a low and ineffective form of magic not to be compared with what a learned magician could accomplish with God's aid. Because there was no consensus on whether witches should be tolerated or persecuted, or even on whether they could really fly, perform magic, or harm anyone, historians have come to speak of this period as one of open discussion when various opinions on witchcraft could be expressed without fear of punishment.

But despite their differences, all writers on the subject of witchcraft after 1500 agreed that witches were women — a sharp departure from earlier practice. Until the late 1400s, men were as likely as women to be charged with witchcraft; but by 1500, the sex-specificity of witches was so widely accepted that it was implicitly assumed in texts about witches. Almost nobody saw a need to address it as an issue, much less explain why it was so. Why were women suddenly singled out as witches?

*Why Witches Were Women*

There are five common explanations for the sex-specificity of the witch hunts: the tradition of misogyny; women's participation in folk healing; changing perceptions of female nature; changes in women's economic and family roles; and changing ideas about women's social behavior. Each of these explanations touches on relationships among women, nature, and magic or explores ways in which women's changing roles related to broader social changes during the period in question. Each deserves a closer look.

The first and oldest approach to explaining the categorization of witches as women is to cite the Judeo-Christian tradition of misogyny.[27] Historians of the nineteenth and early twentieth centuries blame the witch hunts on religious zeal and popular superstition. The church, they point out, equated women and their bodies with sin, carnality, and spiritual death; and in feudal society, women were extremely repressed.

These traditions fused, so the argument goes, in the concept of the modern witch.

The two historians who best exemplify this approach are Joseph Hansen and Nikolaus Paulus.[28] Both concentrate on the earliest treatise on the modern witch, Kramer and Sprenger's *Malleus*, but come to different conclusions. The *Malleus* claims that women rather than men become witches because they are weaker, less intelligent, and so lascivious that they fall easy prey to temptation. According to Hansen, the clerical asceticism of the authors is responsible for this view. He points out that Kramer and Sprenger belonged to the fifteenth-century Dominican reform movement, which propagated celibacy, venerated the Virgin Mary, equated sexuality in women with sin and death, and disparaged the institution of marriage for representing a worldly lifestyle of questionable value. By contrast, Paulus maintains that the *Malleus* is influenced less by clerical misogyny than by deep-rooted popular and classical beliefs in female powers of sorcery, including the use of poison and the evil eye. He argues that misogyny in later treatises on witchcraft has the same popular and classical origins.

Both studies are flawed by the authors' implicit belief in the superiority of modern Renaissance thinking to the superstitions of the Middle Ages. Both writers present the concept of the female witch as a continuation of medieval clerical or popular misogyny into early modern times. Neither explores the impact of early modern humanist and Protestant ideas on the concept of witchcraft and the victimization of women. Hansen in particular ascribes too much importance to the *Malleus*. While its authors were indeed clerical ascetics, the humanists and Protestants who wrote on witches developed equally misogynist arguments. Both Hansen and Nikolaus make the mistake of assuming that women were perceived and treated in the same abusive manner during the medieval and early modern periods, ignoring evidence to the contrary. Although misogyny may appear superficially the same over time, it plays different roles in different societies at different times. Therefore, it is not enough to label the concept of the modern witch "misogynist" and leave it at that; in order to understand the particular nature of early modern misogyny, we need to explore why women were so feared in the early modern period that they were singled out as witches. For this, we must relate prevailing ideas about women in early modern Europe to other social and cultural phenomena.

The second major explanation for the sex-specificity of the modern witch, proffered by Romantic historians, feminists of the 1970s, and some anthropologists, is that many women in early modern Germany embraced traditional folk beliefs attuned to nature and akin to witch-craft.[29] In this view, witches and folk magic are traced to a golden age undisturbed by feudal hierarchies and capitalist alienation. Women practiced a folk magic based on a pagan holistic outlook on the world that clashed with Christian beliefs and the emerging rationalistic world view. Like their counterparts in primitive cultures today, witches organized to defend age-old values of purity and harmony with nature against the modern forces of church and state. In the ensuing struggle, witches were systematically exterminated.

Although it may be true that many alleged witches behaved in socially unacceptable ways derived from older cultural norms or traditions such as folk magic, the existence of an organized opposition to Christianity in defense of a magical folk tradition has not been demonstrated. Carlo Ginzburg makes perhaps the strongest case that witch trials amounted to a clash between Christian and pre-Christian cultures in his study of sixteenth-century Inquisitorial proceedings against Friulian peasants involved in a fertility cult.[30] Friulian villagers believed that some of their members were endowed with special magical powers enabling them to do battle with evil spirits in order to secure a good harvest. But the Friulians regarded their cult as perfectly consistent with Christianity; despite the Inquisition, they continued to practice it along with Christianity for decades after witchcraft proceedings began. Moreover, men and women alike performed the cult's rituals and were endowed with its magical powers. Similarly, trial records show that many alleged witches in France, Germany, Austria, and Switzerland practiced folk magic, but regarded it as entirely consistent with Christian belief, and admitted only under duress to practicing the heresy of witchcraft. Often, their first accusers were their male counterparts in their own communities, although when these traditional "wise men" were accused of similar practices, they were seldom prosecuted. Evidently, those who practiced traditional folk magic in early modern Europe were not rebelling against Christianity; and they were often considered dangerous only when they were women. It was less the practice of folk magic itself, then, than some kind of female behavior — perhaps associated with it — that offended both the witches' accusers at the community level (particularly their male counterparts) and the Christian authorities.

The third explanation for the sex-specificity of witches in the early modern period derives from psychology, dialectical materialism, and the history of ideas.[31] During the period of the witch hunts, so the argument goes, women came to represent a premodern, subsistence-based social order that was giving way to a new society based on producing for profit. Because woman is always "the other" in patriarchal society, she was identified with nature as the field of projection for all the problems emerging in the process of capitalization and civilization. In particular, woman represented chaotic nature's resistance to scientific inquiry and technical domination. In his sketches, for example, Hans Baldung Grien associates the female body with untamed nature and libidinal reservoirs within, which threaten an emerging civilized order characterized by self-control, alienation from the body, and the sublimation of aggression.[32]

The strength of this approach lies in its placement of the witch hunts in a social and historical context that emphasizes changing perceptions of women. The importance of social behavior is stressed: the female witch is associated with erotic, uncivilized behavior that violates emerging social codes. But the argument fails to show that the equation of women with chaotic nature had a broad enough impact to actually influence the witch trials. Moreover, it reduces women to passive objects of history. Like men, women are active participants in social change; therefore, any explanation of the witch hunts in terms of changing ideas about women must be complemented by studies on women's changing roles and reactions to social change.

A fourth group of scholars argues that women were generally better-off in the Middle Ages than in early modern Europe, and that their worsening social situation contributed to their persecution as witches.[33] In her excellent study *Working Women in Renaissance Germany*, Merry E. Wiesner suggests that conditions deteriorated for sixteenth-century urban women in the workplace. For example, the number of well-paid jobs open to women declined as women's labor outside the household was gradually reduced to bywork. In some towns, only poor women were allowed to work at all (and only because authorities wanted to avoid paying them poor relief). One reason for the decline of women in the trades was the spread of the putting-out system of production in early modern Europe. As putting-out entrepreneurs crowded independent artisans from the marketplace, journeymen agitated against competition from women for the few master positions left. By the seventeenth century, women in Germany were completely barred from the guilds.[34]

The putting-out system and the rise of a money economy adversely affected rural women as well. Women in the countryside were increasingly forced to work as wage laborers (usually spinners) at substandard wages in order to supplement household income and help pay the rent, which was now due in money.[35] Helen Berger has studied how poor rural working women were connected to witchcraft in early modern England.[36] Most alleged witches were "spinsters," rural female spinners whom the new weaving looms had forced out of the weaving trade and into piecework at low wages. Most were married to poor agricultural laborers. Their status as wage laborers placed them on the social and economic margins of the traditional community, and brought them into conflict with farmers' and yeomen's wives, who also spun for a living but owned their own wool and were therefore paid more by the piecework entrepreneurs. Alienated and oppressed, the spinsters vented their dissatisfaction through ill-tempered, socially inappropriate behavior. Local communities saw the fate of the spinsters as a latent threat and resented their defiant attitudes. Shunned and suspect within their own communities, the spinsters were prone to charges of witchcraft. Similar circumstances appear to have led to accusations of witchcraft in Germany.[37]

New restrictions were placed on women in their traditional profession of midwifery. Midwives were no longer allowed to form guilds. Instead, they were required to report to the municipal physician, and to notify the authorities when clients had abortions, used birth control, or gave birth to illegitimate children. Midwives suspected of noncompliance were sometimes accused of witchcraft. Female folk healers, who assisted in birth control, were subject to increasing repression, including accusations of witchcraft. Female cultural traditions — such as women's festivities surrounding childbirth — were sometimes restricted or forbidden.[38]

Changes in demographics and marriage patterns contributed to deteriorating conditions for women in the early modern period. Although there was strong pressure to marry, growing numbers of women never married or were left widowed. According to Brian Levack, the percentage of widows among women rose in some places from an average of 10 percent to 20 percent in the Middle Ages to as high as 30 percent in the early modern period because of wars and plagues (which usually claimed more victims among men than among women). By the seventeenth century, the percentage of women who never married had grown from 5 percent to 10 percent, and in some places to as high as 20 percent. At the same time, the average age of first marriage was rising.[39] Protestantism refused to acknowledge common-law marriage, and formal marriage required establishing a household and therefore owning a house, which few could afford. Moreover, couples tended to delay marriage in order to defer the costs of rearing children.

Although it was growing more difficult for women to find a marriage partner and establish a household, alternatives to marriage for women were declining. In Protestant regions, women could no longer elect to join a convent, and lay or semi-religious living arrangements for single women (such as the Beguine communities) were under attack from the guilds, which resented their special economic privileges.[40] Hamstrung by restrictions on their legal rights, women found it increasingly difficult to support themselves without a husband. Wiesner has shown that under the influence of Roman law, ordinances regarding women (notably the *Constitutio criminalis Carolina*) were changed in some areas to reflect supposed female frailty. Women were now prohibited from carrying arms or conducting legal transactions on their own, without the support of their husbands.[41] The right of widows in particular to continue running their husbands' farms or businesses was restricted or abolished.[42]

Data from trial records indicate that most alleged witches were poor and single.[43] Some were homeless or itinerant, but most belonged to the working poor in the countryside. Many were unmarried and middle-aged or older, although in some areas most were younger or married. It appears, however, that economic vulnerability was a more important constant in allegations of witchcraft than the marital status or age of the accused. Why were poor women in particular accused of witchcraft?

The fifth and most popular explanation for the sex-specificity of witchcraft attempts to answer this question. Scholars in this group argue that witchcraft is tied to the collapse of traditional community structures in the early modern period.[44] Before the sixteenth century, the frail, disabled, and impoverished who existed on the margins of rural communities were sometimes thought by virtue of their very marginality to possess innate supernatural powers. Feared for their powers, they were often provided with charitable services by the community, a form of welfare that functioned to reinforce community norms without persecuting deviancy.[45]

In the sixteenth century, this mechanism broke down under the impact of incipient capitalism, rising individualism, and a new Protestant ethic that blamed paupers for their own predicament. At a time when women made up a growing percentage of the poor, the community lost its willingness to support its marginal populations; this led to bitter conflicts between haves and havenots, and to charges of witchcraft leveled by the better-off against poor women in particular.

Using English trial records, historians have reconstructed the likely sequence of events leading to charges of witchcraft. A poor woman asks a neighbor or acquaintance to perform a service to which she feels entitled, and is denied. She retaliates with a curse, invoking her only form of protection — the supernatural powers traditionally attributed to her as a marginal, impoverished member of the community. At first, her curse is dismissed as powerless cant; but when a mishap befalls the accursed, he or she grows alarmed and accuses the poor woman of witchcraft.

The problem with this interpretation is that it treats women as mere objects of social processes rather than as historical subjects. But it does provide a useful description of the alleged witch's typical behavior: quarrelsome and ill-tempered, she frequently cursed and scolded when she did not get her way. Deprived of resources such as property and family support, she resorted to her only remaining recourse, her power of language. Although her threats and curses were no longer enough to assure her marginal existence, they were still powerful enough to provoke her own persecution as a witch.

Trial records from Scotland reveal a wide variety of responses by women accused of witchcraft to the allegations against them. Some bowed before their accusers and meekly accepted their fate; others — impelled by ego — even welcomed the charges, reveling in their newfound identities as witches.[46] But many of those arrested as witches responded with angry threats and curses, the very sort of proud defiance that had led to the allegations against them.[47] Of course, the alleged witch had every reason for anger and resentment. A poor social pariah to begin with, she now faced prison, trial, torture, and execution for things she had not done. Her one power left was the power of her voice: with her sharp tongue and rich vocabulary, she displayed a spirited character that would not be cowed or bowed. Socially dependent because of her miserable condition, she refused to be socially subservient. Ultimately, her scolding and cursing were forms of self-defense and social resistance.

But those who denied the allegations against them and condemned their accusers damned themselves as surely as those who confessed. During the period of the witch trials, strong language no longer provided a viable defense. Instead of producing the grudging acceptance it once did, a sharp tongue now worked against the alleged witch. If a woman refused to accept social ostracism and discrimination because she was poor, single, disabled, or otherwise an outsider, she only maligned herself, intensifying the prejudice against her. Her cursing and scolding were deemed inappropriate, and her open defiance was believed to confirm her identity as a witch. Attitudes toward female behavior were clearly changing — but how and why?

## Redefining Gender

While charges of witchcraft originated at the local level, their collective implications were much broader. In Germany, witch trials were not conducted by the local community, but rather by the law faculty of the nearest university. During her trial, the behavior of an accused woman was assessed a second time by the learned judges and university doctors who conducted the witch trials. Most came from the urban upper and middle classes, and their notions of family and womanhood differed sharply from those of the uneducated peasants who testified before them. For an educated man in sixteenth-century Germany, the ideal woman was chaste, pious, married, silent in public, and submissive to her husband. She never cursed or scolded. The self-assertiveness of alleged witches is likely to have appalled the courts, confirming the allegations and influencing the conception of modern witchcraft.

No studies exist to show how the feminine ideal formulated in Protestant and humanist writings influenced educated thinking about witches. Recent research has overlooked writers such as Martin Luther, Hans Sachs, and Paul Rebhun, focusing instead on how popular magic, local trial records, or the social situation and community relations of the accused women defined the modern witch. The views of the educated elite who sat in judgment of women accused of witchcraft and determined whether they were witches have been largely ignored. Researchers often assume that the concept of the witch has been sufficiently delineated, and that its gender aspect did not significantly change in learned texts during the period of the witch hunts. Although scholars readily acknowledge the misogynist impulses in writings such as Kramer and Sprenger's *Malleus*, they have tended to regard this misogyny as too commonplace to warrant further attention.

Behind such assumptions lies a tendency to view witches primarily in terms of their biological sex rather than their socially constructed gender. Some scholars assume that "women are women" across the ages, and that their social activities are governed by female imperatives that are natural, biologically determined, and distinct from those of men. For example, G. R. Quaife argues that many alleged witches enjoyed fantasizing about the devil, and Hans Peter Duerr claims that women witches may have used unguents and broomsticks for masturbation. E. William Monter hypothesizes that women turned to witchcraft to compensate for their physical weakness, and that witchcraft was therefore the female counterpart to male criminal violence.[48] Yet we have no evidence that women practiced witchcraft in order to satisfy sexual urges, or that women felt weaker than men and therefore turned to sorcery. Such views are based on male fantasies about female sexuality and the male projection of women as weak. These examples — and many more could be cited — have one thing in common: they evaluate women accused of witchcraft in terms of their sex, employing male stereotypes of female nature and sexuality.

The alternative is to evaluate women in terms of their socially constructed gender. I argue in this study that the concept of modern witchcraft is linked to changing notions of female gender in sixteenth-century humanist and Protestant thought. But before turning to the texts in question, I will outline the theoretical basis of my approach with a brief discussion of gender.

Gender identities are informed by social power relationships that assign masculinity to the social subject and femininity to its defining margin. Therefore, gender relates not only to men, women, and the social forms of their relationships (such as marriage and family), but also to more general social relationships (such as forms of education and modes of production). These relationships are expressed in gendered cultural symbols and given meaning in gender-related normative contexts. As Theresa de Lauretis puts it, "The construction of gender is both the product and the process of its representation."[49] The relationship between gender and its cultural representation is especially important for the analysis of literary texts, because the text represents and creates particular gender relations.

Gender theory deconstructs not only "natural" hierarchies and "natural" male and female identities, but also categories such as love, desire, and sexuality, which are often thought of as essential entities. In exploring sexuality as a gendered construct, feminist theorists have drawn on Michel Foucault's concept of discourse and on the deconstruction of unitary concepts of meaning by Jacques Derrida. In Foucault's sense, "discourse" refers not only to words and texts, but to all kinds of social expressions, including theory, imagery, institutions, and interpersonal relations. Discourses produce social meaning and social identities that are always ideological. Ideology is more than the economically motivated production of false consciousness by central state institutions: it is dispersed and created discursively everywhere and functions to constitute concrete individuals as subjects.

Simone de Beauvoir's ground-breaking study *The Second Sex* (1949) revealed that "woman" is a construct always positioned as "the other" that defines the subject "man." Derrida's deconstructionist method exposes the same sort of dualist exclusion as the constituting principle of meaning and truth in Western thought: each unitary concept is based on the negation and repression of another unitary concept. Feminist theorists point to the importance of gender in this process. "Often, in patriarchal discourse," Joan Wallach Scott notes, "sexual difference (the contrast masculine/feminine) serves to encode or establish meanings that are literally unrelated to gender or the body."[50] Gender relations not only signify relations of power, they validate them ideologically. For example, in the early modern period the relationship of subject to magistrate was often explained in terms of the relationship of wife to husband. The metaphor served to validate the social hierarchy of power within the community: because the subordinate relationship of wife to husband was believed to be divinely instituted and therefore part of the "natural" order, the corresponding subordinate relationship of subject to magistrate was above question.[51]

Like the construction of gender, the construction of meaning is always relational, which has critical implications for the reading of literary texts or for any form of cultural expression. For example, terms such as "woman," "eros," and "sexuality" cannot be read literally as biological categories or functions, but rather should be deconstructed within their gendered social and historical contexts. The same goes for the concept of witchcraft.

The concept of gender and the production of meaning in discursive fields collapse several important assumptions in Western thought about truth, meaning, and the position of subversion. Absolute truth or meaning is always informed by political power, and power as well as the dictation of repressive norms are not restricted to central institutions such as the state. Instead, power forms what Scott calls "dispersed constellations of unequal relationships, discursively constituted in social 'fields of force.' "[52] Accordingly, there is no exact location for subversion, which can occur anywhere. Moreover, subversion is an integral part of the conflictual process of establishing meaning, which occurs everywhere: in the family, in literary texts, in social institutions, and in the organization of material production. "Contests about meaning," as Scott puts it, "involve the introduction of new oppositions, the reversal of hierarchies, the attempt to expose repressed terms, to challenge the natural status of seemingly dichotomous pairs."[53] Subversion, then, is part of the creation of new social norms and new forms of oppression. This cycle of oppression is broken only when the challenge to a "natural" status of meaning is connected with a conscious political and cultural practice that breaks through the discursive and material processes that engender social identities and validate unequal relationships.[54]

## Changing Gender Roles

With this theoretical framework in mind, I will now outline the changing characteristics of normative gender in the early modern period. Women within the medieval household (or "familia") were subordinate to men, but played roles that were interdependent with (rather than separate from) those of men. Their subsidiary roles were designed to preserve a social order in which the aristocratic, clerical, and burgher/ peasant estates were seen as hierarchical but interdependent, with each estate equally necessary to the good of the whole. In order to preserve both the integrity of each estate and the "estate" of marriage itself, women in some parts of medieval Germany were able to assume many of the economic and legal responsibilities normally reserved to men — that is, if the head of household was absent or died without a male heir.[55] Ordained and lay religious communities offered alternatives to marriage for women; in some regions, aristocratic abbesses could even attain the status of feudal lords. The medieval notion of female "subsidiarity" enforced female subservience to men within household and polity, but reserved to women — at least in some areas and under some circumstances — the opportunity to assume an authority normally reserved to men.

Such independent, powerful positions for women contradicted the new idea of gender "complementarity," which assigned to each sex a distinct sphere of activity and prohibited women from playing male roles under any circumstances. Based on reinterpretations of the scriptures, particularly Genesis and the Pauline letters, university-educated men of the urban upper classes assigned the sexes to two distinct social arenas: men to a "public" or "political" sphere, and women to a "private" sphere. As head of the household, the man had absolute dominion over everything and everybody within it. He represented the household before the magistrate and enjoyed free access to and mobility in the public and political marketplace. The woman, on the other hand, was enclosed within the domestic sphere and assigned the roles of managing the household, bearing and raising children, and morally edifying her family. Husband and wife were seen in their separate spheres and roles as necessary complements to one another, each perfecting the other. The hierarchical complementarity of husband and wife was projected onto society at large, providing a model for the relationship of subject to magistrate.

The new ideal was formulated primarily by male professionals (such as lawyers, physicians, Protestant clergymen, and court or municipal officials) with links to urban magistrates. The humanist and Protestant discourse they developed was designed to give meaning to their new social roles as courtiers and civil servants. The new nature of their work as professionals meant that the husband worked outside the home away from his wife and children. Therefore, the shared work and household duties characteristic of the medieval "familia" no longer prevailed. The marital relationship needed reformulation: the husband was assigned the task of providing for the household and representing it in public, and the wife assumed sole responsibility for household management and raising the children. As female subsidiarity gave way to complementarity, the behavior expected of women changed: the female assertiveness still tolerated in the Middle Ages gave way to silent submissiveness — at least ideally.

The ideal of complementarity, with its separation of public from private, bore little semblance to reality for the vast majority of sixteenth-century couples, whose household practices remained intermeshed with their public activities. Out of social and economic necessity, women continued to play a wide variety of roles in early modern Europe.[56] Most women worked in one way or another outside of the household, either doing piecework for putting-out entrepreneurs, housework for others as low-paid domestic servants, or more respectable but underpaid work in the increasingly institutionalized areas of health care, children's education, and attending to orphans. Although most women continued to work, the new complementary ideals of gender affected how their work was viewed. Work based on education and formal training performed by university-educated professionals or by skilled artisans was highly valued and came to be seen as masculine, while work based on informal training (such as piecework and domestic service) and unpaid work doing household chores and raising children was devalued and came to be seen as feminine and inferior.

As standards of comportment for women changed, conflict and confusion ensued. Women did not always accept abrogation of what many regarded as their traditional rights. In some areas, women insisted before municipal officials on their right to inherit property, conduct business, enter certain professions, and represent themselves before the law.[57] As Lyndal Roper has shown for Augsburg, women whose husbands failed to perform their economic duties took them to court, demanding that they play roles based on older concepts of gender interdependence. Marriage courts often supported such traditional demands when the survival of the household was at stake, acting more like their medieval counterparts than like early modern institutions.[58] On the other hand, a woman pursuing her traditional rights might appeal as a weak and helpless woman to the male magistrate for aid, thereby validating the new complementary ideas about gender.

Literate women from the urban patriciate and aristocracy sometimes addressed the issue of changing gender relations in writing. Unlike their male counterparts, they were not interested in redefining marital relationships. Instead, they demanded equal access to education, and the right enjoyed by men of their rank to write, study art, and develop historical role models by representing the heroic deeds of women next to those of men.[59] For most such women, marriage was incompatible with a female heroic identity. Some imagined heroic women living in solitary cells surrounded by books, or invented utopian female societies.[60] The most radical writers, realizing that women deprived of a right to property were forced into marriage for survival, identified their legal situation as the main obstacle to female independence. The legal and economic barriers seemed so insurmountable that more moderate writers advocated integrating a heroic female identity into the complementary marriage. By improving her husband morally, they argued, an educated woman not only created a harmonious marriage, she performed a service to the state.[61]

The convent sometimes provided more opportunity than marriage for developing a heroic female identity. In 1524, the humanist abbess Caritas Pirckheimer refused demands by the Nuremberg city council that she close her convent and persuade its nuns to marry. Her resistance succeeded because the nuns knew that they could not count on finding marriage partners, and that without the convent's support they might land in the city's poorhouse. Moreover, the convent practiced an Erasmian spirituality, and many of its nuns were actively engaged in humanist studies. Their intellectual interests spawned a spiritual independence that enabled the nuns to survive as a community in complete religious isolation, without outside support. In a letter to her brother Willibald, Caritas's sister Clara captures the heroic humanist spirit of the convent when she says that even if denied access to a Catholic priest, all she would need for her spiritual survival would be books with which to pursue her studies.[62]

Protestant women activists often gave a unique twist to female identity within marriage. In her *Apology* (*Entschuldigung*, 1524), Katharina Schützin defends her marriage to the priest Matthias Zell, a leader of the Reformation in Strasbourg. Nowhere does she appeal to traditional hierarchies within marriage, nor does she advocate the complementary roles of men and women so important to Protestant thought. Instead, she says that she had been quite content as a single woman, and married a priest only in order to contribute to reform by example. Men, she argues, cannot live celibate, and if unmarried will only seduce and ruin innocent women. By marrying a priest, a woman saves him from whoring and destroying women's lives, and thereby improves the community. Like many religious women, Schützin justifies her public stand by appealing to her spiritual equality with men as a Christian, which forms the basis of her new marital identity: if she and her husband were both crucified for their beliefs, she asserts, they would die as equals on their crosses while exchanging comforting words.

The shift from the subsidiary role of women to complementarity was rife with conflict and contradiction in the dynamic social and historical process that creates hegemony. In order to understand why women were branded as witches, we must examine the new discourse of marital complementarity in sixteenth-century texts written by humanist and Protestant men of the urban upper and middle classes, bearing in mind its context in the process of conflict and change surrounding the creation of new gender norms. Kramer and Sprenger developed the first gender-specific concept of the modern witch in their *Malleus*, published almost a century before the great witch craze. Even though it took decades to develop a social consensus on the nature of witches and what to do about them, few after the *Malleus* was published questioned the fact that

women were witches or saw a need to explain why. The Protestants —
particularly Luther, Sachs, and Rebhun — were the exceptions. Their
writings reflect an entirely new discourse on modern witches, influenced
not only by theoretical views on magic and witchcraft, but also by a new
set of moral and religious values derived from the Lutheran concept
of marriage. Designed to educate lay audiences, their texts discuss the
witch in terms of concrete roles women were now expected to play
within family and society, including mandatory marriage and strict relegation to housework. Protestantism's new moral imperatives for women
led to discrimination against single women and may have contributed to
their victimization as alleged witches in the great witch craze after 1560.

# Chapter Two

# The *Malleus maleficarum*:
# Witches as Wanton Women

I N THE EARLY fifteenth century, Inquisitors searching for heretics in
the mountains of France and Switzerland stumbled upon peasants
who practiced sorcery and believed in night-flying spirits. Attributing their pre-Christian folk beliefs to diabolical influence, the Inquisitors announced that they had discovered a new and dangerous heretical
sect of witches. From 1435 until about 1500, the new heresy of witchcraft was persecuted in a series of trials scattered across Europe. Three
things distinguished this first wave of witch hunts from the great witch
craze after 1560: relatively few were tried; witch trials in Germany were
rare; and, perhaps most important, men were accused of witchcraft as
frequently as women. As late as 1484, Pope Innocent VIII made no
distinction between the sexes when, in his bull *Summis desiderantes affectibus*, he officially warned of the dangers of witchcraft.

The publication in 1487 of the *Malleus maleficarum* (*The Hammer of
Witchcraft*)[1] marked a watershed in the history of the witch hunts: for the
first time, a work on the heresy of witchcraft argued that most witches
were women. The *Malleus* was written primarily by Heinrich Kramer
(1430–1505), with assistance from Jakob Sprenger (1436–1495).[2] Both
were erudite Dominicans influential within their order and within the
Vatican. As such, they traveled in some of the most conservative circles of
the period. The Vatican rewarded Sprenger's zealous pursuit of monastic
reform and Kramer's unwavering support for papal supremacy by nam-
ing both men papal Inquisitors for southern Germany. Inspired by the
theological and political views of their order, with its long tradition of
persecuting heretics, and vexed by Kramer's failure to convict alleged
witches in Innsbruck in 1485, the two Inquisitors set about writing an
encyclopedic handbook on witchcraft.

*Redefining Witchcraft*

Kramer and Sprenger drew on earlier Inquisition manuals for both
the structure of their book and its name. The term "malleus" ("ham-

ILLUSTRATION: Anonymous woodcut, *Devil Seducing Witch*, ca. 1489

31

mer") derives from the cognomen "malleus haereticorum" assigned by the Catholic church to its foremost fighters against heresy, such as St. Jerome. In 1420, the term was first used in the title of a book (the *Malleus iudeorum*, a work against heresy by the German Inquisitor Johann of Frankfurt).[3] By using the term "malleus" in the title of their treatise on witchcraft, the authors explicitly invoked the authority of the Inquisition.

In three separate parts, the *Malleus* explains the nature of witches, the harm they do, and the best way to prosecute them. Designed for use by priests and judges, it contains such items as sample sermons against witchcraft and step-by-step instructions for putting witches on trial. Many early editions also contain three supporting documents: Innocent VIII's 1484 bull *Summis desiderantes affectibus*; a letter from Emperor Maximilian I dated 6 November 1486; and a letter of endorsement from faculty members at the University of Cologne. Although Maximilian's letter is now missing and the Cologne faculty endorsement was partly forged, all three documents lent the *Malleus* the air of highest authority.[4]

The *Malleus* was a resounding success. Altogether, there were between twenty-five and thirty-five editions during the period of the witch hunts; at least eight appeared by 1500 and thirteen by 1520, ten of them in Germany alone (in Speyer, Strasbourg, Cologne, and Nuremberg).[5] The early proliferation of *Malleus* editions and their availability in city libraries may partly explain the hiatus of reprints in the German regions between 1520 and 1580.[6] Finally reprinted again in Frankfurt in 1580, the *Malleus* deeply influenced both the Protestant and the Catholic instigators of the great witch hunts in the late sixteenth and early seventeenth centuries.

Several factors contributed to the *Malleus*'s success. The authors were well known and well connected in scholastic circles, and their book added to an already lively discussion on the subject of witchcraft. Authors as diverse as the Dominican Johannes Nider (*Formicarius*, 1437), the progressive physician Johann Hartlieb (*Puch aller vepotten kunst*, 1456), and the humanist Matthias Widman von Kemnat (*Chronik*, 1475) had already reported on witch trials, mostly in Switzerland. Therefore, the *Malleus* is likely to have enjoyed an educated reading audience that extended well beyond the priests and judges for whom it was intended. In addition, even though the *Malleus* was not translated into German until the eighteenth century, many of its ideas were made available to those unversed in Latin. For example, at the request of the city of Nuremberg, Kramer provided a manuscript (the *Nuremberg Hammer of Witchcraft*, 1491) with trial instructions in both Latin and German so that municipal judges with no knowledge of Latin could refer to it in prosecuting witches.[7]

Kramer and Sprenger present the *Malleus* as a compilation of older writings on witchcraft by church fathers and the philosophers of antiquity (especially Aristotle). Eager to impute their views to acknowledged authorities, they claim that the novelty of the *Malleus* lies only in its encyclopedic character. But their views on witches were really quite new — and sometimes conflicted with church doctrine. For example, the *Malleus* posits that (1) witches exist and disbelief in their existence is heresy; (2) witchcraft involves harmful sorcery; (3) witches should be prosecuted under secular law; (4) the only sure remedy against witchcraft is to exterminate witches; (5) witches tend to be women, not men; and (6) the witch's pact with the devil is explicitly sexual.

By insisting on the existence of witches and equating skepticism on the subject with heresy, Kramer and Sprenger break with long-standing Catholic tradition. According to the *Canon episcopi* recorded by Regino of Prüm in 906, belief in sorcery and night-flying spirits is mere superstition.[8] Kramer and Sprenger argue that the *Canon episcopi* does not apply to the new, formerly unknown heresy of modern witchcraft. While admitting that modern witches may seem similar to the sorceresses and night-flying spirits described in the old *Canon*, Kramer and Sprenger claim that witches are unique; their evil exceeds "all other sin which God has ever permitted."[9] Although this position was never officially sanctioned by the church, Kramer and Sprenger attempt to create the impression that it was by associating it with official documents such as Innocent VIII's 1484 papal bull and the partially forged Cologne faculty endorsement, and by using a scholastic style of argumentation that appeals to authoritative evidence.[10]

Kramer and Sprenger were the first to raise harmful sorcery to the criminal status of heresy. "Maleficium" (harmful sorcery) was originally a term used in secular law to describe folk magic damaging to people or property. Before the *Malleus*, the terms "malefica" ("female witch") and "maleficus" (its masculine counterpart) were rarely used in theological discourse for practitioners of sorcery or magic.[11] Kramer and Sprenger chose the term "malefica" to describe the modern witch because "maleficium" was her main activity. They claim that "malefica," the designation for the female witch, derives not only from "doing evil" ("malefacere"), but also from "thinking evil about the faith" ("male de fide sentire"), and that therefore a witch's sorcery implies her heretical beliefs.[12]

Traditionally, harmful sorcery was considered a secular offense, not a spiritual one. Because it involved personal or property damage, it fell under the jurisdiction of the secular authorities, who used different standards and methods of criminal prosecution than did the Inquisition. This changed in the fifteenth century with the discovery of modern witchcraft: because witches were alleged to serve the devil, their sorcery now implied heresy. If harmful sorcery is a crime on the order of heresy, Kramer and Sprenger argue, then the secular judges who prosecute it must do so with the same vigor as would the Inquisition in prosecuting a heretic. The *Malleus* urges them to adopt torture, leading questions, the admission of denunciation as valid evidence, and other Inquisitorial practices designed to achieve swift results. Moreover, the authors insist that the death penalty for convicted witches is the only sure remedy against witchcraft. They maintain that the lesser penalty of banishment prescribed by the *Canon episcopi* for those convicted of harmful sorcery does not apply to the new breed of witches, whose unprecedented evil justifies capital punishment.[13]

### The Female Witch

Perhaps the most striking of Kramer and Sprenger's novel assertions about witches is that they tend to be women. The title of their treatise already implies this proposition — the term "maleficarum" refers to "female evildoers." Although earlier writers on witchcraft, including Jordanes de Bergamo (*Quaestio de strigis*, 1460) and Girolamo Visconti (*An strie sint velut heretice iudicande*, 1460), had also used the feminine form for witches in the titles of their works, none had argued that witches were specifically women. Even texts written shortly before the *Malleus*, such as Matthias Widman von Kemnat's *Chronik* (1475), Stefan Lanzkranna's *Hymelstrasz* (1484), and Pope Innocent VIII's *Summis desiderantes affectibus* (1484), speak of men and women equally as members of the new sect of witches. Witch trials involving predominately women were still so rare at the time of the *Malleus* that when they discuss specific cases of witchcraft, Kramer and Sprenger often choose male subjects. Yet they assume throughout their work that most witches are women.

They justify this view at length in a section called, "Why is it that Women are Chiefly Addicted to Evil Superstitions?" According to Kramer and Sprenger, sexuality is the key to witchcraft, and God has given the devil power over sexuality, the lowest and least divine of human qualities. God permits witchcraft in order to highlight His own supreme goodness against its diabolical evil, and to test His subjects and reward them if they endure their afflictions like Job. For his part, the devil employs witchcraft as a way of showing his contempt for God by seducing the least worthy of His subjects — women, especially impoverished women. Assuming the shape of an incubus (a demon in human form), the devil easily finds sexual partners, because women are prone to their own carnal desires. A woman's seduction seals her pact with Satan: she renounces God and serves the devil, giving him her soul and bearing his children, who grow up to be witches. Older women who no longer bear children pander to the devil by inciting sexual longing in younger women and delivering them to Satan.

According to Kramer and Sprenger, the devil's main objective in witchcraft is to obstruct marital procreation by making married men impotent. The devil cannot directly tempt a married man, because marriage is protected by its sacramental nature; therefore, he uses the witch to do so. After seducing a married man, the witch becomes jealous of his wife and enchants the man's penis so that he cannot have sexual intercourse with his spouse. Impotence and childlessness are thus products of witchcraft, which is designed to prevent the creation of new souls for the Lord.

Kramer and Sprenger maintain that women are by nature inclined to become witches. Women are either very virtuous (like Mary) or extremely wicked (like Eve). Because of her virginity, Mary does not share the natural inclination of women to waver in their faith. The authors distinguish here between the special, gender-neutral nature of virgins and the female nature of other women, a distinction based on Augustine's speculation that before the Fall, reproduction occurred by virgin birth without sexual intercourse. After the Fall, Eve's sin was inscribed in the female body as a mark of corruption symbolized by the loss of the hymen, whereas men, thanks to Adam's lesser role in the events leading to the Fall, did not lose their resemblance to divine perfection.[14] As a result, virgins are less corrupt than other women; like men (and unlike women), they are rational and intelligent.[15]

Kramer and Sprenger present an array of observations from the Bible, the church fathers, and the poets and philosophers of antiquity to support their contention that women are by nature greedy, unintelligent, and governed by passions. They argue that the evil of women stems from their physical and mental imperfections, a notion derived from Aristotle's theory that matter, perfection, and spirituality are purely expressed in the male body alone, and that women are misbegotten males produced by defective sperm.[16] Women speak the language of idiots, Aristotle contends; like slaves, they are incapable of governing themselves or developing into the "zoon politicon."[17] Thomas Aquinas adapted these views to Christianity, arguing that because woman is less perfect than man, she is but an indirect image of God and an appendix to man. Citing such views, Kramer and Sprenger find that women are "intellectually like children," credulous and impressionable, and therefore easily fall prey to the devil. They claim that the word "femina" derives from "feminus" ("faithlessness"). "Since [women] are feebler both in mind and body," the *Malleus* concludes, "it is not surprising that they should come more [than men] under the spell of witchcraft."[18]

Lack of intelligence prevents women not only from distinguishing good from evil, but from remembering the rules of behavior. Amoral and undisciplined, women are governed primarily by passion. "And indeed," Kramer and Sprenger declare, "just as through the first defect in their intelligence women are more prone to abjure the faith; so through their second defect of inordinate affections and passions they search for, brood over, and inflict various vengeances, either by witchcraft, or by some other means."[19] The envy, passion, and carnality of women lead them to wage daily war on their spouses. In support of this view, Kramer and Sprenger cite stories about contrary wives, from Socrates's Xanthippe to the bad wife ("böses wîp") of medieval lore. In one story, a man looking for the body of his drowned wife walks upstream from the point where she fell into the river. When asked why, he replies that she was so contrary in life that she likely floated up the river instead of down it. Such evil, domineering wives turn the proper order of things upside down, rendering men helpless. The husband who resists must fear for his life — his wife "will prepare poison for him, and consult seers and soothsayers," according to the Greek philosopher Theophrastus, "and will become a witch," add Kramer and Sprenger.[20] Governed as they are by their emotions, women naturally seek to dominate their husbands, thereby reversing the divinely ordained hierarchy. If resisted, they will resort to any means necessary to get their way, including witchcraft. "Wherefore it is no wonder that so great a number of witches exist in this sex," concludes the *Malleus*.[21]

Domineering wives are not the only dangerous women; any woman who fails to get pregnant by her husband, or who feels betrayed by her husband or lover, turns into a raging fury. Moreover, women battle ferociously with each other in their competition for male attention. Women's constant search for sexual partners and their jealousy of competitors lead them into witchcraft. "And truly the most powerful cause which contributes to the increase of witches," the *Malleus* contends, "is the woeful rivalry between married folk and unmarried women and men."[22] This rivalry is so powerful that it has caused the downfall of empires such as Troy, and "therefore it is no wonder if the world now suffers through the malice of women."[23]

Women succeed in corrupting men, Kramer and Sprenger maintain, because they are so "beautiful to look at" and "contaminating to the touch," with sweet voices that "entice passersby and kill them . . . by emptying their purses, consuming their strength, and causing them to forsake God."[24] By their very nature, women are like vampires who suck the lifeblood from men, depriving them of their strength, spirit, intellect, and belongings. Kramer and Sprenger agree with Cato that "if the world could be rid of women, we should not be without God in our intercourse."[25] Women obstruct men's way to salvation; without them, there would be divine intercourse among perfect males. A woman is a curse worse than the devil, Kramer and Sprenger argue, because the devil only tempted Eve, whereas Eve seduced Adam and therefore bears full responsibility for the Fall. In a woman's heart malice reigns, "and her hands are as bands for binding; for when they place their hands on a creature to bewitch it, then with the help of the devil they perform their design."[26]

Because women are governed by uncontrollable lust, the *Malleus* concludes, "it is no matter for wonder that there are more women than men found infected with the heresy of witchcraft."[27] The few men who practice sorcery specialize in practical forms (such as bewitching weapons and protecting the body from battlefield wounds), whereas women practice all kinds of deleterious magic.[28] Although men may fall victim to witches, most are spared by divine grace from becoming witches themselves, "for since God was willing to be born and suffer for us, therefore He has granted to men this privilege."[29] Kramer and Sprenger argue that the Savior died for men, but that women (by nature corrupt) fall from divine grace as soon as they lose their virginity.

Kramer and Sprenger develop a powerful gender-specific theory of witchcraft based on a hierarchical and dualistic view of the world. Everything exists in pairs of opposites: God and Satan, Mary and Eve, and men (or virgins) and women. Each positive principle in a pair is delineated by its negative pole. Perfection is defined not as the integration or preservation of opposites, but rather as the extermination of the negative element in a polar pair. Because women are the negative counterpart to men, they corrupt male perfection through witchcraft and must be destroyed.[30]

### The Malleus *and Its Sources*

Such views on how women corrupt male perfection are not new. Kramer and Sprenger select old arguments from the long tradition of Western misogynist writings, then combine them to produce new meanings. In particular, they borrow from Johannes Dominicus's *Lectiones super ecclesiastes* (1380) and Johannes Nider's *Formicarius* (1435) and *Preceptorium divinae legis* (1475).

In his *Lectiones*, Johannes Dominicus lists the vices of women alphabetically — animal greed ("avidum animal"), bestial foolishness ("bestiale baratrum insipidum"), carnal desire ("concuspiscentia carnis"), and so forth. Each vice attributed to women is documented with quotes from the Bible and the authors of antiquity.[31] In the medieval tradition of associating certain kinds of magic with women (especially love potions and the evil eye), Dominicus lists sorcery as a female vice. Women resort to sorcery, he explains, because — like Eve — they are carefree of spirit and easily influenced by demons, or because their weakness of body and mind leaves them no other means of protecting themselves. But nowhere does Dominicus mention diabolical witchcraft or relate sorcery to female sexuality.

Kramer and Sprenger reiterate Dominicus's alphabetical list of female vices, but use it to prove that women practice witchcraft.[32] They cite the references Dominicus makes to the writings of the church fathers and authors of antiquity as authoritative evidence that women are witches, even though neither Dominicus nor his sources make any mention of witchcraft. Each vice on Dominicus's list is turned into new evidence of witchcraft: female faithlessness is its root, female weakness leads women to it, female passion explains why women resort to it, and female insubordination is a prelude to it. Although Dominicus stresses the carnality of women, Kramer and Sprenger are the first to connect it to witchcraft.

Johannes Nider wrote on modern witchcraft based on his experience of witch trials in Switzerland. His *Formicarius* (1435) compares witch-

craft to whoring (fornication) and idolatry (its spiritual counterpart). He
notes that the Israelites fornicated with the Moabite women upon reach-
ing Shittim, then worshipped the Moabite god Baal (Numbers 25:1–3).
For Nider, such passages from the Bible prove that women are deceptive
and dangerous, and can seduce men into idolatry and witchcraft.[33] But
Nider stresses women's powers of deception rather than their carnal desires. Like Joan of Arc, the witches Nider describes dress and bear arms
like men and pretend to be in contact with God. For Nider, the deceptive female behavior that is characteristic of a witch lies in the transgression of gender roles, which reverses the divine order. He equates
witchcraft not with female carnality, but rather with female presump-
tion, deception, and rebellion.

In his *Preceptorium divinae legis* (1475), Nider attributes female sorcery
to the credulity, impressionability, and loquaciousness of women. These
three characteristics make women easy prey for the devil, Nider maintains, and lead them to betray their knowledge of the evil arts to other
women. Like Dominicus, Nider draws on the medieval tradition of
blaming female sorcery on the characteristic weaknesses of women. But
he never attributes witchcraft to female carnality, nor does he ever identify women as the principal practitioners of witchcraft; for him, both
sexes participate equally in this crime.

Kramer and Sprenger do something quite different. Although they
copy Nider's discussion of female deception nearly word for word, they
shift its emphasis to carnality, arguing that it shows how "the word
woman is used to mean the lust of the flesh" and how even "a good
woman is subject to carnal lust."[34] The notion that women are more
carnal than men is very old; but Kramer and Sprenger were the first to
claim that women rather than men became witches, and that this was
because of their carnal female nature. The *Malleus* imputes an unprecedented intensity and depravity to female sexuality when it suggests that
women readily consort with the devil, and that all witchcraft stems from
fornication with him. The power of a witch's sexuality, symbolized by
her sexual union with Satan, distinguishes the modern witch from medieval sorceresses, who did not owe their magical powers to fornication
with the devil.

Another novel argument made by Kramer and Sprenger is that sexual
rivalries breed witchcraft. The authors could draw on several traditions
to support this contention. Sorcery in antiquity and the Middle Ages
included love potions and other magical means of stimulating passion or

causing male impotence. In fact, most sorcery trials well into the fifteenth century involved accusations of this sort. Kramer himself learned of such practices during his interrogations of alleged witches in Innsbruck in 1485.[35] But love magic was not associated with diabolical witchcraft until the *Malleus*. For example, the devil never appears in the Innsbruck interrogation records, and therefore Kramer failed to convince local authorities that the suspects were guilty of diabolical witchcraft.

The notion that marriage is a precarious institution in constant danger of sexual subversion has deep roots in Christian asceticism. In the late Middle Ages, the Dominican adherents of monastic asceticism insisted on the dangers of profligate sex, even within marriage. For example, Johannes Nider suggests that complete abstinence from sex is the best way to ensure salvation for a married couple.[36] Kramer and Sprenger apply such views to their witchcraft theory, arguing that sharing sexual pleasure places a husband and wife in as much danger as an adulterous couple: undisciplined sex will make the wife a witch and bewitch the husband.

The threat posed by witches to the institution of marriage is central to Kramer and Sprenger's theory of witchcraft. The worst damage that witches can do is to prevent married men from fathering children, thereby destroying the principal religious justification for marriage itself. By preventing procreation within marriage, witches stymy the generation of new souls for the Lord and new subjects for the sovereign, posing a terrible danger to church and state. Spiritual and secular authorities, Kramer and Sprenger argue, therefore ought to cooperate in rooting out the evil of witchcraft.

The witch threatens the social order not only by suppressing fertility, but also by challenging established authority. In their view of the modern witch, Kramer and Sprenger conflate two older images of women — the lascivious woman who corrupts men through sexual passion, and the contrary, domineering bad wife. The witch combines features of both: she seduces men with her wanton sexuality, bewitching them and rendering them impotent; and she dominates men through willful displays of arrogant self-assertion. The witch threatens the divinely ordained social order not only by interrupting procreation, but also by projecting a world turned upside down in which the prescribed social and gender hierarchies of the medieval order are reversed. In the medieval imagination, God ordained a social system in which men were to rule women, just as nobles were to rule peasants. The proliferation of witches identified by Kramer and Sprenger undermines the divine order symbolized by the subordination of women to men, destroying the hierarchical basis of traditional society itself. In identifying the threat witches pose to social coherence and authority, Kramer and Sprenger develop the first comprehensive social theory of witchcraft.

Although the *Malleus* was designed for use by well-educated men (such as priests and trial judges), it contains sample sermons that are directed at audiences of ordinary, uneducated women. The *Malleus*'s homilies on the nature of women and witches follow a long tradition in the Dominican and Franciscan mendicant orders of imparting marital advice to women. Traditionally, such sermons listed female vices and used the topos of the shrewish wife in order to discourage inappropriate female behavior. By linking the shrew (or bad wife) to the modern witch, the *Malleus* is the first work to address the subject of witchcraft in educating women. After the *Malleus* was published, the bad wife was commonly linked to witchcraft in didactic plays designed for uneducated audiences.

With rare exceptions, sermons in the mendicant tradition of educating ordinary women emphasized the positive aspects of married life, such as the help a capable wife could give her husband in accumulating wealth. By the time of the *Malleus*, such positive attitudes toward marriage were converging with the new humanistic notion of marriage as the primary form of social organization, an idea introduced to Germany by the provost of Bamberg, Albrecht von Eyb, in his *Ehebüchlein* (1472).[37] But although the *Malleus* owes the form of some of its sermons to the mendicant tradition of educating women, its authors were not particularly interested in women's education. Never — not even in their sample sermons directed toward women — do Kramer and Sprenger discuss what women might do to overcome their alleged inclination toward witchery. According to the *Malleus*, the only way a woman can avoid succumbing to her passions — and becoming a witch — is to embrace a life of devout chastity in religious retreat. But the monastic life is reserved to the spiritually gifted few. Therefore, most women are doomed to become witches, who cannot be redeemed; and the only recourse open to the authorities is to ferret out and exterminate all witches.

*Witches and the Apocalypse*

There is no mistaking the urgency of the *Malleus*'s message: a rising plague of witches threatens to unravel the very fabric of God's holy order in a catastrophe of apocalyptic proportions. "And so in this twilight and evening of the world," Kramer and Sprenger write, "when sin is flourishing on every side and in every place, when charity is growing cold, the evil of witches and their iniquities superabound."[38] Kramer and Sprenger predict the imminent arrival of the apocalypse foretold in the Bible. With the world nearing its end, they see witches "depopulating the whole of Christianity" in the service of the coming Antichrist.[39]

In the fifteenth century, this was not a farfetched conclusion: apocalyptic explanations provided a framework for understanding the changes and discoveries that no longer fit into the medieval concept of the social and spiritual "ordo." The new social mobility of peasants, the growing financial power of urban merchants, and even the discovery of America were all believed to signal the approaching end of the world.[40] Apocalyptic imagery often projected a world turned upside down in which gender roles were reversed and women ruled men. Accordingly, the *Malleus* warns of an invading army of female witches — often in the form of domineering wives and concubines — whose final aim is to destroy Christianity.

Kramer and Sprenger cite Hildegard of Bingen to lend authority to their vision.[41] In the twelfth century, Hildegard had described her own age as a "female era" in which temporal and spiritual authorities — especially the pope and the emperor — lacked courage and purpose, failings commonly ascribed to women. As she saw it, the failings of her age could be traced to inappropriate male behavior, particularly the sinful worldliness of clerics and princes.

Kramer and Sprenger see a similar corruption of authority in their own age, but attribute it to the seductive powers of witchcraft. Men in the modern age, they claim, act foolishly because they are enchanted by women witches, particularly "the concubines of the great."[42] These most wicked of women share the three special vices of lust, ambition, and infidelity, which lead them to aspire to power through men. By claiming that the concubines of the great are particularly inclined to practice witchcraft, Kramer and Sprenger adopt a new line of argument: witches not only deny God and seek to dominate men, they threaten to usurp power. Enticed by sexuality, the mighty fall under the spell of witches disguised as concubines, who protect their powerful patrons and use them to spread witchcraft and destroy the faith.[43]

Next to the concubines of the great, the most wicked and dangerous of witches are the midwives.[44] According to Kramer and Sprenger, midwives deprive the Lord of new souls by encouraging women to use birth control and obtain abortions. If all else fails, they induce miscarriages and even eat the newborn or offer them to the devil. By killing and devouring infants or delivering them to Satan, midwives steal new souls from the Lord and consign them to the devil, a crime so abhorrent that the authors conclude their discussion of midwives with the observation that "no one does more harm to the Catholic faith than midwives."[45]

Whether as a bad wife who dominates her husband, a concubine who seduces those in power, or a midwife who sabotages childbirth and slaughters the newborn, the female witch turns the world upside down. The topos of a world turned upside down traditionally served a variety of purposes.[46] In the *Malleus*, it serves to malign women's sexuality, to condemn women's pursuit of authority, and to criminalize women's use of birth control. By contrast, inappropriate male behavior (such as appeasing one's wife or surrendering to the charms of a woman) is not demonized in the *Malleus*; instead, it serves by negative example to teach men to dominate women. The *Malleus* is designed not to educate women, but rather to show men how to prevent the spread of witchcraft by disciplining and intimidating women. The authors' apocalyptic imagery in connection with the plague of witches is an important part of this educational mission.

Kramer and Sprenger maintain that witches target not only the family and the state, but also the traditional symbol of male power, the penis. Their repeated assertions that witches strive to make the penis vanish are designed to teach men that lechery places them in grave danger of bewitchment, which in turn may lead to impotence and the sensation of castration.[47] Witches cannot really castrate men through sorcery, the authors admit; but — with the devil's help — witches can create the illusion of castration. Drawing on Augustine's interpretation of Aristotle, Kramer and Sprenger explain how the sensation of castration comes about. Certain mental images, they argue, are stored in the memory. Sinful thoughts (especially sexual fantasies) introduce the devil into the mind, allowing him to conjure up old mental images or to impose new ones that appear quite real. Possessed by the devil, the unfortunate victim of witchcraft believes himself castrated — "he can see and feel nothing but [his own] smooth body with its surface interrupted by no genital organ."[48]

By losing his penis — the symbol of his preeminence in the divine order of things — a man is rendered a nobody within his androcentric frame of reference. In the medieval ideology of gender, which was based on Aristotle's notion that women are the product of defective sperm and that men alone embody human perfection, genitals had a very different social significance for men than they did for women.[49] For women, a smooth body without genitals was considered virginal and uncorrupted, with its hymen intact and its vagina closed and invisible. A virginal body was a positive asset associated with such masculine qualities as reason, intelligence, and devotion to the faith. By contrast, a man without his penis became like a woman — a social nonentity. Castration through bewitchment went beyond impotence to strike at the very core of male social and spiritual identity, which is why Kramer and Sprenger emphasize its danger. They go so far as to tell of witches who keep enchanted penises as pets, placing them in bird's nests or boxes, "where they move themselves like living members, and eat oats and corn, as has been seen by many."[50]

Kramer and Sprenger's relation of witchcraft to the apocalypse stems from their interpretation of apocalyptic passages from the Bible. According to the *Malleus*, the plague of modern witches is part of the battle between good and evil that precedes the Final Judgment. Satan uses his witches to steal souls from the Lord, knowing that the more he can steal, the longer it will take to reach the number of saved souls needed for the Day of Judgment to arrive. Therefore, it is the duty of the virtuous to thwart the activities of witches and prevent Satan from corrupting souls. In His divine wisdom, God has not only saved men from becoming witches, He has made some of them immune to the temptations and afflictions of witchcraft. These are the judges and Inquisitors, the men who lead the battle against Satan and his legions of witches. As the secular and clerical representatives of the divinely ordained "ordo," they wage a lonely, heroic struggle against Satan's army of lascivious women in the final stages of a cooling, dying world.

### Kramer's Actual Witch Trial Experience

Kramer and Sprenger declare in the *Malleus* that their gender-specific description of the modern witch is based on their actual experience of witches on trial for their crimes. But one should treat their claim with caution. The early mass trials of women, particularly those in Italy and Germany in the late 1480s, have not been fully researched and in some cases are not attested except in Kramer and Sprenger's own accounts.[51] Sprenger never actually participated in a witch trial; and trial records suggest that Kramer exaggerated his success as a witch hunter and brought preconceived notions about the wicked ways of women to his own proceedings against alleged witches.

In the *Malleus*, Kramer claims to have tried nearly one hundred women suspected of witchcraft in Constance and Innsbruck, and to have sentenced half of them to burn at the stake. But only one incident is confirmed by another source — the execution of eight women in Ravensburg (near Constance) in 1484. In a letter responding to an inquiry from Archduke Sigismund of Tirol, town officials explain that Kramer came to Ravensburg equipped with papal bulls and other official documents supporting his mission, and began to preach about the dangers of witchcraft, encouraging citizens to name suspected witches.[52] Finally, eight women were convicted and burned at the stake with the approval of city authorities, who supported Kramer's contention that they had fornicated with the devil. It appears that even before Kramer's arrival, the educated elite in the area near Constance were familiar with the concept of the modern witch and were prepared to see alleged witches prosecuted and put to death. Although we do not know much about other trials in the area, in his *De laniis et pythonicis mulieribus* (1489), Ulrich Molitor portrays the mayor of Constance, Conrad Schatz, as a fervent believer in the dangers of witchcraft; and the abbot of the nearby Weingarten monastery was rewarded by Pope Innocent VIII for his support of witch trials.[53] One reason for this zeal may be the proximity of Constance to the Swiss witch-hunting grounds, where diabolical witchcraft was considered a reality much earlier than in most of Germany. A good indication of Swiss influence on witch hunts in the area is the use by the Ravensburg officials of the Swiss term "hechsen" to denote witches.

It is evident from the trial descriptions in the *Malleus* that two of the eight convicted women confessed to elements of witchcraft (copulating with the devil and conjuring up a hailstorm) only after torture. Particularly revealing is Kramer's characterization of Agnes Bader, whose vehement insistence on her innocence during her first trial strikes him as "not quite like a woman, but [rather showing] a male spirit."[54] After the application of torture during her second trial, Bader reveals her true female character when she weakens and finally breaks, confessing to her practice of diabolical witchcraft.

In 1485, Kramer moved his witch-hunting activities to Innsbruck, where he interrogated about fifty women suspected of witchcraft.[55] But

his proceedings were abruptly halted by Bishop Georg Golser of Bressa-
none, who expelled the Inquisitor from town. Golser objected to Kramer's ruthless abuse of his authority, refusing to believe that there could
be so many witches in his diocese. In fact, records from Kramer's proceedings reveal a striking disparity between the original accusations
against the arrested women and the charges of diabolical witchcraft
leveled by Kramer himself.[56] Originally, most of the women were accused of practicing love magic and thereby causing illness in their victims or (in one case) even death. Most accusations could be traced to
conflicts within the community; many came from jilted lovers or betrayed spouses, and others resulted from envy or old feuds. None of the
accusations contained the slightest hint of diabolism, which convinced
Golser that none of the cases involved witchcraft and that the accused
women should be released.

Kramer saw it differently: shocked by the apparent promiscuity of the
accused and by their attitudes of defiance, he interpreted their extramarital affairs in themselves as signs of diabolism and witchcraft. For
example, in the case of Helena Scheuberin — a woman charged with
practicing love magic — Kramer gives several reasons for suspecting her
of witchcraft: though married, she was promiscuous and had a bad reputation; she was accused of sorcery and of associating with other sorceresses; and she questioned his authority as Inquisitor and therefore
that of the Catholic church. But Kramer based his case against Scheuberin primarily on her sexual behavior. During her initial interrogation,
he asked such detailed questions about her sex life that the bishop's
representative was appalled and ordered him to stop.

Bishop Golser was especially worried about the community's reaction
to Kramer's prosecutorial ruthlessness. The accused women complained
about the slanderous tone of Kramer's sermons, which they held responsible for their arrest; Helena Scheuberin was especially outspoken, cursing Kramer at the doors of the church. The lawyer Johann Merwais
opened the accused women's defense by charging the Inquisitor with
using improper methods of interrogation, such as asking leading questions. Apparently, the defendants carried clout within their community:
Golser was so afraid that their outraged friends and families would con-
front the Inquisitor and disturb the peace that he ordered all of the
accused to be set free, over Kramer's strenuous objections. Archduke
Sigismund of Tirol, who consulted and concurred with Golser on the
matter, agreed to cover the trial costs, putting an end to the whole affair.

The incident finished Kramer's career as a witch hunter, but motivated him to write a book designed to educate obstinate officials about the dangers of witchcraft.

Kramer's witch trial experience provided him with valuable materials for the second part of his *Malleus*, which describes the various kinds of witchcraft. His knowledge of cases in which love sorcery was related to extramarital affairs may have contributed to his theory that marital and sexual relations give rise to witchcraft. His trial observations may also have convinced him that greed and poverty are partly to blame for witchcraft, a notion that appears in the first two parts of the *Malleus*. Apparently, some of the alleged witches Kramer faced confessed that they had turned to sorcery because they needed or wanted such items as milk and butter.

But Kramer and Sprenger drew more from scholastic theories on the evil of women than from actual trial experience. In the second part of their book, the authors give many examples of male witchery, including medieval stories about monks practicing magic. They also rely heavily on the confessions of Staedelin, a man who was accused of witchcraft in early fifteenth-century Switzerland. In resorting to accounts of male witchcraft to prove their point, Kramer and Sprenger implicitly admit that Kramer's actual trial experience was not enough to support his views on witchcraft — including his contention that most witches are women.

Rather than drawing his conclusions from the trial evidence, Kramer seems to have prosecuted women as witches because he already believed they were. The trial records reveal that his whole approach to the witchcraft proceedings in Constance and Innsbruck was influenced by his conviction — in accordance with scholastic theory — that women are by nature evil and corrupt. His notion of female carnality influenced his interpretation of magical practices on the part of the accused, steering his attention toward their sexual behavior. But the outcome of the Innsbruck proceedings shows that many communities were not yet ready to accept his modern definition of the female witch.

Kramer's and Sprenger's political views complemented their theological prejudices against women and helped to shape their attitudes toward gender and witchcraft. Kramer, an ardent advocate of papal supremacy, was actively involved in the dispute over the authenticity of the Donation of Constantine. The discovery fifty years earlier that the supposed bequest was in fact a forgery had raised serious questions about the legality of papal powers in the secular realm. Kramer's support for the papacy led to his involvement in heresy cases: he attributed the embattled state of the Catholic church to heresy and witchcraft. A staunch Dominican, Kramer saw himself as a "hound of heaven" ("domini cane") whose "barking" kept the wolves of heresy and witchcraft away from the flock of Christ's sheep. In 1474, he was named papal Inquisitor for the region in Germany between the Alps and the Rhine.

Sprenger, the prior of the Dominican monastery in Cologne, enthusiastically supported conservative church reform. Appointed by his order to supervise the Dominican reform movement in Germany, he advocated monasticism and strict observance of clerical celibacy and asceticism. In accordance with his belief in celibacy, Sprenger founded the first Rosary Confraternity in Germany. In 1480, he was named dean of the University of Cologne, a bastion of scholasticism against the new ideas of humanism. His position helped him get a letter of endorsement for the *Malleus* from the Cologne faculty, albeit partly forged. In 1481, he was named papal Inquisitor for the Rhine region. He joined Kramer to write the *Malleus* out of a shared commitment to papal supremacy and ascetic monastic reform at a time when the Holy See was under growing attack from humanists, theologians, and popular social and religious movements. The two Inquisitors formed an alliance based on the belief that women witches were responsible for the social and religious changes they feared. By proving the existence of witchcraft, the *Malleus* was designed to reaffirm the need for the entire political and spiritual apparatus of the church.

The *Malleus* laid the foundations for the gender-specific discourse that informed subsequent works on witchcraft. After the *Malleus* was published, no work on the subject of witchcraft during the entire history of the European witch hunts challenged the assumption that women are more likely than men to be witches. Although few German writers agreed entirely with the *Malleus*, nearly all identified witches with women, including such disparate writers as Ulrich Molitor (*De laniis et phytonicis mulieribus*, 1489), Thomas Murner (*De pythonico contracto*, 1499 and *Narrenbeschwörung*, 1512), Martin Plantsch (*Opusculum de sagis maleficis*, 1505), Johann Trithemius (*Antipalus maleficiorum* and *Liber octo quaestionum*, 1508), Agrippa von Nettesheim (*De incertitudine et vanitate scientiarum*, 1526), and Johann Spreter (*Hexenbüchlein*, 1540). Very few of these authors saw a need to explain why women are witches; and of those who did, only a few (for example, Johann Trithemius) attributed witchery to female sexuality. Instead, most offered the older medieval explanation that women resort to sorcery because of their weakness of body and mind. Still, all accepted as intuitively correct the *Malleus*'s gender-specific notion of modern witchcraft. With the publication of the *Malleus*, a general consensus was established in early modern Germany on the evil nature of women as witches.

# Chapter Three

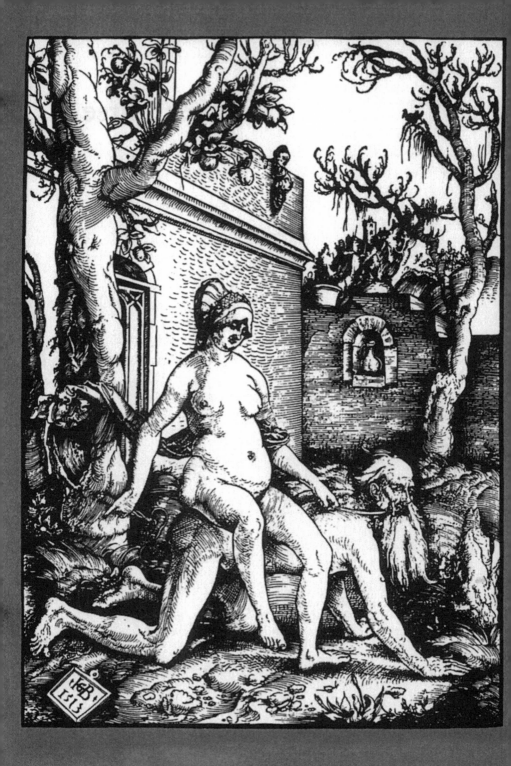

# Martin Luther: Witches and Fearless Housewives

ARTIN LUTHER (1483–1546) reached maturity well after the concept of the female witch had been established. Whether he ever read the *Malleus maleficarum* (1487) by Heinrich Kramer and Jakob Sprenger is a matter of conjecture, but he is known to have studied Geiler von Kaisersberg's sermons on witchcraft (*Emeis*, 1508).[1] During Luther's lifetime, witch trials were rare. In 1540, a witch trial was held in Wittenberg — Luther's principal residence — and four accused witches were burned at the stake. It is unknown whether Luther was involved in the trial or witnessed the executions.

Luther was the first writer since Kramer and Sprenger to reevaluate the gender-specificity of witches and to offer a new explanation for it. It may seem surprising that Luther contributed to the discussion of witchcraft, because he never specialized in witch sermons or explored witchcraft in a treatise. Historians of the European witch hunts, from the pioneers Wilhelm Gottlieb Soldan and Heinrich Heppe to the present day, have neglected or misunderstood Luther's views on witchcraft. Soldan and Heppe maintain that Luther overlooked the importance of the subject, and more recent historians contend that he was an uncritical believer in witchcraft who said nothing new on the subject.[2] This persistent view is largely based on the analysis of Luther's texts on witchcraft by Nikolaus Paulus in 1910.[3] Partisan Catholic in tone, Paulus's study presents Luther as an unoriginal, credulous believer in witches and the need for their persecution.

This traditional assessment of Luther's views on witchcraft does not stand up under scrutiny. In his sermons and teachings — particularly those on idolatry and marriage — Luther frequently refers to witchcraft, which he treats as part of daily Christian life. Far from merely reiterating well-established views on witches, Luther was the first to link the concept of witchcraft to the role of women as housewives. His redefinition

ILLUSTRATION: Hans Baldung Grien, *Phyllis and Aristotle*, 1513

53

of the witch as a foil for the proper housewife has broad ramifications for
the modern understanding of witches and women alike.

At first glance, Luther's references to witches appear quite conventional. He uses a variety of well-worn Latin terms for them, including
"maga," "saga," "malefica," "incantrica," "venefica," and "pythonissa,"
along with the less familiar "daemonum ancilla" and "haliora." His most
frequent German term for the witch is "Zewberin," but he also uses
"Hexe," "Teuffelshure," "Teuffels Pfeffin," and "Teuffels Prophetin." In
accordance with the conventional belief that witches were recognizable
only by their evil actions, Luther rarely offers a physical description.[4]

Luther names nine practices commonly attributed to witches, including the four key practices of harmful sorcery, secret meetings, the devil's
pact, and flying at night. But some of these practices, says Luther, are
attributed to witches in error. He maintains that witches exist and that
the devil practices harmful sorcery through them, which God permits in
order to test believers and avenge the faith. But Luther doubts whether
witches really fly on broomsticks, turn into animals, or bear children to
the devil, and he ascribes practices such as convening for feasts, fornicating with demons, and bargaining with the devil not only to witches, but
to other practitioners of folk magic as well, all of whom he roundly
condemns.[5] In general, his assessment of witches and their activities
is quite consistent with such orthodox demonologies as Kramer and
Sprenger's *Malleus maleficarum.*

Like the *Malleus,* Luther insists that most witches are women, and he
cites the Scriptures to support his view, particularly Paul's epistle to the
Galatians. In Galatians 3:1, Paul chastises his listeners for erring from
the path of righteousness. "Who hath bewitched you," he asks, "that ye
should not obey the truth?"[6] Luther uses this passage to explain what
Paul meant by "bewitched," a term derived from "badchaino" in the
original Greek. Luther claims that "badchaino" has two separate meanings: to envy, and to enchant with the evil eye. Since female witches are
known to enchant with the evil eye and to envy mothers with beautiful
children, Luther concludes that "badchaino" refers to the female practice of bewitching young children, and that its proper Latin translation is
therefore "fascinare" ("to bewitch"). By implying that Paul was referring
to the evils of modern witchcraft in his epistle to the Galatians, Luther
ascribes a timelessness to the female witch that validates his own age's
belief in her.

Again drawing on Paul's epistle to the Galatians, Luther explains the word for witchcraft ("veneficium") as a female practice. Since the Greek word "pharmachion" used by Paul means both poison and medication, Luther argues that a woman preparing medication is a "pharmaceutria veneficia," a "poisoning sorceress," or witch. As a predominately female practice, "veneficium" is therefore the appropriate term for witchcraft.[7] Luther alludes here not only to the medieval view that sorcery includes the use of poison, but to ordinances prohibiting women from pursuing the pharmaceutical profession.[8] In Luther's day, women who continued their traditional practice of preparing medicines were suspected of witchcraft. Luther claims that Paul deliberately chose to discuss female witchcraft because he was aware of the bodily harm women witches inflict on men, babies, and cattle through their magical arts. "It is clear on the authority of so great an apostle," he concludes, "that those sorceries are not unreal but are able to work harm."[9]

 Like Kramer and Sprenger, Luther demands that witches be executed swiftly, and he gives several reasons for doing so. First, he claims that the Bible calls for it; he translates Exodus 22:18 as, "You shall not allow witches to live."[10] Second, in accordance with secular law, Luther maintains that the damage done by witches calls for their capital punishment. For example, in his *Table Talks* (*Tischreden*, 1536–1540), Luther reacts to the alleged theft of milk and butter by witches and to their supposed role in spreading disease by angrily declaring that he would personally burn them at the stake if he could.[11] Third, Luther calls for executing witches "not for stealing milk, but rather for their blasphemy in strengthening the devil and his sacraments and churches against Christ."[12] With this argument, Luther verges on declaring witchcraft a heresy, a view that influenced the Protestant laws on heresy and witchcraft defined by Philipp Melanchthon in his Wittenberg church ordinances of 1552.[13] Finally, Luther calls for executing witches as a deterrent to others. For example, in his *Table Talks*, Luther discusses the case of an alleged witch ("Zauberin") who was accused of poisoning her husband; he demands that she be put to death "so that others are deterred from such diabolical undertakings."[14]

At first glance, Luther's concept of witchcraft seems to coincide with the orthodox views on witches expressed in Kramer and Sprenger's *Malleus*. Drawing on the authority of the Scriptures and influenced by folk belief, Luther argues that witches are predominately women who practice harmful sorcery, make a pact with the devil, and engage in other practices traditionally attributed to the "malefica" or "Zauberin." Like

Kramer and Sprenger, he charges witches with lese majesty against God ("crimen laesae maiestate divine"), a crime that combines blasphemy with treason and is punishable by death.[15]

But Luther's argument that executing witches will deter others from witchery is strikingly inconsistent with the views on witchcraft expressed in the *Malleus*. Kramer and Sprenger argue that because women are impelled by wanton sexuality, they are driven by their very nature to become witches. By contrast, Luther's advocacy of deterrence suggests that women do not become witches by nature, but rather choose whether to practice witchcraft. Starting from the premise of free choice, Luther develops a theory of women and witchcraft that is utterly at odds with orthodox Catholicism. His novel approach to the subject begins with his conception of witchcraft as idolatry.

## The Idolatry of Witchcraft

The rituals of sixteenth-century folk magic were similar to such semi-magical rites of Catholicism as brandishing rosaries against the devil. Through their respective rituals, both folk magic and Catholicism imputed to objects and spirits the power to benefit or protect a supplicant; and both belief systems endowed with spiritual powers the vocational practitioners of their rituals (such as priests or the traditional "wise women" who practiced folk magic). Because those in need of help were encouraged to seek the ritual support of the church, it probably seemed quite reasonable to many of them to seek additional assistance from practitioners of folk magic. Whether one paid a priest or a wise woman to cure disease or to ward off witches and demons mattered little.

By condemning all ritual as idolatry, Luther not only attacked the basis of folk magic, he challenged orthodox Catholicism. In his *Decem praecepta Wittenbergensi praedicata populo* (1518) and his sermons on Galatians (1519 and 1535), Luther argues that clerical office, religious ceremony, and pious works neither save from temptation nor guarantee redemption. "There is no one of us who is not bewitched rather often by false opinions," he insists.[16] "Idolatry reigns in each human until he is healed by grace in the faith of Jesus Christ."[17] Because nobody can count on receiving God's grace, the only remedy is humility and a continual striving for religious perfection in daily life. Rituals (whether religious or magical) are signs of idolatry, not redemption, which can only come from within.

Luther distinguishes between spiritual idolatry (such as the worship of saints and other orthodox Catholic practices) and physical idolatry (including witchcraft and astrology).[18] Both are based, he says, on a bargain for immediate personal gain: witches make a deal with the devil, and those who worship the saints hope for succor from a God whose nature is misunderstood. Luther sees a foolish human dependence on earthly goods and satisfactions as the reason for both kinds of idolatry; but spiritual idolatry — for example, the Catholic practice of selling dispensations — is worse for him than such physical idolatry as witchcraft. Although self-gratification through witchcraft may be foolish and idolatrous, Luther sees it as understandably human. The devil, he says, is far more interested in corrupting the spirit and intellect through papist teachings than in deluding the senses through witchcraft. Therefore, Luther devotes more time to exposing the spiritual idolatry of orthodox Catholicism than to denouncing the physical idolatry of witchcraft.

Luther's views on witchcraft and idolatry represent a complete revision of orthodox theology. If Luther's devil can corrupt even the most pious and exalted of prelates, then he is not only more powerful than the devil of orthodox Catholicism, but also more democratic. This democratic element, inherent in Luther's criticism of religious ritual, is at the heart of Luther's theology. But Luther's insistence on universal corruptibility places more demands on Christians than does Catholicism. In Luther's view, the individual assumes an added burden of responsibility for his actions: because the rites of confession no longer suffice to redeem the sinner, he or she must overcome the devil's temptations every minute of every day. And, because it is therefore so easy for the devil to corrupt even the most devout, Luther sees idolatry — and witchcraft — as widespread practices.[19]

The size of the problem posed by witchcraft depends on the spiritual state of society, according to Luther: at times when the level of spirituality is low, people are more likely to resort to witchcraft than at times when many have found God's grace. In his early sermons, Luther warns that witchcraft is rampant, but later he finds that the Reformation has nearly wiped it out. Finally, he rediscovers it among Anabaptists and rebellious peasants, whom he accuses of appointing as "prophetesses and priestesses" women "who are known among Christians as devil's whores," a typical description of witches.[20]

Luther's identification of magical practices with idolatry coincides with medieval doctrine; the *Canon episcopi* of 906 presents a similar point of view. But the *Canon* was directed against a pre-Christian religious belief in night-flying spirits, whereas Luther attributes witchcraft not to pagan beliefs, but rather to a spiritual deficiency at the core of all ritual: the lack of courage to place oneself entirely in the hands of God. For Luther, the idolatry of witchcraft stems from a lack of faith in God, a far cry from Kramer and Sprenger's view that witchcraft stems from female sexuality. Whereas witchery in women appears inevitable in the *Malleus*, Luther calls on every Christian to decide for him- or herself whether to give in to fear and resort to magic or to overcome fear through trust in God. But if Luther sees all Christians as susceptible to idolatry, why does he insist that witchcraft is a predominately female practice?

### God's Housewife

One of Luther's most interesting references to female witchcraft appears in a sermon delivered after his return to Wittenberg from exile in 1522. Citing 1 Peter 3:1–7 on the role of women in marriage, Luther calls on wives to "deport themselves in such a way in the matter of gestures and conduct that they entice their husbands to believe."[21] A wife should do more for her husband than bear and raise his children, Luther argues: through exemplary conduct, she should "entice" him (Luther uses the term "reytzen," with its sexual innuendo) into abiding by the faith. Through humility, submission, and the inner beauty of her soul, a woman has the power to seduce men into righteous behavior. At the same time, a woman's husband should respect her subordinate position and not mistreat her. Not only is she physically weaker than he, a woman lacks the mental faculties necessary to deal with life's adversities, and therefore her husband should take care of her and educate her as though she were a child.

Luther punctuates his prescription for virtuous marital relations with a telling remark on the origins of female witchcraft. "It is commonly the nature of women," he declares, "to be afraid of everything. This is why they busy themselves so much with witchcraft and superstitions and run hither and thither, uttering a magic formula here and a magic formula there."[22] According to Luther, women are by nature fearful; they practice witchcraft in order to overcome their fears, but this only binds them all the more to their fearful nature. A woman can free herself from fear only if she accepts her weakness and becomes an obedient wife who trusts in God. "For since she then knows what her condition in life is and that her condition is pleasing to God," Luther concludes, "what does she have to fear?"[23]

There is no attempt here to relate witchcraft to female sexuality or lust. Luther does not adopt the view presented by Kramer and Sprenger that the root of female witchcraft is carnality. In fact, Luther is not very interested in the sexual aspect of witchcraft. Even his rare remarks on the subject are at odds with the *Malleus*: he does not attribute witchcraft to fornication with the devil, and he maintains that demons seduce men as well as women. Seldom does he ascribe male impotence to witchcraft.[24]

In his commentary on Genesis, Luther explains that sexuality was originally a noble human activity that men and women engaged in as equals for the sake of procreation.[25] But after the Fall, sexuality was poisoned by passion and lost its nobility. Eve's sin deprived women of their equality with men, and in punishment women were subordinated to men, confined to the household, and forced to suffer in perpetuity the pain of childbirth. For their part, men were subjected to the punishment of sustaining their families through hard labor. For Luther, sexuality is part of the God-given nature of human beings; it is the means for establishing the most important institution on earth, the family. Therefore, it cannot be the origin of witchcraft.

Luther's revaluation of sexuality leads him to take a fresh look at Genesis 6:2 ("That the sons of God saw the daughters of men that they were fair; and they took them wives of all which they chose"). In orthodox Catholic theology, the "sons of God" were seen as fallen angels who were seduced by earthly women, leading to the race of giants and the Great Flood. For orthodox Catholics, this disastrous sequence of events, known as the Second Fall, shows the danger inherent in female sexuality; the *Malleus* goes so far as to infer from the passage sexual contact between the devil and witches.[26] But Luther translates the terms "filii Dei" in the Vulgate not as "sons of God," but rather as "God's children" ("kinder Gottes") in the sense that we are all children of God.[27] For Luther, the passage demonstrates not that fallen angels spawned a race of giants, but rather that ordinary men strayed from the path of righteousness by allowing lust to guide their choice of women. Their spiritual degeneration ignited God's wrath and caused the Great Flood. Luther thus abandons the traditional focus on female sexuality as the root cause of the Second Fall, instead blaming it on the foolishness of men who use women to satisfy their desires.

In his 1535 sermon on Galatians, Luther explicitly rejects the notion that witchcraft stems from carnality, even correcting Paul's view on the matter. "Among the works of the flesh Paul numbers witchcraft," Luther states, "which, as everyone knows, is not a work caused by the desires of the flesh, but is an abuse or imitation of idolatry."[28] In rejecting the idea that witchcraft stems from female carnality, Luther revolutionizes the traditional notion of female nature. In the medieval clerical tradition, women were thought to have inherited the wicked, lascivious nature of the temptress Eve. The temptations of the world were represented in medieval German allegory as "Lady World" ("vrô welt"), a lovely woman filled with vitality whose beautiful visage conceals a hideous, worm-eaten skeleton. In the image of "Lady World," woman is bound by her carnal nature to a seductive and egoistic life-force that obscures the deadly, transient nature of the world and obstructs ascetic spiritual self-realization. Luther replaces the voracious sexuality of woman as eternal temptress with another side of her nature, her moral virtue and talent for piety, qualities reserved in the medieval view to the exceptional few women who lived celibate lives in religious retreat. Luther takes the novel view that women in general — not just the celibate few, but married women in particular — radiate an innate morality that is highly seductive in a positive way, stimulating men to abide by the faith. As God's house-wife, every married woman is divinely ordained to educate her husband in moral virtue by displaying humility and submission in marriage.

Nevertheless, Luther adopts the medieval clerical view of women as physically and intellectually inferior to men. Although he maintains that men and women are spiritually equal before God, Luther assumes that they are unequal on earth. In Luther's view, women are the weaker sex, and their subordinate position is unalterable, a view that precludes even the narrow window of opportunity granted to a celibate few women by the orthodox Catholic church. In orthodox thought, virgins who deny their female sexuality share men's superior spiritual and intellectual qualities (such as the ability to reason), and are therefore entitled to privileges normally reserved to men. Luther's emphasis on family and his concomitant acceptance of sexuality lead him to reject both the demon-ization of the libidinal woman and the accordance of male privileges to the virginal nun. The traditional clerical fear of female sexuality so evi-dent in the *Malleus* is entirely absent from Luther's writings; but in prescribing for women the divinely ordained role of housewife, Luther places them in a confined, controlled context informed by subordination to men.

### Women's Weakness and Witchcraft

For Luther, it is not her sexuality, but rather her inherent female weakness of body and mind that leads a woman to become a witch.

"Who can count all the foolish, ridiculous, wrong, senseless, and su-
perstitious things that women deal in?" Luther declares. "From their
mother Eve, it has been natural for them to be deceived and made fools
of."[29] Luther depicts Eve not as the dangerous temptress that haunted
the medieval imagination, but rather as a simpleton whose female foolishness provided an opening for the devil.[30] Women practice witchcraft
because they inherit Eve's foolishness. "On witches," Luther maintains,
" . . . [w]hy does the law stress women more than men? . . . Because of
Eve."[31] Unlike Kramer and Sprenger, Luther does not link women's
proclivity for folly to aggressive female passions such as lust, rage, ambition, or a thirst for revenge. For Luther, witchcraft is rooted in women's
mental deficiency rather than in a female will to power.

According to Luther, women resort to witchcraft because they are by
nature too weak and foolish to control their passions. But he sees female
passion as docile and domesticated, not wild and menacing like the untamed sexuality that so frightened Kramer and Sprenger. "Wives are
easily seduced to sorcery," Luther asserts, "because of their excessive
love for their children and their dependence on earthly satisfaction."
Women resort to witchcraft in order to cure their beloved children
from disease. Luther condemns such foolishness, warning women not to
overdo their laudable concern for their children, and counseling them
instead to "seek natural remedies and pray to God in simple faith and full
of creed."[32]

Luther advises women to overcome their inborn fear and excessive
love, and to passively accept their fates as housewives. "If your child dies,
if you become ill," he intones, "be of good cheer; commit it to God. You
are in a condition pleasing to God; what better lot could you desire?"[33]
Luther's advice to women is simple: instead of resorting to witchcraft,
trust in God's plan. Although women are weak in mind and body and
therefore prone to natural fears and strong feelings, if they accept their
divinely ordained role as housewives and use their inherent moral power
within marriage, they will be protected. In order to abstain from witchcraft, women need not deny their sexuality, as Kramer and Sprenger
suggest in the *Malleus*; but they must overcome the temptation to try to
solve their own problems, and instead entrust their fates to God. In
effect, they must deny their qualities as women and their abilities as
human beings.

In a way, Luther's ideal Christian woman is a nun turned housewife:
she must be a loving wife and mother, but she must also refrain from

loving too much. Her emotional balancing act demands a Herculean effort at self-restraint like that demanded of women who enter the convent. But the Catholic ideal of virginal asceticism was never intended for women in general; it was only intended for the select few who were called to a life of devotion to God. The overwhelming majority of women were not expected to live up to the ideal — indeed, marriage was seen as a necessary refuge for the spiritually weak. By contrast, the Lutheran feminine ideal places a tremendous burden on every woman, compelling her to decide anew each day whether she will remain a good Christian. If she does not choose of her own free will to obey her husband and trust in God, Luther argues, "she will not be helped in any other way. For you will accomplish nothing with blows; they will not make a woman pious and submissive. If you beat one devil out of her, you will beat two into her."[34] In Luther's view, women are not evil by nature, but rather by choice: if a woman refuses to marry, or if her married behavior is inappropriate because she loves her family so much that she resorts to magic to protect it, then she renounces the inner moral power that is part of her nature. By refusing to be God's housewife, she becomes a modern witch.

Too weak and foolish to resist their fears, Luther argues, women turn away from God and seek their own sinful solutions to their problems. But what attracts women to witchcraft in particular rather than to other means of solving their problems? For an answer, Luther turns to the history of magic, which he explores in his sermon for Epiphany in 1522.

The magical arts, Luther says, stem from the observation of nature, which can reveal many useful secrets. In early Arab and Persian societies, magic was refined to a learned art, and the Middle East is still its home — the Jews and gypsies, Luther claims, are renowned for their magical skills.[35] Unfortunately, the Fall tainted human reason by associating it with the vain aspiration to divine knowledge. The study of nature was subsequently corrupted by the excessive use of reason, allowing Satan to seduce magicians into joining him in his vain attempts to imitate God. In their overweening pride, these magicians became the wizards and philosophers who give magic a bad name.[36]

Reason, Luther argues, is by no means entirely corrupt. In its natural state, it has two positive components: the common sense that a peasant needs to work his fields, and the divine knowledge that prophets possess when God speaks through them. In Luther's view, magic — as a divinely inspired force — is distinct from diabolical witchcraft in that it is based on the positive elements of natural reason. Luther does not follow Kramer and Sprenger in subsuming all magical practices under witchcraft. Instead, he distinguishes between witches and learned magicians according to the amount of natural reason found in their art.

Luther's understanding of the magical arts implies that diabolical witchcraft — as opposed to magic based on natural reason — holds a special attraction for women in particular because women are irrational. Among the mental defects women inherit from Eve, argues Luther, is their limited ability to reason. Those who embrace sorcery must be deficient in reason, and those who are most deficient in this area are known to be women. In their fear, women resort to witchcraft out of an intellectual deficiency inherited from Eve: their incapacity for rational reflection and judgment.

*The Aging of the Witch*

One might expect that women who refuse to be God's housewives and instead resort to witchcraft would be relatively young. But not all witches are young, according to Luther; next to "the little wives [who] are easily seduced to sorcery because of their excessive love for their children" are many "old women or others who dabble in the same [magical] arts, such as making a pact with the devil."[37] In fact, Luther often depicts the witch as an old woman ("vetula") — in contrast to Kramer and Sprenger, who describe witches of all ages, but who regard women between the ages of twelve and twenty (in their most fertile years) as the most likely to become witches.[38]

Luther's image of the aging witch is part of a trend in sixteenth-century literature. Especially in vernacular texts — such as Thomas Murner's *Narrenbeschwörung* (1512) and Hans Sachs's *Der teüffel mit dem alten Weyb* (1545) — witches grew rapidly older. In a parallel development, the beautiful but bad wife of medieval lore turns in the fifteenth and sixteenth centuries into an ugly old hag whose repulsive appearance may have been designed to reflect the moral ugliness of wicked female behavior.[39] Another reason for the aging of witches and bad wives may be the frequent association in texts of antiquity and the Middle Ages of old women with magic. And as the activities of women in the early modern period were increasingly restricted to bearing and rearing children, women who were past menopause may have come to be seen as useless and ugly, like a witch or a bad wife.

For Luther, the advanced age of the witch is associated with her infertility. In his first sermon on Galatians (1519), Luther claims that old women past their childbearing years are consumed with envy whenever they see the beautiful children of younger women. Out of spite, they cast a fatal spell on the children, which incites their mothers to resort to witchcraft in order to protect their children.[40] Whereas the witches in Kramer and Sprenger's *Malleus* are preoccupied with orgiastic sex, Luther's witches are obsessed with motherhood: some are spiteful old women who long for children despite their age and infertility, and others are devoted young mothers who love their children too much. In Luther's writings, the root cause of witchcraft shifts from wanton female sexuality to women's preoccupation with motherhood — with their failure to reproduce or with their desire to protect their offspring.

In Luther's view, motherhood is based on marriage, the most sacred of Protestant institutions. Out of spite and envy, Luther's old witches seek to undermine marriage by sowing discord between husband and wife. The real culprit, of course, is the devil, who creates the illusion that matrimony is a state of sheer bliss sustained by perpetual passion.[41] Satan's use of the witch to subvert marriage is illustrated in a German folktale known as "The Devil and the Old Woman" (*Der Teufel und das alte Weib*). In the tale, the devil sets out to destroy a long and happy marriage with the help of an old woman who is often described as a witch.[42] Through lies and deceit, the old hag provokes a bitter quarrel between husband and wife, which in some versions of the tale leads to the death of one partner.

Luther uses the devil-and-old-woman story to illustrate various aspects of his doctrine, such as the work and daily prayer it takes to maintain a healthy marriage, or the importance of preserving the social peace by thwarting the devil's efforts to disturb it.[43] Marital disorder, Luther argues, can reach beyond the household to disrupt the peace of the entire community. In one version of the devil-and-old-woman tale, Luther connects the marital discord caused by the lies of old women to the activities of sectarians and rebellious peasants, thereby showing how witches help the devil undermine the foundations of the Christian state.[44] As Luther sees it, relationships within family and society mirror the hierarchical relationship of each Christian to God. Therefore, any disruption of family unity threatens the very foundations of social and spiritual stability. Luther uses the devil-and-old-woman tale to fortify all three pillars of Protestant society: family, Christian community, and state. Luther's modern witch, whether in the form of a recalcitrant housewife, an envious old woman who bewitches children, or an old hag who helps the devil disrupt marriages, conspires against the family to disturb the social peace.

## Luther and the Modern Witch

Luther's notion that witchcraft undermines the divinely ordained social order coincides with views expressed in Kramer and Sprenger's *Malleus*. Indeed, few of the practices Luther attributes to witches are new; most, including the disruption of marriage and the evil spells witches cast on children, are contained in learned demonologies or drawn from popular belief. Even Luther's admonitions to women to eschew magic and to obey their husbands are anticipated in humanist texts on marriage, such as Desiderius Erasmus's colloquy *Uxor mempsiqamos* (1523) although Erasmus does not specifically refer to witchcraft.[45]

Unlike Kramer and Sprenger, however, Luther largely ignores the witch's more esoteric practices, such as bargaining with the devil and stealing souls for him. By stressing instead the concrete harm done by witches — such as stealing food, spreading disease, and disrupting marriages — Luther feeds the popular fear of witches. In turn, he feeds from it — his didactic and often anecdotal use of the witchcraft theme suggests that the concept of modern witchcraft was already well understood, and that witches were widely feared.

Luther was the first to discuss witchcraft in the context of educating women about their roles as housewives. For Luther, women are informed by the weakness of body and mind they inherit from Eve. Their weakness gives rise to their natural fear of the ills that may befall them or their families; but it also produces, according to Luther, an inherent sense of morality in women. A woman derives her moral power not from her own experience or from her intellectual efforts to distinguish good from evil, but rather from her inner nature. A woman's moral power is therefore — paradoxically — a measure not of strength, but of her hereditary weakness as a woman. Accordingly, she uses her moral power not on her own behalf, but rather in service to her family: its primary purpose is the moral edification of her husband, which a woman accomplishes by playing her role as obedient wife. This includes bearing and raising children, although a mother must not love her children too much, for doing so could tempt her to resort to witchcraft in order to protect them. She must eliminate all egoistic impulses, subordinating herself to the needs of her husband and children; and she must exercise supreme self-discipline in order to overcome her natural fear of harm to her family and herself, trusting completely in God.

Luther adopts the orthodox Catholic premise that women are weak in mind and body, but the consequences he draws from it clash with the views on women presented by Kramer and Sprenger. When Luther refers to a woman's innate female morality and uses the term "entice" ("reytzen") to describe it, he alludes to the orthodox Catholic concept of the evil, uncontrollable power of female sexuality, but redefines it in a positive way. A woman's sublimated sexuality becomes her divinely imbued moral power to educate her husband and children in proper deportment within family and society. The ideal woman is no longer a virginal nun who denies her sexuality, but rather a housewife who uses her sexual power to train her husband and to raise her children to be good neighbors, citizens, and Christians. Luther's feminine ideal was anticipated in the urban literature of the late Middle Ages, especially by city preachers faced with the need to advise the women in their congregations on how to live a pious secular life.[46] But Luther was the first to present the family unit as the primary site of religious self-realization, supplanting in spiritual importance even the monastic life.

With his shift in focus from female carnality to a woman's role as wife and mother, Luther redefines not only the ideal woman, but also her evil counterpart, the female witch. No longer the sexual vampire portrayed by Kramer and Sprenger, the witch is the inverse of Luther's obedient, restrained housewife—a nagging shrew who refuses to obey her husband, a mother who loves her children so obsessively that she resorts to magic on their behalf, or an unmarried old woman who casts spells on children and disrupts marriages. No longer does a woman become a witch by virtue of her innate carnality; now she has a choice in the matter, and when she chooses to become a witch, she renounces the benevolent moral power that is part of her nature.

Luther introduces several new and intriguing elements to the discourse of female witchcraft: (1) women practice witchcraft out of irrational fear and excessive love for their children, both of which are innate female qualities; (2) women have the innate moral power—and duty—as obedient, God-fearing housewives to educate their families in proper social and religious deportment; and (3) women have the power to choose between becoming good housewives and serving the devil. In linking witchcraft to women's roles as housewives, Luther takes the definition of witchcraft a step further than do Kramer and Sprenger. The *Malleus* attacks alleged witches for a wide range of gender-specific activities; Kramer and Sprenger consider all women (except for nuns) potential witches. By contrast, Luther conflates witchcraft with a woman's failure as wife and mother, or with her attempts to sabotage marriage and family. He narrows the focus of attention to women's specific performance as housewives. The family role Luther prescribes for women — the education of husband and children — is distinct from and complementary to the family role of men, partly because it is based on a woman's specifically female (and, by implication, sexual) nature. Luther's concept of witchcraft is designed to educate women to accept their new complementary roles as housewives, and to discipline those who fail to do so by branding them as witches. Luther's views — perhaps modified and mediated by Protestant writers such as Paul Rebhun and Hans Sachs — likely influenced attitudes toward women and witches prevalent among the educated elite who presided over witch trials and determined their outcomes.

# Chapter Four

# Paul Rebhun: Witches
# and Bad Wives

Paul Rebhun (1505–1546) joined the Lutheran church in the 1520s. A native of Austria, he studied in Wittenberg under Philipp Melanchthon, and may have heard Martin Luther's sermons and lectures. He then moved to Saxony, where he taught at the Latin school in Zwickau. He became the Lutheran pastor of Plauen and later of Oelsnitz, and held the post of superintendent for the Lutheran church in the Vogtsberg district. Sometime before 1538, while still a teacher, Rebhun wrote his *Wedding Play Based on the Wedding at Cana* (*Ein Hochzeit Spiel auff die Hochzeit zu Cana*).[1]

Rebhun was motivated in his professional life by a deep desire to spread the teachings of Lutheranism, including Luther's teachings on marriage. According to Luther, women are by nature irrational and prone to their emotions. They are susceptible to an excessive love for their children and to an overblown fear of what may befall them. Only within marriage can a woman overcome her fears and other deficiencies; the ideal housewife submits to the superior wisdom of her husband, entrusting her fate to God. By contrast, women who try to control their own fates — by resorting to witchcraft or other forms of idolatry — reveal the contrary, self-assertive character of shrews. The counterpart to God's fearless housewives are the frightened shrews who embrace witchcraft. Implicit in the Lutheran concept of marriage is the notion that witches and shrewish wives are closely related.

The proverbial shrew (or bad wife) has nebulous origins in medieval folklore. In their *Malleus maleficarum* (1487), Heinrich Kramer and Jakob Sprenger draw on folktales about shrewish wives to illustrate the contrary, unruly nature of witches. Luther uses another folklore figure to depict the modern witch — the old woman who serves the devil by disrupting marriages. In the sixteenth century, these well-known folklore figures — the shrew and the old hag — were combined in the works of

Illustration: Hans Schäuffelein, *Diaper Washer*, ca. 1536 (print). Credit: Kunstsammlungen der Veste Coburg

Paul Rebhun and Hans Sachs to represent the modern witch. Before turning to Rebhun's *Wedding at Cana*, I will briefly examine the folklore figures of the shrewish wife and the meddling old hag.

## The Bad Wife

In this study, I use the terms "shrew" and "bad wife" interchangeably to capture the meaning of the Early New High German term "böses wîp." In the late medieval and early modern periods, the term "böse" had two meanings: (1) "evil" in a calculated or theological sense, and (2) "bad" in the sense of the antonym for "biderbe" (meaning "exercising good or appropriate behavior").[2] Although the "böses wîp" was evil at times, she was primarily characterized by improper, unpleasant behavior. Therefore, the English word "bad" seems to describe her best. The term "wîp" refers to women in general, but the "böses wîp" tale typically centered on marriage. Even when the "böses wîp" was not married, she was usually associated with the violation of behavioral codes for married women.[3] Therefore, the best working translation for the term "böses wîp" seems to be "bad wife," with "shrew" an acceptable alternative.

Dating at least to the thirteenth century, the "bad wife" topos spans the late medieval and early modern eras, addressing tensions in gender relations during both periods. The bad wife is a woman who insists on having her own way. Her obstinacy is characterized by self-centered actions, resistance to her husband, and rebellion against marital codes. In her later manifestations, the bad wife violates social codes extending beyond marriage.

The bad wife first appears in the tale of a beautiful aristocratic woman who refuses to show her husband the proper deference. Despite beatings and incarceration, she remains proud and defiant. Finally, she is abandoned by her friends. In her isolation, she confronts death and repents; the devils that had possessed her are driven out, and she is restored to virtue. She pledges submission to her husband and promises to atone for her sins by devoting herself to reforming other wayward wives.

The story's happy ending vanishes when city burghers adopt the tale in the fourteenth and fifteenth centuries. The bad wife refuses to change her behavior, which leads to her destruction. For example, in Johannes Pauli's collection of folktales *Humor and Seriousness* (*Schimpf und Ernst*, 1533), there is a story called "Evil Adelheid" ("Diu übel Adelheit") in which the bad wife habitually does the opposite of what her husband tells her. After deliberately ignoring his warnings not to go down a dangerous path, she falls into a body of water and drowns.

In the course of the fifteenth century, the bad wife grows ever feistier—she begins to return her husband's blows to the point of beating him up. Sometimes she even takes on the devil himself, fighting off whole armies of his demons. As she seeks to dominate her husband, the "battle for the pants" begins. The bad wife's success in subordinating her husband is symbolized by the transfer of male power symbols (pants, swords, house keys, or money purses) from husband to wife. She begins to "wear the pants in the house," becoming a "she-man" ("Siemann").

Although the unruly aristocratic wife of the Middle Ages was beautiful, the wayward wife of the city burgher is invariably ugly and often old. Her repulsive appearance may serve to highlight the evil of her ways, or to suggest that defiance and disobedience make women unattractive in the eyes of men, no matter how beautiful they may actually be.[4] The bad wife's advanced age may signify her unworthiness at a time when the value of women was increasingly measured in terms of their ability to reproduce. The infertile old woman who has usually outlived her husband appears not only superfluous but dangerous—lacking a male master, she is potentially out of control.

In sixteenth-century vernacular literature, the bad wife increasingly comes to resemble the modern witch. The 1533 edition of Johannes Pauli's *Humor and Seriousness* contains a replication of a woodcut showing witches preparing a magic ointment. Silvia Schmitz suggests that these witches illustrate the evil of the shrewish wives featured in Pauli's selection of stories. Pauli's obsession with the bad wife, she argues, reflects his unease with a changing world and his longing for moral and religious revival. As a Franciscan monk with orthodox views, Pauli sees the licentious behavior of women as both symptomatic of and contributing to growing turmoil in the world. For Pauli, throngs of vicious, lascivious women use their womanly wiles to seduce men. Poisoned by female sexuality, their victims abandon reason and allow their drives to govern their actions, thereby destabilizing the world order. Social and spiritual order can be restored, Pauli believes, only if men control their libidos and distance themselves emotionally from women, or else beat them into submission.[5]

As Schmitz points out, Pauli's notion that women corrupt men through their lascivious behavior resembles the views on witchcraft expressed by Kramer and Sprenger in their *Malleus*. Like Kramer and Sprenger's modern witch, the bad wives in the stories Pauli selects perform magic and are driven by vanity, rebelliousness, and insatiable lust. But Pauli's bad wives remain fundamentally different from the modern witch: their magical abilities derive from folk practices and are not associated with the devil's pact, a vital characteristic of the modern witch. Moreover, Pauli never uses terms for witches to describe the unruly women in his stories, and the 1533 edition of his *Humor and Seriousness* — with its suggestive woodcut of witches preparing a potion — was published after his death. The woodcut of witches could not have been his idea, and is probably attributable to his publisher, Bartholomeus Grüninger.

## The Devil and the Old Woman

The bad wife first meets the modern witch in late fifteenth- and early sixteenth-century versions of a tale called "The Devil and the Old Woman" ("Der Teufel und das alte Weib"). This popular story from the Middle Ages was found in many of the "exempla" collections that provided priests with materials for sermons. In its traditional rendition, the tale opens with an angry Satan venting his frustration over thirty or forty years of vain attempts to disrupt the marriage of a pious couple. In one final attempt, he transforms himself into a wealthy and handsome young man, then waits at a crossroads until an old washerwoman passes by. He makes a deal with her, promising her money or a pair of red shoes if she can sow discord between the pious husband and his wife. The old woman goes to the husband and accuses his wife of infidelity, then goes to the wife with the same mendacious story about her husband. She convinces the wife to use sorcery in order to regain her husband's love, and to cut off a lock of his hair while he sleeps. Meanwhile, she warns the husband that his wife is plotting to kill him in his sleep. A nocturnal confrontation follows in which the wife is severely beaten or killed. In the end, the old woman's lies are usually discovered and she is punished; but in some versions of the tale, she collects her reward from the devil, who is so afraid of her power that he flees. In either case, the tale is designed to illustrate the proverb that a treacherous tongue is worse than the devil, and to ridicule superstition while reinforcing marital fidelity.[6]

The story was widely known in the fifteenth and sixteenth centuries. The Nuremberg Dominican Johann Herolt (*Premptuarium exemplorum*, 1480), the Strasbourg Franciscan Geiler von Kaisersberg (*Das Buch von den Sünden des Munds*, 1518), the Dutch humanist Desiderius Erasmus (*Ecclesiastes*, 1535), and the Lutheran minister Philipp Melanchthon (*Kirchenordnung*, 1552) all tell versions of the story. In the late fifteenth century, the story underwent an important modification in an anonymous drama called *Here Begins a Good Shrovetide Play* (*Hie hebt an ain guot vasnachtspil*, 1494). In this play, a young knight marries a beautiful lady, and Lucifer orders his subordinate Sathanas to destroy the marriage. Sathanas sends a lecherous priest to the young lady, but to no avail. Sathanas then turns for help to an old sorceress ("alte zaubrarin") and makes a pact with her to destroy the marriage. The sorceress goes to the lady and promises her happiness in exchange for food and clothing. The lady agrees, and the sorceress tells her that her husband has taken a mistress. Enraged, the lady announces her intention henceforth to do as she pleases and to give in to the lecherous priest. Her maids restrain her, however, arguing that giving away food and clothing to the old woman would constitute bad household management, and warning her that her honor will be destroyed if she allows the old woman to turn her into a bad wife. Husband and wife are finally reconciled, and an enraged Sathanas demands his money back from the old woman. With the help of three friends, the old sorceress overcomes Sathanas and his army of demons, but is so badly wounded in the fray that she goes to a doctor. The physician who treats her gets into an argument with his wife, who fears that the old woman will not pay him. Enraged by his wife's obstinacy, the doctor gives her the sorceress's shoes and closes the play with a tirade against bad wives.[7]

Two novel elements emerge in this version of the devil-and-old-woman tale. First, the hag does more than merely spread lies: she persuades the wife to mismanage her household and to become a shrew by asserting herself against her husband. The moral of the story is no longer directed against lies and slander, but rather against disobedience, household mismanagement, and other practices of bad wives. The other new element in the play is its emphasis on the old woman's sorcery, which is no longer the love sorcery found in earlier versions of the devil-and-old-woman tale. The old woman seems to know the secrets of learned magic; for example, she looks up magic words in books. She meets with other sorceresses to conjure up the devil, then defeats the devil and his minions through her powers of magic. These events refer to a witches' Sabbath — suggesting a prior pact with the devil — and the practice of harmful sorcery, typical of the modern witch. Called "unhuld" and "zaubrarin" (common terms for the witch), the old woman combines key attributes of modern witchcraft — harmful sorcery, the devil's pact, and the witches' Sabbath — with the intentions of a bad wife.

Over the course of the sixteenth century, the devil-and-old-woman tale continued to evolve, with Satan gradually turning into a "marriage devil" ("Eheteufel") who specialized in disrupting wedded life.[8] Usually, the story still ended in reconciliation between husband and wife, but the devil dropped his disguise as a young man, and the old woman no longer dabbled in folk magic and love sorcery, revealing instead the diabolical powers of a witch. The story began to be used in homiletic and other didactic literature to illustrate how Satan tempts married people, and how they can overcome him by ignoring the lies of his servant the witch. Parts of this tale were inserted into plays on marriage. Perhaps most important, the confrontation between the old hag and the wife was greatly expanded, providing a forum for discussing appropriate female behavior.

Elements of the devil-and-old-woman tale surfaced in sixteenth-century witch trials. In their confessions, many accused witches reported that they first encountered the devil disguised as an attractive young man who promised them a pair of red shoes in exchange for sex. However, the shoes never materialized, or else turned to dust by morning. In the Middle Ages, shoes were a common form of payment to prostitutes, and shoes made of red saffron leather were the most expensive, usually reserved for festivals. Although prostitutes were rarely accused of witchcraft, the female witch was known to engage in a special form of prostitution, the sale to the devil of her body and soul in exchange for money or shoes. During interrogation, an accused witch's confession to receiving shoes was considered proof positive of her pact with the devil. The motifs of red shoes and the devil's disguise as a young man could have been introduced either by the accused or by her interrogators — both were almost certainly familiar with the popular story. The appearance of these motifs in witch trial records suggests the importance of the devil-and-old-woman tale in spreading the concept of the modern witch.

Two Protestant writers were among the first to use and develop the changing characters of the devil and the old woman: Paul Rebhun in his *Wedding at Cana* (1538) and Hans Sachs in his Shrovetide play *The Devil with the Old Woman* (*Der teüffel mit dem alten Weyb*, 1545). Their modifications of the devil-and-old-woman tale rapidly caught on; plots making use of the marriage devil and the old hag can be found in Jaspar von Gennep's *Susanna* (1552), Leonhard Culmann's *Isaac und Rebecca* (before 1559), Andreas Musculus's *Wider den Eheteufel* (1556), and Peter Praetorius's *Historia von der Hochzeit Isaac vnd Rebeccae* (1559). These adaptations of the devil-and-old-woman tale were usually dramatizations, many of them Protestant school plays designed for the edification of children or of the laity in general. The modern witch appears in them more often than in any other sixteenth-century genre, suggesting the importance of the devil-and-old-woman tale in popularizing the concept of the modern witch.

What made the devil-and-old-woman tale so suitable for representing the modern witch? Why did a tale originating in the Middle Ages so fascinate Protestant writers? With these questions in mind, I now turn to Paul Rebhun's depiction of the old woman in his *Wedding at Cana*.

*Rebhun's Evangelical Use of Theater*

As a Protestant pastor, teacher, and writer, Paul Rebhun was devoted to spreading Luther's version of the Christian gospel. His dramatic creations reveal his evangelical purpose: all are designed to teach proper Christian behavior in the context of marriage, Christian community, and state. Rebhun based his best-known play, *Susanna* (1535), on the apocryphal story by the same name, and his *Wedding at Cana* contains three characters from the apocryphal work Tobias (the devil Asmodes, the angel Raphael, and Tobias himself). In drawing on the Apocrypha for his stories and characters, Rebhun follows a suggestion made by Luther. In the prefaces to his translations of the Apocrypha, Luther draws a distinction between the historical factuality he ascribes to the Old and New Testaments and what he says is the fictional character of the Apocrypha. As fiction ("geticht") rather than fact ("historie"), the Apocrypha provide useful parables about proper Christian conduct in family and community. According to Luther, the ancient Hebrews used the Apocrypha in plays to teach proper comportment to their young, a practice that influenced the Greeks in their development of early drama. For Luther, drama is historically rooted in religious instruction and therefore capable of transmitting God's word through prophecy ("prophetie").[9]

Rebhun accepted Luther's distinction between biblical "historie" and fictional "geticht." Although his *Wedding at Cana* is based on John 2:1– 10, in his preface to the play he calls elements of it "geticht" (such as the role of Maria—Jesus' mother Mary—as the bride's foster mother). Rebhun says that such "fictitious" elements are designed to "provide a good lesson."[10] In fact, his play was intended for devotional reading as much as for staging; as Paul Casey notes, its long didactic monologues resemble a sermon collection more than a drama.[11] Rebhun closely followed Luther in designing a play that would convey the word of God through "prophetie."

Rebhun was deeply indebted to Lutheranism not only for the evangelical basis of his play, but also for its subject matter — proper Christian behavior in marriage. Drawing on Luther's treatise *On Married Life (Vom ehelichen Leben*, 1522) and on Paul's injunctions on marital relations in Ephesians 5:21–33, Rebhun summarized his views on marriage in a popular sermon known as the *Wedding Sermon on Domestic Peace (Hochzeitspredigt vom Hausfried*, 1546). In it, Rebhun reduces harmonious relations between husband and wife to a simple formula: "Husband, love your wife; wife, obey your husband; this creates domestic peace."[12] Rebhun derives his formula for good marital relations directly from the Pauline doctrine that female obedience as well as male love and patience in marriage are ordained by God, adding the Protestant stipulation that these dictates must be obeyed willingly, and that each individual is responsible directly to God for doing so. Domestic peace, Rebhun reasons, is the basis for social peace as well as peace with God, because a peaceful marriage in which the wife obeys her husband will produce children who grow up to be peaceful neighbors who obey secular and divine authority.[13] His thinking reflects Luther's (and Paul's) notion that a wife's obedience to her husband corresponds to her husband's obedience to secular authority and to the obedience of Christians to God. The family hierarchy both mirrors and reproduces the social and religious order; therefore, any disruption of family is a serious threat to society.

For Luther, a wife's duty to obey her husband is no more important to a successful marriage than a husband's duty to love his wife. Drawing on Ephesians 5:28, Luther calls on a husband to love his wife like his own flesh, an obligation that he sees as primary and unconditional because of Eve's origins in Adam's rib.[14] A husband is just as responsible for domestic peace as is his wife, and evil can find its way into a household through either partner. Accordingly, in the preface to his translation of the apocryphal book Tobias, Luther interprets the devil Asmodes not as a marriage devil, but more broadly as a house devil ("Hausteufel") bent on disrupting the household as a whole.

By contrast, Rebhun regards a wife's obedience to her husband as more important than a man's conjugal love. "For obedience," he argues, "is placed upon the female sex as punishment [for the Fall]. . . . Love, however, is not placed upon man as punishment, but rather to honor and reward preceding obedience."[15] A wife's obedience to her husband is, in Rebhun's view, a primary, unconditional obligation stemming from Eve's original sin, whereas a man's conjugal love is a secondary, contingent factor derived from obedience as its reward. As closely as Rebhun follows Luther's teachings otherwise, he locates the devil's disruptive power in the problematic nature of women alone, not within each individual Christian.

Rebhun sees the devil at work in women who seek equality with men, thereby undermining God's order and threatening hierarchies of church and state. In his *Sermon on Domestic Peace*, Rebhun recapitulates an argument that he says women make to prove the exalted origins of their sex: because Eve emerged from the flesh (Adam's rib), whereas Adam was created from mere dust, the Bible shows that women are superior to men.[16] Rebhun dismisses such arguments as an affront to God reflecting female hubris. "Because they invert His [God's] order in this way," Rebhun charges, "[women] are trying to make a better job of it than He did Himself."[17] His *Wedding at Cana* is specifically designed to show that women's demands for equality with men amount to a dangerous reversal of gender roles bordering on sacrilege.

In the play, a poor young couple plans to marry, but finds itself short of money for the wedding. The groom cannot buy the necessary food and wine, and the bride cannot afford suitable attire. On the advice of two pious older role models (Tobias, the bride's employer, and Maria, mother of Jesus and foster mother of the bride), the groom decides to leave the question of money up to God, and the bride contents herself with the clothes she has and the adornment of her own natural beauty.

Then the marriage devil appears to disrupt the impending wedding. He is confronted by Raphael, the guardian angel of marriage, who beats him up and drives him off. Undaunted, the devil enlists the support of an old woman, but Raphael finds his own human helpmates in Maria and Tobias. On behalf of the devil, the old woman seeks out the bride and tries to convince her not to marry, arguing that marriage will mean her enslavement to her husband. Maria confronts the old woman and convinces the bride to pledge obedience to her husband. The old woman then turns to the groom, who refuses to listen to her. At the ensuing wedding, Jesus marries the young couple and rewards the new husband for his faith in God by changing water into much-needed wine.

Two minor episodes in the play help to define gender roles. First, the disciple Simon arrives too late for the wedding ceremony, because he has had to help his wife with the housework. He is ridiculed and made to sit with the women. In the second episode (which Rebhun relegated to an appendix because he thought it too long to include but too important to omit), Tobias instructs the groom on marriage. He warns him to dominate his wife or else forfeit his manhood by fomenting female rebellion.

The old woman in Rebhun's play is called "Zauberin," "incantatrix," and "wettermacherin," all common terms for the modern witch. She has given herself over to Satan, who exercises complete control over her. "Whatever I inspire her to do [*thu blasen ein*] she does splendidly," the devil declares.[18] She is an expert in magical practices, but her most important characteristic as a modern witch is her bondage to the devil, which is more explicit and insidious than in earlier versions of the devil-and-old-woman tale.

In the original devil-and-old-woman story, the old hag maligns each partner's marital fidelity in an effort to instigate a quarrel, a tactic that leaves unquestioned (and may even reinforce) the notion that a proper wife should submit to her husband. By contrast, the old woman in Rebhun's play seeks to disrupt the impending marriage by challenging its very basis. She openly questions the central tenet of Protestant marriage, a wife's obedience to her husband. Her attack on the institution of marriage — and its concomitant gender norms — is direct, immediate, and threatening. Rebhun adapts the devil-and-old-woman tale to his purposes by taking it to its logical extreme: he makes the old woman a witch who embraces the practices of disobedient, self-assertive shrews and encourages the young bride to resist and subjugate her husband-to-be.

### Long-Suffering Obedience

Rebhun's play begins with Tobias's advice to the bridegroom on disciplining women. According to Tobias, there are four kinds of women: the first is endowed with divine virtue and readily obeys her husband; the second is willing but foolish, and requires good-natured nudging to keep her in place; and the third is an obstinate shrew whom the husband must educate through occasional beatings and the example of his own reasonable behavior. These three kinds of women make good wives.

The fourth kind of woman makes a bad wife, because she can never be beaten into submission. Such women "always go against the flow in order to get their way in the devil's name," Tobias warns.[19] The bad wife defies divine and natural law by "going against the flow," and her willfulness ties her to the devil. Beating one devil out of her, Tobias says, will only beat nine more into her (reminiscent of Luther's admonition that bad wives cannot be saved through beatings). Devoted as she is to the devil, a bad wife will forever undermine marital peace.

Rebhun's marriage devil strives to undermine marital relations by turning women into bad wives. "I goad the wife into rejecting the obedience she owes," he declares, "and instill in her a rebellious spirit."[20] As the devil's agent, the old witch attempts to make a bad wife out of the young bride by turning her against marriage. She points out that married women face the excruciating pain of childbirth and the endless misery of raising children while dealing with lazy, dishonest servants.[21] But the worst thing about marriage, says the witch, "is that the wife must obey her husband in all matters, allowing him alone to be master."[22] The witch reserves most of her invective for the unquestioning obedience a married woman owes to her husband.

Claiming that a woman's subservience in marriage is detrimental to her well-being, the witch offers to teach the young bride how to preserve her vitality in order to grow as old as she herself is. The witch urges the bride to make her husband sexually dependent on her through love magic. She tells her to do as she pleases and never to fear her husband. She should manipulate her husband, says the witch, by giving him the impression that she occasionally does what he wants, but not always; and she should ignore his criticisms, but mercilessly castigate him whenever he himself misbehaves. When he beats her, she should fight back. Even if she is severely injured, the witch points out, in the end her resistance will exhaust her husband, and she will assume her rightful position as "Dr. She-man" ("Doctor Sieman"), master of the household. The only sensible goal for women in marriage, argues the witch, is to "finally become masters, and to do as they please. Otherwise," she warns, "a woman would have to live in fear."[23]

Implicit in the witch's arguments is her assumption that the sexes are equal. According to the witch, marriage is a daily battle of the sexes in which neither side has the initial advantage: if husband and wife have equally strong egos (and there is no reason to suppose that they do not), then neither will voluntarily surrender to the other. The question of dominance in marriage is to be decided not by the divine order of things or the ostensibly weaker nature of women, but rather by the outcome of the concrete, everyday struggle between husbands and wives.

The bride rejects the witch's viewpoint for two reasons. She points out that a wife depends on her husband to support her, which gives him economic leverage over her. Moreover, she says, men are physically stronger than women and can force them to submit. The bride is so fearful of being beaten by her prospective husband that she vows to do anything to please him.

It soon becomes apparent, however, that both the witch and the bride are mistaken. Neither is capable of conducting a rational discussion about marriage, because both are ruled by emotion rather than reason. The witch argues from a position of female egoism grounded in a will to power, and the bride is motivated primarily by fear. In fact, the bride's very fear proves that women are inferior to men, refuting the witch's egalitarian assumptions: unlike her prospective husband, who rationally assesses and confidently dismisses the witch's appeals to emotion, the bride carefully considers them out of fear. Due to her anxious, emotional nature as a woman, the bride lacks the rational faculties needed to properly assess the witch's arguments and to arrive at the appropriate conclusions on her own.

She is rescued by Maria, who scolds the witch for troubling the bride with selfish, egalitarian notions that violate God's law. Instead of backing down, the witch challenges Maria on her own turf, insisting that female equality is consistent with church doctrine. "I do not contradict God's word," she declares, "for I have heard sermons where it was said that man and wife should be one body. I take this to mean that mastery is as proper to women as to men, and that men have taken it by force. This is intolerable, because both of them [men and women] are supposed to be free."[24]

With this argument, the witch touches on a difficult subject in Protestant theology, the notion that husband and wife are equal before God. In his *Sermon on the State of Being Married (Ein Sermon von dem ehlichen Stand,* 1519), Martin Luther compares the relationship between husband and wife to that between God and mankind as one flesh through Christ, an analogy taken directly from Paul (Ephesians 5:21–33).[25] Luther interprets the equality of the sexes to mean that husband and wife are interdependent; in accordance with Pauline doctrine, he assigns different duties and occupations to each gender, establishing a gender-based hierarchy within marriage. But in his treatise *On Married Life* (*Vom ehelichen Leben*, 1522), Luther writes that domestic labor (traditionally women's work and considered of inferior value) is not demeaning for a husband, because any work that is part of marriage is pleasing to God if performed out of conjugal love. "When a father proceeds to wash diapers or to perform some other degrading task for his child," Luther says, " . . . God with all his angels and creatures is smiling, not because he is washing diapers, but because he is doing so in the [Christian] faith."[26]

By invoking pastoral authority for her argument that the sexes are equal, Rebhun's witch points out the tension in Luther's writings between his advocacy of a gender hierarchy and his notions of gender equality. In the early phase of the Reformation, this tension had contradictory effects on its followers. On the one hand, notions of gender equality in some of Paul's and Luther's teachings gave activist Protestant women — such as Katharina Schütz and Argula von Stauffen — the license to speak out publicly on behalf of the new creed.[27] On the other hand, the gender equality implicit in Lutheran teachings made many men very nervous. Just after the publication of Luther's *On Married Life* in 1522, the ducal counsel Diedrich von Werthern reported from Nuremberg to the Duke of Saxony that it had offended some Protestant men in the city. "It would not be good for us poor husbands," he remarked, "if bad wives read it."[28]

They soon had little to worry about. As the Protestant movement established its own regulations and institutions, notions of gender equality fell by the wayside. In Rebhun's play, they have lost any semblance of legitimacy: voiced by the witch — a representative of the devil — they are not even worthy of rebuttal. Maria refuses to debate the witch, dismissing her with the words, "You interpret things to suit yourself but fail to see the wider context."[29] Obedience is the only legitimate precept for women in marriage, and Maria will discuss it only with those who will listen. The witch does not qualify, because — like bad wives everywhere — she makes no effort to discern God's truth. Maria chases the witch away, then returns to lecture the bride about marriage.

Maria stresses the importance of female obedience within marriage, arguing that a wife's submission to her husband is the cornerstone of family, society, and God's holy order. But such pious considerations fail to allay the bride's overwhelming fear of being beaten by her husband. Maria admits that marriage entails hardship — men may be blind and selfish, and they may beat their wives without just cause. In some cases, a wife may report an abusive husband to the authorities; usually, however, she must endure his brutality, hoping to change his behavior through love and patience, and leaving her fate and his punishment in the hands of God.

This formula for dealing with abuse corresponds to the Lutheran demand that women suffer in silence, obeying their husbands and wordlessly enduring whatever injuries their husbands may inflict. According to Luther, each Christian owes obedience to God's representatives in family and society, who in turn answer only to God. In case of abuse by an authority figure, the Christian has no right to protest, but must patiently endure mistreatment, trusting in divine Providence. For Rebhun, women best exemplify this doctrine of "long-suffering obedience" ("leidender Gehorsam"), because they are utterly subservient to male authority on every level: the husband, father, or brother rules over the women within his household, speaks on their behalf before secular authority, and represents God to them in His direct image. A woman's long-suffering obedience to her husband is the key to preserving social peace, because marriage is both a religious arena for demonstrating steadfast Christian faith and a secular arena in which social relations (including deference to authority) are taught and learned.[30]

Rebhun's play redefines good Christian relationships not only between men and women, but also among women themselves. The witch is more than just an advocate of improper marital conduct in women: she represents a kind of relationship among women no longer deemed socially acceptable. In the sixteenth century, many wives visited female practitioners of folk magic in search of love potions to ensure their husbands' fidelity or magical assistance to prevent their spouses from beating them.[31] Lyndal Roper reports that brides in Augsburg touched the doors of their husbands' homes and placed ritual items in the wedding bed to ensure their own dominance in marriage.[32] By denigrating such practices and discouraging women from going to female practitioners of folk magic, Protestantism deprived them of some of the few means they had of coping with a system of marriage that afforded them little or no protection.[33]

In Rebhun's play, the bride turns for counsel and support not to the traditional wise woman (in the form of the rebellious old witch), but rather to a model of Christian comportment — Maria, mother of Jesus. As an older, experienced housewife, Maria teaches the young bride how to conform to the new Protestant ethic of long-suffering obedience, partly through her own example. When Maria approaches her son Jesus for help with the wedding plans, she is rudely rebuffed; but — demonstrating the proper ethic of long-suffering obedience — she refuses to let his insolence bother her. Assuming the proper deference toward men, she assures herself that he must have his reasons.[34] In the end, Jesus does help out with the wedding by turning water into wine, which shows the wisdom of Maria's unquestioning deference to him. She faithfully attends to the duties of a housewife throughout the play and instructs the bride to do likewise. Unlike the traditional Mary of the Catholic church, Maria no longer intercedes between the faithful and their God as the protectress of young brides and women in labor. Instead of alleviating the pangs of childbirth, she justifies them in the name of Eve's sin. As foster mother to the young bride, Maria performs the duty of a Protestant mother by imparting the virtue of long-suffering obedience to her foster daughter.

### The "She-Man" and Manliness

After Maria chases her away, the witch is replaced by the disciple Simon as the most prominent symbol of gender role reversal in the play. Simon misses the wedding ceremony because "he is tied up with women's business," as his fellow disciple Andreas puts it. "His wife ordered him to do something around the house," Andreas says scornfully. When Simon arrives, he admits to the offense, but offers an explanation. "I had to rock the child for her awhile," he says, "because we don't have many servants."[35] Unable to afford domestic help, Simon assists his wife with the child before leaving for the wedding. Luther describes such compassionate male behavior motivated by conjugal love as perfectly acceptable in the eyes of God; by contrast, he says, those who ridicule a husband for helping out with the children fail to see his charitable motives and speak for the devil.[36]

Rebhun does not follow Luther in this matter. Instead of making Simon a model of Protestant male comportment, Rebhun holds him up to ridicule. "Your name befits your deed," taunts Andreas in a punning allusion to "Siemann," the farcical "she-man" character who reverses gender roles. The bridegroom disdainfully tells Simon to go sit with the women, who "always try to be she-men, too."[37] This was harsh punishment and a severe insult, because a sex-segregated seating arrangement (which Rebhun carefully laid out in his stage directions for the fourth act) was an important part of urban wedding rituals in the sixteenth century, one that highlighted the inequality of the sexes and their different marital roles.[38] Revealing his effeminacy, Simon professes indifference. "I get along well with women," he shrugs, "and allow them to rule by night and day."[39]

The women welcome Simon into their midst, because — as the bridegroom points out — they share his she-man character; by nature rebellious, women aspire to male privilege. The effeminate, submissive Simon is the male counterpart to the female witch in Rebhun's play: both are she-men who reverse gender roles and disturb the institution of marriage. By inverting the marital order, the unruly wife and the submissive husband undermine the foundations of the secular and divine hierarchies ordained by God.

The she-man and the witch are burlesque characters taken from Shrovetide plays, which Rebhun identifies with farce ("possen"). Early modern farce often refers to the ambiguity of a world turned upside down, a traditional theme in carnival plays that was frequently represented as gender role reversal, with men dressing up and performing as unruly wives. Such carnival rituals functioned to enforce normative behavior by vilifying or ridiculing social and gender deviancy.[40] In its normative usage, the she-man figure served to warn men not to relax control over the household.[41] For urban artisans in some German cities, marital order was closely tied to social and economic success: only after becoming a master could an artisan marry, and establishing a household was the condition for full citizenship. The inability to establish and maintain a household led to symbolic punishments representing loss of control over women and thereby loss of manhood. For example, male bankrupts in Augsburg "could be made to suffer the indignity of sitting among the womenfolk at weddings, a powerful denigration of their manhood," according to Lyndal Roper.[42]

Similarly, Rebhun uses the Simon episode in his *Wedding at Cana* to castigate men who have lost control over their households. "As a man," Tobias advises the bridegroom, "you should observe moderation in a manly fashion in accordance with your station so that you keep the upper hand."[43] The most important thing to remember about manhood is to keep firm control over the women in one's household. In Rebhun's view, Simon's willingness to help his wife around the house reflects his weakness and subordination to women, costing him his reputation as a man and turning him into an effeminate she-man. Worse yet, his laxity toward women has negative repercussions for the entire community, because it encourages disobedience and misbehavior in other wives. "Such humble behavior causes much harm," Tobias declares. "For God's order is reversed and this also makes trouble for others because such examples encourage the arrogance of bad wives."[44]

Using the virtuous Tobias as his spokesman, Rebhun defines masculinity in terms of the ability to control one's emotions, especially love and anger. Tobias tells the bridegroom that self-control is "particularly . . . a male strength . . . and . . . the task of men."[45] Men are endowed with the strength to control their emotions and should cultivate this ability. By contrast, women have no such ability; in order to control their destructive impulses, they must accept the rational guidance of their loving husbands. Accordingly, Maria propagates the need for women to abandon their fears and submit to the superior wisdom of men. Both male self-control and female obedience are necessary to control chaotic emotional forces and ensure domestic peace. If either is missing, disorder ensues: the bride's fear of beatings by her prospective husband is exploited by the witch to raise doubts about her impending marriage, and Simon's emergence as a she-man in performing household chores for his wife leads to the disruption of the wedding ceremony.

In Ephesians 5:33, Paul stresses the need for husbands to love their wives, and Luther goes so far as to suggest that God smiles on husbands who perform household chores out of conjugal love.[46] Rebhun echoes Paul's enjoinder to husbands to love their wives, but uses the Simon episode in his play to put it into perspective. By helping his wife with the housework, Simon makes the mistake of loving her too much. Like a woman, he is overwhelmed by excessive emotion, displaying a lack of manly self-control. The Simon episode is a warning to men not to take their Pauline duty to love their wives to excess, but rather — as Tobias urges — to "observe moderation in a manly fashion" by restraining their feelings through the use of the rational judgment God has bestowed upon them as men.

Although Simon is ridiculed, he is tolerated, whereas his female counterpart — the witch — is chased away by Maria. Female gender transgression is more of a threat than its male counterpart, because the witch aspires to the level of men, whereas Simon displays no such unseemly arrogance. To the contrary, as a she-man he descends to the level of women, an act so blatantly foolish and contrary to self-interest that it seems ridiculous — even the waiter who seats him at the women's table calls it "a good joke."[47] Simon's gender role transgression is treated as

something "that everyone can laugh at . . . with nothing more to it,"
Rebhun's definition of a farce ("possen") in the preface to his play.[48]
Although Simon can be lightly dismissed, his counterpart the witch is no
laughing matter. A witch must swiftly be eliminated, because she aspires
to a status above her natural condition: the power and privilege reserved
to men in accordance with their position in the divinely ordered scheme
of things.

*Economic Roles and Social Peace*

Jesus' miraculous transformation of water into wine is tied metaphor-
ically in *The Wedding at Cana* to marriage: obedience to God and trust in
divine Providence, Rebhun says in the play's conclusion, transforms the
troubled waters of married life into sweet wine. Marriage stands for
worldly tribulations of all kinds in a society increasingly informed by a
money economy. Lack of money provides the devil with the opening he
needs to tempt the young couple. In the course of the play, however,
money increasingly becomes the bridegroom's concern alone. Providing
for household needs — such as food and wine at the wedding — is associated with male activity in the public sphere.

Initially, the lack of money poses an equal problem for both bride and
groom. In the second act, the bride worries that she cannot afford a
wedding dress. "As you know," she tells Maria, "I ought to have pretty
clothes that befit the household, as is the common custom these days."[49]
The bride cannot afford to dress the part she is to play in her new social
role as a married woman. Through her moral and social conduct, a
sixteenth-century woman was supposed to represent the honor of her
household ("Hausêre") to the outside world. The bride in *The Wedding
at Cana* needs the proper attire and accessories in order to display her
"Hausêre" before the community. "I would gladly have bought a pearl
necklace," she sighs, "and other things that are good to wear these days
for the honor of the household."[50]

The woman with her dress and strand of pearls was a public symbol of
domestic prosperity. In the cities of early modern Germany, the social
status of a household came to be measured in terms of the clothes and
other items its members wore in public. Some merchants, artisans, and
piecework entrepreneurs could now afford luxury items previously reserved to the aristocracy. Luxurious clothes, hitherto a measure of social
rank, now became an index of prosperity. In order to halt this democratic
trend and to reinforce distinctions by birth and station, sumptuary codes

were strictly enforced in early modern cities. Protestant authorities supported such restrictions, because they saw luxury as a sinful indulgence and a hindrance to true spiritual devotion. Accordingly, the bride in Rebhun's play is torn between conflicting value systems. "I therefore worried for a long time about whether it would be good for me to borrow clothes to wear for the sake of honor," she says. "I would not want them otherwise."[51] Although the bride feels she must try to conform to social expectations by wearing the proper wedding attire, she distinguishes these materialistic externalities from her own sense of self-worth. Through the voice of Maria, Rebhun advises her to forget about outward appearances altogether and to concentrate instead on obeying her husband. The solution to a Christian woman's problems with money is to rise above them. She should focus instead on household matters (such as pleasing her husband), allowing men to take care of such mundane matters as money.

The bridegroom arrives at a parallel solution to the problem of his insolvency. At first he consults his steward, whose advice to penniless young people is to postpone marriage. But the bridegroom rejects this very practical advice, because God commands men to marry "in order to avoid scandal and whoring."[52] Next, the bridegroom tries to borrow money, but is rebuffed; speculators who were eager to bankroll him when he had sufficient collateral funds now offer him little and demand rapid repayment. "Nobody lends money anymore," the bridegroom sighs, "unless assured in advance of profit."[53] Bemoaning the decline of charitable love for one's neighbor, he laments a world gone awry. "Everything ordained by God," he complains, "must always meet with great resistance and hindrance here [on earth] among us."[54]

But because God has commanded men to marry, the bridegroom decides to hold the wedding despite his lack of money, trusting in God to provide the wine he cannot afford. "Because He Himself has ordained the state [of marriage]," the young man declares, "then I will place the matter in His hands. He will give it His blessing."[55] Like his bride — who trusts in her husband to provide for her — the bridegroom puts his faith in a higher authority (God) to provide for him and his household. His faith is rewarded: Jesus attends the wedding and, after observing the young man's steadfast faith in God, changes water into the wine needed for the wedding.

When Jesus enters the play, the bride all but disappears. Jesus focuses his attention on the bridegroom, giving him a wedding present and putting his faith to the test. The man — not the woman — directly relates to God (through Christ) and wins His approval. Similarly, it is the man — and not the woman — who must pay for the wedding, set up the household, and feed his family. But not even he is fully allowed to assert himself in this area. Instead, he must accept his own economic impotence and trust in the higher authority of God.

Rebhun offers here an ideologically charged solution — passive acceptance — to the rising problem of urban poverty in sixteenth-century Germany. Luther espouses the same solution in his treatise *On Married Life*. Declaring that men should marry by the time they are twenty and women by eighteen, Luther advises them to leave it up to God to provide the means to establish a household and support a family. "God makes children," he says, "He will surely feed them as well."[56] Luther's advocacy of passive trust in divine Providence seems designed to pacify the poor and to defuse conflicts arising from economic change. By advocating a similar formula for social peace in his *Wedding at Cana*, Rebhun obviates the need to identify forces of conflict at work in the public sphere.

Instead, Rebhun transfers conflict from the public sphere of competing social and economic interests to the private sphere of competition between the sexes. In his play, he identifies the main danger to the family, Christian community, and God's holy order as the female demand for equality, which he associates with the figure of the modern witch. Men must control their own destructive impulses — as well as those of women — by using their God-given reason and trusting in divine Providence. But because women have no such capacity for rational self-control, they must look to their husbands for guidance, obeying them without question. Only then will order prevail in family and society, in accordance with God's plan. Rebhun's central formula for social peace depends primarily on the long-suffering obedience of women.

### God's Precarious Peace

Despite its importance in Protestant doctrine, the ethic of long-suffering obedience seems precarious in Rebhun's play. Luther teaches that obedience to God is ultimately up to each individual Christian alone. But the bride is clearly incapable of banishing temptation and embracing her duty to obey her husband without outside help. In fact, it takes a concerted effort by Tobias, Maria, and the guardian angel Raphael to rid the community of the witch and to turn the bride to God. The involvement of so many characters suggests the inadequacy of voluntary female obedience as a means of ensuring social peace.

Moreover, in citing sermons to support her claim that women are equal to men, the witch highlights a contradiction within the Protestant theology of marriage itself. Although husband and wife are spiritual equals who must love each other compassionately, they must also arrange themselves in hierarchical order. Rebhun's witch offers a detailed, realistic description of gender inequality and its injustice, and Rebhun's Simon is the model of a husband who behaves compassionately by helping his wife with housework, as advocated by Luther himself. But Simon is roundly ridiculed, and the witch is shown to be a diabolical menace; in using ridiculous or diabolical characters to present the case for gender parity, Rebhun undermines its validity. Still, Rebhun allows voices of protest to be heard — suggesting that they were loud enough in the Protestant community to need to be addressed.

If Rebhun's stand on gender parity in marriage seems in some respects harsher than Luther's, one should remember that Rebhun no longer needed to defend the state of marriage against the former preeminence of monastic life, and that as a pastor and superintendent of schools he was responsible for the spiritual guidance of an increasingly regimented and institutionalized community. Following Luther's lead in denouncing the series of peasant revolts from 1524 to 1526, the Protestant church emerged in the second half of the sixteenth century as an organization that firmly supported secular authority, vigorously condemned any form of social rebellion, and absolutely refused to tolerate other religious groups. In a time of ongoing social and religious upheaval, the peace remained fragile, and a stable family order seemed to Rebhun and others the best way to preserve it. The marital relationship in particular became the paradigm for the relationship between the ruler and the ruled in the centralized absolutist form of government that emerged in early modern Germany. In order to establish stable marital relations, Protestant clergymen placed tremendous demands on their congregations, requiring extreme self-control on the part of men and unquestioning obedience to their husbands on the part of women.

The strict new codes of behavior introduced in Protestant communities caused severe social strains. Recent studies suggest that as gender roles changed in the fifteenth and sixteenth centuries, marriage became a field of conflict.[57] Unfortunately, we have no information regarding Rebhun's pastoral involvement in marriage counseling, and no study has been done of marital conflicts in the Zwickau area, where Rebhun worked most of his life. Lyndal Roper has shown for Augsburg, however, that marital relationships in the sixteenth century were under stress, with conflicts centering on access to household money and the distribution of household work. These conflicts — which often led to wife beating — suggest that men and women had difficulty adjusting to their new marital and economic roles. And Augsburg's Protestant pastors seem to have been rather inept in counseling quarreling couples, usually resorting to sermons on the need for female obedience. Although such efforts failed to resolve marital conflicts, they succeeded in reinforcing a new order of gender. Rebhun's *Wedding at Cana* can be seen as part of this process of teaching men and women to conform to new gender roles.

In his adaptation of the devil-and-old-woman tale, Rebhun incorporates Luther's image of witches as bad wives who undermine God's holy order. Unlike Luther's witch, however, the old woman in Rebhun's play is no longer primarily a practitioner of magic, but rather the embodiment of female disobedience and inappropriate gender behavior. Her notions of gender equality are diabolical and therefore forbidden; women are supposed to obey male authority without question, passively enduring any suffering that strict obedience might entail. Because the witch challenges this principle, she is driven away. Through the characters of the witch and the male she-man, willfulness, impulsiveness, and other forms of self-assertion and emotional expression are branded as excessive and effeminate. Men have the responsibility of controlling them not only within themselves, but also within the women in their households.

# Chapter Five

# Hans Sachs: The Witch Lurking Within

ANS SACHS (1494–1576), a master shoemaker and Meister-
singer in Nuremberg, joined the Lutheran church in the
1520s. For years he studied Reformation theology, acquiring
several collections of Luther's sermons.[1] His works show the influence of
the new Protestant teachings and of his social background as a Nuremberg artisan. Although there is no evidence that Sachs was familiar with
Rebhun's *Wedding at Cana* (1538), many of his works — like Rebhun's —
were devoted to defining the new gender relationships that were emerging in family and society. His concepts of the proper housewife and the
female witch provide insight into sixteenth-century attempts by educated urban men not only to discipline women, but also to control the
impulsive, self-assertive behavior that was associated with women —
even when it appeared in men.

One of Sachs's favorite subjects was the bad wife. Like the witch in
Rebhun's *Wedding at Cana*, the bad wife in Sachs's works strives to undermine the divinely ordained hierarchy of the sexes by subjugating the
husband and making him do the housework. Sachs's bad wife displays
vices such as gluttony and a malicious tongue; her worst quality — listed
first in Sachs's poem "The Twelve Characteristics of a Bad Wife" ("Die
zwölff eygenschafft eynes bosshaftigen weybs," 1530) — is her laziness
and incompetence as a homemaker. In particular, she makes her husband
pay for household items that she could produce herself were she dili-
gent.[2] Managing the household economy assumes central importance
for Sachs in defining the unruly wife and assigning gender roles within
marriage.

Sachs's emphasis on frugality in the household may well reflect his
concern for the urban artisan, whose situation worsened dramatically in
the late fifteenth and early sixteenth centuries. International commerce
enhanced the economic and political power of merchants, allowing them

ILLUSTRATION: Hans Baldung Grien, *Two Weather Witches*, 1523. Credit: Städelsches
Kunstinstitut Frankfurt, photograph (c) Ursula Edelmann, Frankfurt.

to expand a new form of production, the piecework (or putting-out) system. In the piecework system, an entrepreneur (a person with capital, usually a merchant or a successful master artisan) provided raw materials to a skilled artisan and paid him by the piece for the finished product. Piecework entrepreneurs determined the number of items produced as well as their unit price, which gave them growing leverage over the market for the products of artisans. The guilds (or, in Nuremberg's case, the patrician city council) conceded partial control over wages and prices to the piecework entrepreneurs. Through low wages and economies of scale, the new enterprises were able to undercut the prices charged by traditional master artisans, who found themselves in a growing battle for survival not only with the piecework entrepreneurs, but also with each other.[3]

In Sachs's Nuremberg, the threat from piecework enterprises was especially severe, because artisans made up fully 50 percent of the work force.[4] No longer could a journeyman, however skilled, count on becoming a master in his trade; in the course of the sixteenth century, one-third of Nuremberg's artisans were forced into piecework and wage dependency, without hope of ever establishing the self-sufficient household of a master craftsman.[5] Living conditions for pieceworkers and their families were often terrible. In a tract he wrote against greed in 1524, Sachs bitterly criticized the "merchants and piecework entrepreneurs who exploit their laborers and pieceworkers" and force them to "slave away by day and night, barely able to stave off hunger and feed themselves and their wives and children."[6]

Artisans reacted vigorously to the new competitive pressures. Journeymen, seeing their hopes dashed and livelihoods threatened, joined radical movements and figured prominently in the urban uprisings that occurred during the peasant revolts of the 1520s.[7] Others, particularly master artisans, worked through the guilds to protect and strengthen established shops by limiting their number. Training for mastery in a trade was restricted; certification became more difficult and expensive to obtain; and an unwritten code of honor appeared among artisans, comprising strictly enforced rules of morality. In her study on Sachs, Maria E. Müller discusses this code of honor, which circumscribed the values an artisan needed to have in order to survive in his profession — foremost among them frugality.[8] Saving money was vital: for a journeyman, it was the only way to obtain the means to establish an independent shop; and for a master artisan it could mean the difference between solvency and ruin.

Saving money demanded discipline and prudent household management on the part of a wife. The artisan code of honor called for complementary gender roles to be established within the household: the husband was to wield absolute authority in spiritual and financial matters, and his pious and submissive wife was to represent the honor of the household to the outside world.[9] Above all, she was excluded from the workplace and relegated to the home. In a market where work for skilled artisans was growing scarce, women were discouraged from competing. Even work traditionally performed by the wives and daughters of master artisans was restricted — which served to strengthen the authority of the male head of household. The frugality and subservience demanded of the artisan's wife were seen as necessary to the survival and prosperity of the artisan household. The artisan code of honor coincided with Luther's new theology of marriage in affirming the central importance of family, the gender hierarchy within the household, and the division of responsibility between the wife in the domestic sphere and her husband in the workplace.[10]

The emerging money economy demanded not only the accumulation of savings, but also a new economy of human drives through control of affects, increased self-discipline, and delayed gratification.[11] Discipline was demanded of men and women alike. In Sachs's writings, the bad wife has a male counterpart, "the slack husband" ("der lose man"), who drinks and gambles away the family funds. But the bad wife appears much more frequently and is demonized as a modern witch, a character Sachs drew from a wide variety of sources, including farces, popular tales, Shrovetide plays, classical works, sermon collections, and theological writings. More than other early modern German authors, Sachs adopted ideas and materials from various social sectors, but he wove them into a fabric of thought and values suited to his own artisan class.

*The Battle between the Sexes*

Sachs was fascinated by the popular folktale "The Devil and the Old Woman." Within a single year, he used it in three different works: twice in poems (April 1545 and March 1546) and once in a Shrovetide play (November 1545). His play, called *The Devil with the Old Woman* (*Der teüffel mit dem alten Weyb*), features the standard four characters in the devil-and-old-woman tale (husband, wife, devil, and crone) and the usual plot line: the devil recruits an old woman to help him disrupt the conjugal bliss of an old couple; she provokes a marital spat and is rewarded by the devil, who then flees from her, terrified by her power; the couple is reconciled, and the moral of the story is to ignore malicious gossip.

Routine as Sachs's version of the story may seem, it begins with a novel twist: a man appears on stage to announce that he has just had a nightmare, and to ask the audience for help in interpreting it (a hint to look for a moral in the story to come). The man's wife enters the scene and persuades him to disclose his dream. He tells her that in his dream, he had fought with her and she had scratched out his eyes. She admits to having had similar nightmares. Although husband and wife reaffirm their devotion to each other, their dreams reveal the wife's clandestine impulse to reverse the marital hierarchy by brutally beating her husband. The nightmare of female rebellion seems so horribly real that it cannot easily be dismissed — it lingers in the husband's mind.

To reassure her husband, the wife tells him that it was only a dream, and that "a dream is nothing more than fantasy."[12] By appealing to reason in order to calm her husband's fears, the wife confounds traditional gender stereotypes. In the sixteenth century, only men were thought capable of the rational reflection needed to vanquish fear, whereas women were believed to be prone to fear and emotion — and therefore susceptible to the anxiety and melancholy associated with dreams. In diverging from the feminine norm, the wife reveals her unusually virtuous character. She urges her husband to forget his fears and return to the safe, secure realm of daily household routine. "Come home," she tells him, "let's eat the soup."[13] The act of eating soup together — at the time in a large communal bowl — defines the members of the household, reaffirming their gender-based hierarchy and the husband's dominant role as provider. One duty of a sixteenth-century housewife was to preserve and project the honor of the household.[14] By discounting the scandalous nightmare of marital disorder, and by returning to thoughts of household routine, the wife restores the outward propriety of her husband's household.

Early modern notions of witchcraft were based in part on the medieval belief that the devil inhabits the imagination, especially sinful dreams and fantasies.[15] Satan enters the mind, finds a suitable image stored there, and places it before the mind's eye, which then sees it as something real — thereby confusing fantasy with reality. Luther says the devil has the ability to inspire ("blasen") delusions in this way; and the devil in Sachs's play admits that he has inspired ("hab einblasen lassen") nightmares in the married couple for thirty years in hopes of provoking a quarrel.[16] In the sixteenth century, the devil was thought to use delusions to prepare his victims for enchantment by a witch. People who succumb to diabolical delusions were believed to grow morose and melancholy, unable to distinguish dream from reality. The husband at first reacts in this way, but the wife's appeal to reason restores him to sanity, because the devil's power is ineffective when piety prevails in a marriage.

In order to provoke a marital spat between the pious husband and his wife, the devil enlists the help of an old woman. In the traditional devil-and-old-woman tale, he strikes a deal with an old washerwoman who happens to be passing by. But the old hag who appears in Sachs's play is already devoted to the devil. Even before she is asked, she volunteers to bring the couple to blows, promising that "they shall beat each other even during the day when the sun is shining," an allusion to the couple's battles in their nightmares.[17] Well aware that the devil is infusing dreams of disorder into the minds of husband and wife, the old woman — like a good servant — anticipates her master's wishes by offering to turn these dreams into reality. When the devil offers her his patronage, the hag reminds him that "I am already yours."[18] She displays all four characteristics of the modern witch: she uses harmful sorcery to disrupt marriages, already has a pact with the devil, conspires with demons and witches, and carries a pitchfork — a device used by witches for flying at night — with which she ultimately beats her master. Sachs calls her "Hex," "Unhuld," and "Wettermacherin," all popular terms for the modern witch.

The old woman displays the character of a witch: she is arrogant, self-assured, and ultimately more powerful than her master. When it is time for the devil to pay her, he is so enthralled by the spectacle of husband and wife fighting that he forgets about her. Infuriated, she draws a magic circle and forces him to appear before her. Fearing her power, the devil submits. "I don't dare fight you," he declares; "you are much too harsh and evil for me."[19] The conventional relationship between devil and witch is inverted: she gains the upper hand because she is so evil ("boess"), a reference to the domineering character of the bad wife. Afraid to come near her, the devil hands over the promised shoes on a long stick that is peeled so that she cannot creep up under the bark to ensnare him, as he claims three old women once did.[20] He alludes here to a popular tale called "The Bad Wife and the Devils" ("Das böse Weib und die Teufel") in which bad wives subdue the devil. Like them, the witch becomes a bad wife bent on dominating her master.

Despite his precautions, the devil does not escape unscathed. After snatching up the proffered shoes, the witch beats her patron out the door with her pitchfork, an episode reminiscent of Sachs's later Shrovetide play *The Devil Took an Old Woman in Marriage (Der Teufel nam ein alt Weib zu der Eh*, 1557). In this play, the devil is again beaten with a pitchfork by a witch who threatens to join three other old women to capture him. In a caricature of Protestant marriage ideals, the devil chooses the witch to be his wife because he finds her so compatible with him. He vows to love, honor, and support her magical practices, and the wedding party resembles a witches' Sabbath.

The new husband is immediately subjugated by his wife and forced to obey her every command, with disastrous results for the household: she squanders the money he gives her on her lazy female friends. Not only is he forced to obey his wife and do the housework, now he must support a house full of shrewish women as well. Sachs subtly associates these female parasites with Jewish usurers and swindlers when he ends his play by giving thanks that Jews and evil wives have been driven from Nuremberg. "We are happy now," he says, "that this city has no more Jews. . . . No more bad wives are to be found here. . . . Far away with them! wishes Hans Sachs."[21] The misogyny and anti-Semitism in Sachs's play are both rooted in the urban artisan's fear of economic deprivation. The Jew represents the power of commerce that threatens to ruin the artisan in the marketplace, and the bad wife stands for the household waste that threatens his prosperity at home. Although Jews and bad wives have supposedly long been banished from Nuremberg, the economic ruin they stand for remains so present a danger that Sachs devotes much of his play to describing and denouncing it.

Nuremberg had indeed expelled its Jews — in 1498, long before Sachs wrote his play. Arguing that Jews were dangerous usurers who owned too much Christian property, the city council applied for an imperial permit to expel them — and to confiscate their valuable lands. Emperor Maximilian granted the request in exchange for a handsome sum realized from the sale of confiscated Jewish property.[22] By 1519, Jews had been similarly expelled from most German cities; still, they remained firmly associated in the popular mind with usurious practices. Anti-Semitism among urban artisans was often connected to demands for social reform and criticism of the financial schemes of merchants, aristocrats, and clergymen.[23] Jews became scapegoats for economic threats of all sorts, including the danger posed by the new piecework entrepreneurs.

Jews made good targets for urban anger because they represented things un-Christian. Similarly, bad wives were targeted because their behavior was considered un-Christian; in particular, their reversal of the prescribed gender hierarchy was thought to lead to the destruction of household prosperity. The devil's fear of the witch in Sachs's Shrovetide plays is based not so much on the witch's magical powers as on her disruption of household order and the financial ruin it entails for household and community alike. Urban fears of downward social mobility brought on by a developing money economy are projected in Sachs's plays onto both the Jew and the female witch.

The witch's domination of the devil in Sachs's plays seems to contradict the servility to Satan ascribed to her by Heinrich Kramer and Jakob Sprenger in their *Malleus maleficarum* (1487). But the witch's rebellion against her own master is the logical extension of her servitude to him. Her proud display of power over the devil shows her hubris, the devil's own chief vice, reflecting her continued bondage to him. Moreover, the witch's powers of magic are illusory—in the sixteenth century, the devil was believed to work through witches to delude his victims into thinking that they were bewitched.[24] By terrifying her diabolical master with his own illusory powers, the witch makes both him and herself look ridiculous. The more she shares the devil's delusions of the power of her own witchcraft, the more indebted she is to him, and the more ludicrous both appear. The inversion of power between devil and witch not only intensifies the diabolical and ridiculous sides of the witch's character, it uniquely qualifies her to faithfully execute Satan's plans as his loyal servant.

Nevertheless, witches were widely feared in early modern Germany for their harmful magic and for the threat they posed to God's holy order. Kramer and Sprenger projected an apocalyptic spiritual struggle under way between the Lord's servants and Satan's legions of witches; and Martin Luther sharply condemned witches for their harmful magic, warning against its corrupting influence on women. By contrast, Sachs did not seem particularly worried by the magical powers of witches or by the spiritual threat they posed. He seems much more concerned in his works with the precarious position of the urban artisan and the witch's disastrous effect on it through her reversal of gender roles. This raises an interesting question: Were witches nothing more to Sachs than a literary figure for gender role reversal? Did Sachs really believe in witches?

## Witches and Self-Control

Concern about witches was slight in Nuremberg during the early period of the witch hunts (1435 to 1500). By 1491, however, interest in the problem of witchcraft had grown, and the city council requested judicial advice on how to prosecute witches. In response, the papal Inquisitor Heinrich Kramer supplied a vernacular version of his theories on witchcraft, known as the *Nuremberg Hammer of Witchcraft* (1491). But Kramer's fervent belief in the reality of witches found little resonance in Nuremberg, and witch trials there were rare during Sachs's lifetime. Before 1560, there were occasional sorcery trials against both men and women (mostly involving the use of love magic), but seldom were charges of witchcraft brought.

One exception involved three women accused in 1536 of harmful sorcery. One of them, Adelheit Schneiderin, had been hired by a farmer to heal his cows through sorcery. When the cows failed to recover, the angry farmer brought charges of witchcraft against her. Under torture, she confessed to the key practices of witchcraft: flying at night, practicing harmful sorcery, copulating with the devil, and participating in a witches' Sabbath (involving the other two women charged with her). Due to the unusual nature of the accusation, the city council sought advice from lawyers and theologians representing a wide range of views on witchcraft. Liberal counsel prevailed, and the women were not prosecuted for witchcraft, although the case led the city council to impose new laws forbidding consultation with practitioners of folk magic.

The argument that carried the day was most clearly formulated by the lawyer Johann Hepstein, who maintained that witchcraft was purely a product of the imagination.[25] This view, based on church doctrine with origins in the *Canon episcopi* recorded in 906 by Regino of Prüm, coincided with views stated by Sachs five years before the trial in his poem "An Amazing Conversation among Five Witches" ("Ein wunderlich gesprech von fünff Unhulden," 1531). In the poem, five witches appear to a traveler in a nightmare induced by the devil. All five are ugly and old, and each practices a different kind of magic. The first makes men impotent; the second causes lumbago and dries up the milk of cows; the third finds stolen goods and conjures up the devil; the fourth produces bad weather and is married to the devil; and the fifth transforms herself into animals, rides a goat through the air at night, and steals wine and food from cellars. When the traveler awakens, he realizes that it was all just a dream, and that witchcraft is mere illusion. Those who practice or believe in it are liars and idolaters deluded by the devil, and the best protection against it is faith in God. "If you acknowledge God in faith," Sachs concludes, "no spirit can harm you."[26]

Like the lawyer Hepstein, Sachs discounts the reality of witchcraft, calling it a figment of the imagination induced by the devil. But Sachs takes his argument a step further. Asserting that love sorcery is a hoax, he claims that witches "cannot force anybody to love. Whoever lets love overwhelm him has only himself to blame for behaving half like a fool."[27] Because emotions are generated within each individual, they can be controlled by an act of will. Therefore, the fool for love is his own victim, and love sickness can be cured only through individual self-control, not through witchcraft.

Sachs's emphasis here on self-control reinforces a tendency identified by Norbert Elias: the shift in human behavior in the early modern period toward disciplining drives and affects.[28] Elias adduces documentary evidence — such as early modern table manners — to show that the "civilized" behavior we take for granted today was only gradually imposed in a historical process of learning social self-control. By denying the reality of witchcraft, Sachs contributes to what Elias calls "the civilizing process" in two ways. First, he dissociates the affects (drives and emotions) from magical external causes (such as witchcraft) and relocates their origins within the individual. Second, he demands that individuals — at least insofar as they are men — control their own emotions. For example, he associates love-stricken behavior with foolishness, thereby implying that manifestations of love are shameful and should be repressed. By subsuming love and other drives and emotions under the will of the individual instead of attributing them to sorcery and witchcraft, Sachs demystifies the human affects while internalizing their control.

Accordingly, Sachs joins Luther in dismissing the sexual potency of witches that so frightened Kramer and Sprenger. But Sachs goes beyond Luther when he contends that love — and the sexual drives associated with it — are subject to self-control. For Luther, the passions associated with love can be controlled only within the framework of marriage. Luther believes that husband and wife should practice sex to avoid the temptation of philandering, in accordance with Pauline doctrine (1 Corinthians 7:1–6). By contrast, Sachs suggests that the individual should subject love to strict self-control; he makes no mention of relaxing control under any circumstances, not even within marriage. By emphasizing individual self-discipline, Sachs seems to weaken the Lutheran doctrine of utter dependence on the will of God through the institutions of marriage, Christian community, and state. Sachs takes a tentative step here in the civilizing process toward dissociating the individual from his social and religious context and placing him in the isolation of what Elias calls the "homo clausus," the segregated male with his egocentric world view.[29]

In his poem on the five witches, Sachs is not entirely consistent in denying the reality of witchcraft — he asserts that the devil can make a woman into a witch by getting her to deny her faith, and he claims that witches acting on behalf of grain speculators cause bad weather.[30] The spread of a money economy in the sixteenth century was accompanied by inflation whenever bad harvests pushed up grain prices. The connection of harvests to the money economy and growing centralized markets was poorly understood, fostering a belief that witches generated bad weather for the sake of speculation — the number of witchcraft accusations tended to rise whenever harvests were bad. The view of witches that Sachs presents is thus an ambivalent one. On the one hand, he demystifies the drives and affects associated with witchcraft by attributing them to the individual; on the other hand, he ascribes certain conflicts and crises to witchcraft, particularly ones with social and economic origins.

For the most part, however, Sachs maintains the belief that magical practices are illusory and foolish. In one story, a man who tries to conjure up witches is beaten by practical jokers ("Das unhulden pannen," 1550); in another, a man who uses love magic is rewarded with a beating from his wife ("Der alt buler mit der zauberey," 1554). Still other stories ridicule night-flying and similar practices commonly ascribed to witches.[31] For Sachs, harmful magic is effective only when used by mythical figures, such as Circe of classical antiquity (who transforms people into animals in *Die göttin Circe*, 1550) or a Danish witch at the time of Christ (who transforms people into animals in *König Frote in Denmarck kam durch eine alte hexen um*, 1547). Only once — in his story "The Battle with the Bad Wife" ("Der kampf mit dem poesen weib," 1541) — does Sachs attribute genuine powers of magic to a figure akin to the modern witch. In the story, a peasant discovers a woman fornicating with a priest. He insults her, and she challenges him to a duel in which she is mortally wounded. Before dying, she avenges herself by murdering her foe in a hailstorm conjured up with the help of her friends. The play ends with a warning to beware of bad wives who corrupt the Protestant ideals of marriage.

However, Sachs usually depicts magical practices as harmless. Even the most wicked of his witch figures rarely do real damage, and any harm done is reversed by the end of the story. For example, in *The Devil with the Old Woman*, the couple is reconciled in the end; the prescribed marital hierarchy is restored, and marital disorder returns to the illusory dream world from whence it came. Similarly, in *The Devil Took an Old Woman in Marriage*, Sachs concludes by proclaiming that Nuremberg is free of Jews and witches. The proper gender hierarchy is restored, and "pious wives . . . are subordinated to their husbands."[32] The reversal of gender relations through witchcraft teaches by negative example how to reaffirm moral boundaries.

At times, Sachs goes so far as to use the devil and the witch to state expressly his own point of view. In his "Conversation of the Old Witch with the Devil" ("Gesprech der alten hexen mit dem dewffel," 1553), the devil meets with a witch to compare the relative sinfulness of unmarried cohabitation with clerical greed and sloth. The devil and witch come to the conclusion that these sins are equally wicked. Sachs uses the unholy pair to express the importance that he as a Protestant attaches to officially sanctioned marriage. Similarly, in "The Ill-Fated Courtship that Was Prattled Away" ("Von der unglückhafften, verschwatzten Bulschafft," 1552), the devil and the witch prevent a young woman's sweetheart from marrying her. She had allowed young men to visit her at night, and although the visits were innocent, they ruined her reputation; the reader is to infer that she deserves what she gets. Sachs uses the devil and witch here to express his opinion that young women should remain hidden inside the home and shielded from public view, in accordance with new Protestant educational ideals.[33]

In Sachs's writings, the witch figure does not serve to condemn the practice of magic, which is never taken particularly seriously. Nor is there much emphasis on her sinful transgression of God's holy order. Instead, she is primarily a metaphor for disturbed relations within the home, especially the reversal of the gender hierarchy with its attendant threat to prosperity in household and community. These forces of disruption are situated for Sachs in the feminine gender, particularly in the diabolical relationship between wicked witch and bad wife.

### The Witch within the Wife

In the beginning of Sachs's play *The Devil with the Old Woman*, the wife's behavior appears more rational than her husband's. But after the witch spreads her lies, the situation is reversed: the husband becomes the rational one who at first refuses to listen to the witch, whereas the wife is the one who appears weak and gullible, allowing her emotions to be manipulated. Sachs returns here to the traditional distinction made by philosophers and theologians since antiquity between rational male superiority and irrational female weakness.[34] Although both parties grow violent during the ensuing quarrel, Sachs reserves to the husband the voice of virtue and reason in the play's closing lines. In drawing the proper conclusions from the events in the play, the husband shows sober analysis and rational reflection. By contrast, his wife loses the initiative to her husband, becoming passive and voiceless as he speaks for them both.

Instead of solving problems as she did at first, the wife becomes part of the problem by associating with the witch and listening to her slanderous allegations against the husband. "It was not in vain that I dreamt today that my wife scratched out my eyes," the husband later muses, noting that her anticipated attack did in fact materialize. He charitably places blame on the old witch for turning his "pious wife away from me with her false counsel," but the wife is also at fault for having listened to the witch at all.[35] The conflict ultimately originates in the close advisory relationship between wife and witch.

Immediately after talking with the witch, the wife abandons her former prudence and vows to make her husband suffer. "He shall not have a wife in me," she declares, "but rather a devil for as long as I live!"[36] Her identification with the devil transforms her into a bad wife. In his *Origin of Bad Wives* (*Ursprung der bösen Weiber*, 1554), Sachs explains that the first bad wife was a defiant woman who joined carnival festivities without her husband's knowledge, then chose a devil's costume and frightened him so badly that he pledged eternal obedience to her. Similarly, the wife in Sachs's Shrovetide play becomes a bad wife by assuming the identity of the devil and reversing the traditional gender hierarchy.

Transformed into a shrew, the wife fills the house with bestial growls, falling upon her husband like a wildcat and opening deep wounds with her claws. Her animal quality is shared by the witch, who is denigrated as "mare" ("stute, merha") and "bitch" ("breckin").[37] Sachs outlines the animal nature of women in "The Fourfold Nature of a Woman" ("Die vier natur einer frawen," 1562), based on a poem by the Greek author Phocylides.[38] A woman, he says, is by nature as lusty as a pig, as noisy as a barking dog, and as recalcitrant as an unbridled horse; but she can also be as industrious as a honeybee. According to Sachs, each woman has a different combination of these four animal qualities, making her highly unpredictable. The only way to control her is to instruct her from an early age in the art of home economics so that her "honeybee" character as an industrious housewife flourishes at the expense of her less desirable qualities.

These qualities — carnality, obstinacy, and a malicious tongue — are the primary characteristics of a bad wife or witch. Every woman is torn between the domesticated and rebellious sides of her nature. The four-fold nature of women poses a problem for Sachs, making even the best of housewives potential shrews who threaten domestic harmony. In Sachs's play *The Devil with the Old Woman*, the latent evil in the wife's character explains her husband's concern regarding her hidden intentions as well as her own sudden shift from demure prudence to malevolent aggression: by appealing to her vanity and curiosity (which Sachs considers to be elements of a woman's flawed nature), the witch releases the bad wife inside her.

The witch serves to bring out the wife's worst qualities because she represents them herself as the inversion of a good housewife. Hidden within every woman is the potential for evil. In Sachs's "Ill-Fated Courtship," a companion points out to the suitor of the lovely, demure young Eva how evil and dangerous she will be "when she is old, angry, and cranky." "Old dogs are hard to make behave," he says, "and they are plagued by arrogance and are chock full of secret tricks. It would be too bad if you should be murdered because of it."[39] Behind a woman's sweet, docile exterior lurks the nature of a malevolent, dangerous bitch. Youth, beauty, and virtue in a woman merely conceal the evil visage of an ugly old hag, reminiscent of the medieval representation of "Lady World" ("vrô welt") as a vibrant, beautiful woman on the outside with the horrible face of death underneath. Lurking within every housewife is an angry old witch ready to pounce on her unsuspecting husband. Her arrogance, obstinacy, and voracious appetites — all part of her fourfold animal nature as a woman — must be suppressed if her marriage is to succeed and her household to prosper. In sixteenth-century Nuremberg, newlyweds spent their first two years living with the bride's parents, a custom designed to help young wives suppress their egos and become prudent housewives.[40]

Waste, slander, gluttony, rebellion, and other practices that Sachs considered dysfunctional are not limited in his view to women alone. According to Sachs, men and women alike indulge in these practices, which threaten not only individual households, but also the welfare and prosperity of the entire community. In medieval allegory, the dual nature of women symbolized by Lady World stood for the tendency of both sexes to indulge in mundane pleasures, selfishly enjoying the present and forgetting about the hereafter. Similarly, the fourfold nature Sachs ascribes to women, symbolized by the witch hidden within, stands for universal human vices that undermine urban peace and prosperity. Sachs's male characters often share such qualities as greed, mendacity, and deception. "Tsk, tsk, who would trust a man?" the witch asks the wife, raising doubts about her husband. " . . . He well knows how to conceal the scoundrel within him."[41] But Sachs does not attribute the husband's negative qualities to his masculine gender, leaving the female sex alone to represent the flaws in human nature.

Like female foibles, human vices in general lead in Sachs's view to social chaos and economic ruin. Sachs projects the tension and uncertainty he sees in social relations onto the battle between the sexes or (more specifically) onto the conflict between good and evil within women. For Sachs, resolving conflicts and restoring social peace means establishing control over the human drives within oneself and others, particularly women. One way of doing so is to raise women to be obedient wives and prudent housekeepers; the other is to monitor one's own feelings and exercise self-restraint. At the end of the play, the husband admonishes the audience not to believe blithely whatever it hears. "Instead, calmly and carefully find out for yourselves whether it is lies or the truth," he advises. "Nobody should fly off the handle so quickly and angrily over mere words if he wishes to avoid what happened to us."[42] Using the husband as his spokesman, Sachs advocates taking personal responsibility for one's actions, and moderating impulsive, egoistic behavior through reason and self-discipline.

### Disciplining Women

Although Sachs associates self-discipline with men and egoistic impulsiveness with women, it does not necessarily follow for him that women are unable to cultivate and exercise self-control. Sachs's female characters are by nature unpredictable and therefore rightly—in his view—subordinated to male rule, but they can also be rational and energetic, as the wife in *The Devil with the Old Woman* shows. In this regard, Sachs differs from Luther and Rebhun, for whom women are by nature utterly passive and entirely irrational by virtue of their weakness inherited from Eve.

In his *Debate between Jupiter and Juno* (*Kampff-gesprech zwischen Juppiter unnd Juno*, 1534), Sachs explores the question of gender equality. The hermaphrodite Tiresias is chosen as judge to decide whether men or women should govern the world. He is so impressed with the political and intellectual prowess of women like Juno that he would rule in their favor, were it not for the fact that it would contravene divine and imperial law. Acknowledging that the moral, rational, and physical excellence of women qualifies them to rule in place of men, Tiresias reluctantly decides against them because "God in the beginning gave precedence, dominion, and governance to men," as Emperor Justinian confirmed in his code. "I cannot in the end break the divine and imperial law," he concludes.[43]

For Sachs, the authority of men to rule women does not derive from the inherent superiority attributed to men by Luther and Rebhun; because human nature is imperfect, men can be as flawed and ambivalent as women. Instead, the male right to rule stems from laws established by church and state. And—unlike Rebhun—Sachs does not equate the female demand for gender equality with diabolism. Juno's arguments are carefully and respectfully weighed, and she is portrayed as a good housewife, not the modern witch that Rebhun makes the old hag out to be for demanding equality with men in his *Wedding at Cana*.

But female rationality does not make women equal to men. For Sachs, a rational woman is one who understands and accepts her subordinate place within the household, obeying her husband and practicing frugality. If her husband acts irrationally, her role as a prudent housewife is to remind him of his masculinity by appealing to his reason. It is not to challenge his authority; gender role reversal results in a diaper-washing husband supporting a lazy wife, leading to financial ruin. Arrogant women who refuse to stay at home compete with men for the dwindling number of spots in the work force, with disastrous consequences for the entire urban economy.

Sachs concurs with Luther and Rebhun that the witch projects the egoism and irrational emotionality characteristic of women. These female qualities are disruptive and dangerous to family, community, and God's holy order. Because women are by nature weaker than men, affects in women must be controlled by means of the authority imposed by men, whereas men are able to restrain their own affects by exercising self-control. A wife must therefore obey her husband, following his guidance in all matters.

Although Sachs agrees with Rebhun and Luther on the need for a gender hierarchy, he stresses secular rather than spiritual reasons for it. Luther and Rebhun see male self-control and female obedience as ordained by God to serve the goal of spiritual peace on earth. By contrast, Sachs advocates self-control in men and subservience in women because they lead to financial success. The divinely ordained gender hierarchy is not an end in itself for Sachs, but rather the means by which a household may survive and prosper. As an urban artisan, Sachs is primarily concerned with economic changes that threaten the welfare of his estate, and he therefore castigates female behavior that might further erode its already precarious position.

By combining the figure of the bad wife with that of the modern witch, Sachs transforms the latter into a household truant and social renegade while mystifying and demonizing the former. As she merges with the witch, Sachs's shrew becomes a field of projection for anxieties about economic disorder within the individual household as well as within the urban community at large. At the same time, the characteristics of modern witchcraft that so alarmed the likes of Kramer and Sprenger (harmful sorcery, conspiratorial meetings, the devil's pact, and flying at night) are reduced to the status of hilariously incredible caricature. Although Sachs refused to take witchcraft seriously, he was alarmed by the precarious economic position of his own artisan estate in sixteenth-century Germany. By using the image of the witch to project his anxieties onto the dangerous household practices of rebellious wives, he contributed to the hysteria of the great witch hunts after 1560.

# Chapter Six

# Burning the Witch
# to Tame the Shrew

M UCH HAS BEEN written about the European witch trials, and therefore much is known about the tens of thousands who were executed as witches from 1435 to 1750. Most of the victims were women, and many were illiterate peasants — as were most of their accusers. By contrast, those in the judicial apparatus were university-trained men from the urban middle and upper classes. People from disparate backgrounds with clashing ideas about what constituted appropriate behavior for women faced each other in court. Trial records suggest that behavior deemed inappropriate on the part of the accused women led to their conviction as witches. It therefore seems likely that changing notions about gender roles — especially within the early modern urban elite — informed the definition of the modern witch. In this study, I have explored the connection between the new feminine ideal in early modern Europe and the persecution of women as witches.

The texts on witchcraft that I have examined were written by influential members of the early modern urban elite in Germany. The authors were university-trained or self-educated; four of them (Heinrich Kramer, Jakob Sprenger, Martin Luther, and Paul Rebhun) had theological backgrounds, and the fifth (Hans Sachs) was an urban artisan. In their works, they present a complex and changing view of the witch that varies according to each author's background, religious convictions, and political interests. These differences are most visibly expressed in the spiritual revolution of Protestantism, but they also relate to the emergence of a modern society with its money economy, division of labor, and restructuring of human drives. Despite differences among them, however, each of the authors I have examined regards witchcraft as a serious threat to the social and spiritual order, and all agree that witches are women.

*From Wanton Woman to Bad Wife*

In their *Malleus maleficarum* (1487), Heinrich Kramer and Jakob Sprenger establish the first gender-specific definition of the modern

ILLUSTRATION: Anonymous woodcut, *Three Witches Being Burned Alive*, ca. 1555 witch. Because of the weak, lascivious nature that women inherit from Eve, the authors argue, most modern witches ("modernis malefici") are women — and most women tend to become modern witches. The authors seem obsessed with the female body, especially the womb, which they describe as a voracious, insatiable animal. Womb, woman, and witch represent libidinal drives standing in the way of ascetic spiritual self-realization. Therefore, the authors see little use for and much danger in women; even virtuous wives may give in to their sexual appetites and become witches. There is only one effective remedy for witchcraft: killing all witches.

Kramer and Sprenger were conservative Dominicans committed to papal supremacy and monastic asceticism. Although their narrow view of witchcraft and female sexuality found little resonance in the eighty years following the publication of the Malleus, their gender-specific definition of witchcraft was seldom questioned. The Protestant writers Martin Luther, Paul Rebhun, and Hans Sachs shared Kramer and Sprenger's belief — based on the traditional Christian view of women — that witches were women because women were physically, spiritually, and intellectually inferior to men. Unlike the authors of the Malleus, however, Luther and his followers never attributed witchcraft to female sexuality. Instead, they redefined the modern witch in terms of new family values associated with Protestantism and the urban artisan estate.

The notion expressed in the Malleus that women are cursed with a wicked, insatiable sexuality is foreign to Protestant thinking. For Martin Luther, humanity has been endowed with sexuality by God for the purpose of establishing the most important institution on earth, the family. Rejecting the Catholic church's emphasis on monasticism, Luther defines the family as the primary setting for spiritual self-realization. A woman's highest duty before God is therefore to her husband and children. Her role as wife and mother is to "entice" ("reytzen" — a word that suggests the moral and educational value of a woman's sexual appeal) her husband to behave morally, and to raise her children to be good Christians and obedient citizens. She accomplishes both objectives through her own exemplary behavior as a virtuous, submissive housewife.

In his sermons and treatises, Luther offers a novel explanation for female witchcraft: by nature weak and irrational, women are driven to witchcraft as a means of coping with their fears. Instead of trusting in God, they turn to the idolatry of witchcraft for a solution to their problems. Luther calls on women to turn instead to God for support and to their husbands for guidance. Those who give in to their fears and take matters into their own hands by practicing witchcraft disobey God, displaying the contrary, rebellious character of a bad wife. The counterpart to God's ideal housewife is the fearful shrew who becomes a witch.

In his *Wedding Play Based on the Wedding at Cana* (*Ein Hochzeit Spiel auff die Hochzeit zu Cana*, 1538), Paul Rebhun elaborates on the character of the bad wife in Luther's definition of the modern witch. By negative example, Rebhun's witch — and her "she-man" counterpart Simon — teach both sexes that emotional behavior and egoistic aspirations are typically feminine and subject to repression. But the lessons for men are different than those for women. Men learn that the impulsive, egoistic behavior typical of women and witches is inferior to the male virtue of rational self-control. Women are taught that because egoism is part of their nature, they can control it only by submitting to the authority of men. Women are expected to follow the guidance of their husbands, and men are supposed to monitor and restrain their own feelings as well as those of their wives. If men abuse their authority, then women must patiently endure whatever suffering their submission entails, in accordance with the principle of long-suffering obedience ("leidender Gehorsam").

Like Rebhun, Hans Sachs creates a literary figure that is both bad wife and modern witch. The witch in his play *The Devil with the Old Woman* (*Der teüffel mit dem alten Weyb*, 1545) provokes a fight between a husband and a wife, releasing dangerous egoistic impulses within their marriage, particularly within the wife. Sachs emphasizes that a successful marriage and a peaceful community depend on exercising control over the irrational impulses in human nature, especially those in women. As Sachs sees it, a man whose wife ruins him financially through household mismanagement has nobody to blame but himself, because he has failed to exercise control over the irrational impulses that are part of her nature. Sachs suggests two ways of controlling ruinous impulses: educating women to obedience and frugality, and taking responsibility for one's own actions in order to exercise self-control.

Sachs demystifies witchcraft by discounting its magical power and attributing its supposed effects — such as love-sickness — to feelings that are subject to the human will. But Sachs creates a new myth of the witch as a dangerous, destructive shrew who subverts both the individual household and the community at large. More clearly than in Rebhun's play, the modern witch in Sachs's works is internalized as the evil side of human nature. She lurks in every household as the wicked alter ego within women, ready to pounce on men.

But for Sachs — and even for Rebhun — irrational emotionality is not limited to women. Both authors call on men to exercise strict control over their own feelings as well as over those of their wives. Sachs's often humorous portrayal of the modern witch functions to support the repression of the affects by offering readers and audiences an emotional outlet: they compensate for restricting their own egoistic impulses (the lesson implicit in Sachs's works) by releasing them vicariously through the characters of devil and witch, husband and wife as they battle it out in scenes full of emotional outbursts and physical violence.[1] The pleasure that readers and audiences take in their own vicarious release of pent-up emotions informs the burlesque humor in Sachs's works. But Sachs's humor is always tempered by the message that the impulsive, self-assertive behavior of his characters is typical of women and witches, and therefore taboo. Rebhun's burlesque treatment of the effeminate "she-man" in his play functions in a similarly paradoxical way: it teaches self-restraint while providing emotional release.

## The Role of the Witch in the "Civilizing Process"

The most striking thing about the witch in Luther, Rebhun, and Sachs is that she is no longer associated primarily with sins of the spirit — such as consorting with the devil and practicing diabolical magic. Instead, she is now associated with sins of her gender — transgressions against the new feminine ideal of the submissive housewife. In the sixteenth century, the traditional meaning of family as the primary site of production was changing. The subsidiary role of women in supporting (and sometimes assuming) the public and productive functions of men — a role they had played since the Middle Ages — was giving way to their new complementary role in performing a limited set of household functions in the newly emerging private sphere. The meaning of work, gender, family, and marriage was contested in a wide variety of sixteenth-century texts and contexts, including literature on witchcraft.

With the emergence of vernacular literature, the learned concept of the witch entered plays, sermons, and other texts designed to teach ordinary men and women proper gender roles within marriage. The new ideal of femininity projected a chaste married woman subordinate to her husband and limited in her activities to managing the household, educating the children, and representing moral virtue. Her role in public was reduced to projecting the prosperity and propriety of her household; she was prohibited from assuming public functions and largely hidden from public view. Originally restricted to the urban upper and middle classes and to the university-trained elite, this new feminine ideal was widely projected in sermons and didactic literature as the only proper way for women to behave.

The new feminine ideal was largely formulated by a single group, male theologians and artisans from the urban upper and middle classes. The judges and university doctors who presided over witchcraft trials came from this group. It seems logical to assume that they used the new feminine ideal to evaluate the behavior of women accused of witchcraft, even when these women (as was usually the case) came from poor rural backgrounds with very different standards of behavior. The judges — many of whom were undoubtedly familiar with the notions of witchcraft contained in works by Luther, Rebhun, and Sachs — probably found the assertive and aggressive behavior of the alleged witches before them shocking, even diabolical. Under these circumstances, it is hardly surprising that so many of the accused were convicted of witchcraft.

Texts on witchcraft by Luther, Rebhun, and Sachs thus helped set the stage for the persecution as witches of women who failed — for whatever reason — to accept or to perform their roles as demure, obedient housewives. I do not mean to suggest that Protestantism was solely responsible for the new image of the witch as a bad wife. Many authors and artists from a wide variety of religious backgrounds made a similar connection between witch and bad wife, both before and after the Reformation.[2] An analysis of their representations may come to similar conclusions about the link between the gender-specific image of the modern witch and efforts to discipline the behavior of women.

The modern witch engendered in sixteenth-century literature is not linked to women alone. As the negative counterpart to the empowered male gender, the female gender that informs the inverse images of modern witch and proper housewife projects the early modern agenda of its male "other." In *The Civilizing Process*, Norbert Elias describes the early modern process of establishing growing control over the affects (drives and emotions) in men and women alike.[3] As Elias points out, the rising need for affect control came about largely under the impulse of urban change. Life in Germany's towns demanded that men separate their private lives at home from their public roles at work, and their personal feelings and opinions from their public pronouncements in the marketplace or in the municipal halls of power — particularly at court. Early modern towns were therefore centers of civilization where what Elias calls the "threshold of shame" was particularly far advanced, and where the male process of learning emotional self-control thrived.

The towns also produced the educated elite who presided over witch trials. Witch trials may have been occasions for urban judges — appalled at the defiant behavior of many of the poor peasant women on trial — to discipline female self-assertion and to provide an object lesson to women to obey their husbands in long-suffering silence. By extension, men may have learned to control any self-assertive impulses in themselves. In accordance with Elias's theory, the modern witch may have played a "civilizing" role by shaming and frightening both men and women — women into submitting to the authority of their husbands, and men into controlling the behavior of their wives while exercising strict control over themselves.

Maria E. Müller confirms that control exercised by men over women in early modern Europe was at least partly designed to enhance self-control in men.[4] Müller argues that in order to govern successfully at every level (in the home, community, and state), men had to suppress their own drives and affects. Part of a housewife's duty (in accordance with her Lutheran educational mission) was to contribute to her husband's self-control by using her inborn "womanly wiles" — a quality traditionally ascribed to women — to "civilize" him. For this, she needed to control her own affects in isolation from the distracting influences of the outside world so that she could concentrate on observing her husband in order to understand and manipulate his behavior. In her role as observer and manipulator, she provided a model for her children and husband alike: her daughters learned how to behave like good housewives, and her husband and sons learned the skills of a good courtier or civil servant — how to dissemble before authority, and how to observe those in power in order to manipulate them. Controlling the affects in women by turning them into dependable housewives was thus considered a precondition for male success in the early modern marketplace and halls of power. The interdependency of the new, complementary male and female gender roles helps to explain the official hysteria associated with the great wave of witch hunts after 1560: the success of men depended on the proper behavior of women as good housewives.

By associating uncontrolled displays of emotion with the frightening image of the female witch, early modern writers contributed to the "civilizing" of men and women alike. In the writings of Rebhun and Sachs, the shrew represents the drives and affects that needed to be newly managed by men and women if they were to succeed in life, and the witch represents a threat to success that had to be eradicated. In sixteenth-century travel literature, witches find counterparts in the Native American women who sexually seduce Europeans, then kill and eat them (reminiscent of the castration and cannibalism practiced by Kramer and Sprenger's rapacious witches).[5] Like the witch, these native women stood for dangerous drives and affects that had to be controlled, either by eradicating native populations or by placing them in colonial dependency. The link between the persecution of women as witches in early modern Europe and the colonial subjugation of native peoples abroad remains to be explored.

Whatever additional information may emerge on the concept of the modern witch, it seems clear that sixteenth-century gender roles informed the image of the witch, rendering her much more palpable as a threat than Kramer and Sprenger's original vision of the witch as a woman obsessed with her own sexuality. Now every woman, no matter how seemingly demure — even the most faithful of wives, mothers, or daughters — could suddenly turn into a witch. With her pejorative and frightening connotations, the witch entered the average household as the impulsive spirit and potential troublemaker thought to reside within every woman. In the writings of Luther, Rebhun, and especially Sachs, the witch sits like a familiar spirit within, haunting the sphere of gender relations.

# Appendix: Sixteenth-Century Terms for Witches

The concept of the modern witch emerged only gradually in early modern Germany. Due to its novelty, there was no common term for modern witchcraft. To describe the modern witch, writers used terms for practitioners of older forms of heresy and sorcery. In German, witches were called *Hexe*, *Unhulde*, and *Zauberin*; in Latin, they were referred to as *lamia*, *malefica*, *pythonica*, *striga*, and *venefica*. Originally associated with individual aspects of modern witchcraft, each of these terms came to signify all four central practices of the modern witch: (1) performing harmful sorcery; (2) sealing a pact with the devil by copulating with him; (3) meeting secretly with other witches; and (4) flying at night on goats, broomsticks, and other devices.

## Hexe

Although prevalent today, *Hexe* was not always the most common German term for witches. It derives from Old High German *hagazussa*, the name for the female spirit in Nordic mythology who straddled the fence separating the world of the gods from that of men. The term *hagazussa* and its derivatives in Old and Middle High German (*hazesse*, *hazus*, and *hezze*) have several distinct connotations, including (1) a female comedian, (2) a slovenly, promiscuous woman, and (3) a cannibalistic, night-flying female spirit. Rarely were these concepts associated with sorcery.

*Hagazussa* and its derivatives all but vanished from usage in the thirteenth and fourteenth centuries, only to reappear in the fifteenth century in connection with the witch hunts in Switzerland. Records from a 1419 Swiss trial show the first use of the term *Hexereye* for witchcraft. By the late fifteenth century, variations of the term *Hexe* (including *Hex*, *Heckse*, and *Haxe*) were used to denote the modern witch in Switzerland and neighboring German-speaking regions, such as Alsace and the area near Constance. Outside of southwestern Germany, however, the term

Hexe seldom appears in witch trial records. More common are *Unhulde* and *Zauberin*, or such regional terms as *Kunstfruw* and *Töwersche* (northern Germany), *Trutte* (Bavaria), and *Weidlerin* (eastern Germany).

Though absent from most German witch trial records, the term *Hexe* found its way into many early modern legal treatises and literary texts on witchcraft. Because the first witch trials involving German speakers occurred in Switzerland and southwestern Germany, interest in witchcraft focused on records from these areas, helping to popularize the term *Hexe*. The term first spread across southern Germany, appearing in such works as Geiler von Kaisersberg's *Emeis* (1508) and Ulrich Tengler's *Der neue Layenspiegel* (1511), as well as in many of Hans Sachs's writings (from the 1530s on). Writers elsewhere soon picked up the term, notably Martin Luther.

*Unhulde*

Unlike *Hexe*, the term *Unhulde* and its variations (including *Unhold* and *Unhole*) were in constant use from the Middle Ages on. Originally, *Unhulde* was the name for a malevolent spirit in Nordic mythology. With the spread of Christianity in the early Middle Ages, it came to be associated first with the pagan gods, then with the Christian devil. From the eleventh century on, it was used to describe the night-flying spirits of folk belief, both good and evil. Rarely was it associated with sorcery. In the fifteenth century, it was increasingly used as a term of invective for women, finally becoming the most common sixteenth-century German word for the female witch.

*Zauberin*

In both its Old High German (*Zaubrarin*) and Middle High German (*Zouberærinne*) forms, this term referred to a sorceress. Witchcraft and sorcery have elements in common: like a witch, a sorceress was believed to invoke spirits to perform magic, and her magic was sometimes considered harmful. But sorcery was not associated with other practices of witchcraft—such as flying at night or copulating with the devil—until the fifteenth century, when the term *Zauberin* and its variations (including *Zauberin*, *Zeuberin*, and *Zewberynne*) came to signify the modern witch. The related masculine term *Zauberer* was sometimes applied to men accused of witchcraft, but more often it retained its older connotations of sorcery rather than witchcraft. Only the female form of the term was permanently linked to the modern witch.

## Lamia

The term *lamia* is rooted in ancient mythology. Originally, it was the Greek name for a Libyan serpent goddess. Later, *Lamia* was the name for a minor figure in the Greek and Roman pantheon: a consort to Zeus, she turned into a vampire who preyed on infants after the jealous Hera murdered her children. In the early Middle Ages, the term *lamia* referred to the night-flying spirits of folk belief. After about 1450, *lamia* began to appear in technical treatises on witchcraft, where it referred exclusively to the modern witch. Some fifteenth-century writers derive the term from the completely unrelated word *laniare* ("to lacerate"), because witches, they argue, devour human flesh.

## Malefica

*Malefica* was the most commonly used Latin term for witch in the sixteenth century. It derives from the adjective *maleficus*, used in classical Latin to describe an evildoer. In the Vulgate Bible, the male plural noun *malefici* refers to sorcerers (Exodus 22:18 and Deuteronomy 18:10); similarly, medieval glossaries define the second declension male noun *maleficus* as "sorcerer." The related term *maleficium* appears in legal treatises throughout the Middle Ages, where it refers to harmful sorcery.

Until the fifteenth century, *maleficium* was associated only with sorcery, not with the other practices of modern witchcraft. The female noun form *malefica* was first introduced by Heinrich Kramer and Jakob Sprenger in their *Malleus maleficarum* (1487) to describe the modern witch. They use the male plural form *malefici* for sorcerers in general, but reserve the female form *malefica* for the modern witch—because, they claim, many more women than men are witches.

## Pythonica

The term *pythonica* (or *pythonissa*) derives from "the Pythia," title of the priestess of Apollo at Delphi. In medieval glossaries, a *pythonica* is strictly a soothsayer, without any of the attributes of the modern witch. The term was associated with fortune-telling throughout the fifteenth century, but gradually acquired connotations of modern witchcraft. In the *Malleus*, Kramer and Sprenger use the term *pythonica* to refer to practitioners of magic who predate modern witchcraft. The devil speaks through a *pythonica*, they maintain, and performs feats of magic through her, but he does not use her to seduce men, a practice attributed in the *Malleus* only to the *malefica*, or modern witch. In the sixteenth century, however, German writers dropped the distinction between the *pythonica* and the *malefica*.

## Striga

In Roman folklore, the *striga* (derived from Latin *strix*, or "screech owl") was a birdlike female spirit of the night who was believed to render men impotent and to feed children poisonous milk. Clerical writers used the term in the Middle Ages to describe the night-flying spirits of folk belief. But as in the cases of *Hexe*, *lamia*, and *Unhulde*, a term originally used to describe a mythical female spirit was redefined after 1450 to apply to the real-life modern witch.

Though less common than other terms for witches, *striga* inspired several etymologies and variations that tied it to modern witchcraft. The Inquisitor Bernhard of Como (*Tractatus de strigiis*, 1508) derives the term from the mythological underworld river Styx — because witches, he says, are from hell — and from the Greek word *stigitos* ("sadness") — because witches, through their harmful sorcery, bring sadness. The Roman Dominican Sylvester Prierias (*De mirandis strigimagarum*, 1521) changes the term *striga* into *strigimaga* in order to emphasize the harmful sorcery of witches. The Italian Inquisitor Arnaldus Albertinus (*Tractatus de agnoscendis assertionibus catholicis, et hereticis*, 1540) claims that witches are called *strigae* because they communicate at night by screaming like screech owls. Through such imaginative derivations and word combinations, sixteenth-century writers tailored the term *striga* to fit the new concept of the modern witch, adding connotations of harmful sorcery and diabolical dealings to the term while fortifying its traditional association with night flying.

## Venefica

The term *venefica* is a feminine noun form derived from the adjective *veneficus*, meaning "poisonous" or "magical" in classical Latin. Medieval glossaries retain these meanings in defining the *venefica* as a sorceress adept at the use of poison. Originally, the term was devoid of other connotations of witchcraft, such as flying at night or bargaining with the devil. But the Greek Bible refers to the witch or sorcerer as *pharmacous* — one who deals with medications and poisons (Exodus 22:18 and Deuteronomy 18:10). Perhaps drawing on this connection, sixteenth-century legal treatises ascribe to the *venefica* all the characteristics of the modern witch — in addition to her special qualities as a poisoner.

# Notes

## One. The Modern Witch

1. Heinrich Kramer and Jakob Sprenger, *The Malleus Maleficarum of Heinrich Kramer and James Sprenger*, trans. Montague Summers, p. 47, hereafter abbreviated as Summers, p. 47. The Latin original is: "Omnia per carnalem concupiscentiam, quae quia in eis est insatiabilis." The Latin original follows each translation in the note; here it is taken from Heinrich Kramer and Jakob Sprenger, *Malleus maleficarum* (Lyon), 1:46 (Book 1, Question 6), hereafter abbreviated as *Malleus*, 1:46 (1:6). I use the Lyon edition of the *Malleus* for better readability, because the first (Speyer) edition contains common fifteenth-century Latin abbreviations. The *Malleus maleficarum* might be translated as *The Hammer of Witchcraft*, but I follow the translator Summers's practice of referring to the work by its original Latin title, which I usually shorten to *Malleus*.

2. Summers, p. 47. "Tria sunt insatiabilia, &c.& quartum quod nunquam dicit, Sufficit, scilicet nos vuluae. Unde & cum Daemonibus, causa explendae libidinis se agitant.... Et benedictus altissimus, qui virilem speciem a tanto flagitio vsque in praesens praeseruat." *Malleus*, 1:46 (1:6).

3. Summers, p. 74. "... [M]ala quae a modernis maleficis perpetrantur cuncta alia mala, quae Deus vnquam fieri permisit ... excedunt." *Malleus*, 1:77 (1:14).

4. See Norman Cohn, *Europe's Inner Demons*; and Joseph Hansen, *Zauberwahn, Inquisition und Hexenprozeß im Mittelalter und die Entstehung der großen Hexenverfolgung*, and *Quellen und Untersuchungen zur Geschichte des Hexenwahns und der Hexenverfolgung im Mittelalter.*

5. For lack of a better term, I refer to these areas as "Germany." By using this term, I suggest no more than a general cultural and linguistic affinity among the areas in question; I do not equate them with any of the political, cultural, or linguistic entities known as "Germany" in the nineteenth and twentieth centuries.

6. Brian P. Levack estimates that 60,000 witches were executed (*The Witch-Hunt in Early Modern Europe*, p. 21). G. R. Quaife puts the figure at 200,000 (*Godly Zeal and Furious Rage*, p. 79).

7. Levack, p. 124.

8. Gerhard Schormann, *Hexenprozesse in Deutschland*, pp. 8–16, 71.

9. Schormann (pp. 100–123) offers an overview of general explanations for the witch hunts and the state of research into witch trials in early modern Germany. The most influential studies are H. C. Erik Midelfort's *Witch Hunting in Southwestern Germany, 1582–1684*; and E. William Monter's *Witchcraft in France and Switzerland*. Newer studies include, for Bavaria, Wolfgang Behringer, *Hexenverfolgung in Bayern*; Michael Kunze, *Die Straße ins Feuer*; and Christel Beyer, *"Hexen-Leut, so zu Würzburg gerichtet"*; for northern and eastern Germany,

Christian Degn, Hartmut Lehmann, and Dagmar Unverhau, eds., *Hexenprozesse*; and, for the lower Rhine, Irene Franken and Ina Hoerner, *Hexen*.

10. Cohn, p. 226.

11. For a discussion of changing legal procedures in sorcery cases from the High Middle Ages to the eighteenth century, see Schormann; Richard Kieckhefer, *European Witch Trials*; and Siegfried Leutenbauer, *Hexerei und Zaubereidelikt in der Literatur von 1450 bis 1550*.

12. Hansen, *Quellen*, pp. 25, 137.

13. *Malleus*, 1:119 (2:1). In a letter from a Ravensburg town official, only eight executions are documented. The letter is reprinted in Karl Otto Müller, "Heinrich Institoris, der Verfasser des Hexenhammers," p. 400.

14. Kieckhefer, p. 145; Hansen, *Quellen*, p. 596.

15. There were an additional seventy-five trials for sorcery in Germany during the fifteenth century. Kieckhefer, pp. 123–147.

16. See Wolfgang Ziegeler, *Möglichkeiten der Kritik am Hexen- und Zauberwesen im ausgehenden Mittelalter*, pp. 82–111.

17. There were ten editions of the *Malleus* in Germany from 1487 to 1520, all in Latin. Joseph Hansen, "Der *Malleus maleficarum*, seine Druckausgaben und die gefälschte Kölner Approbation vom Jahre 1487," pp. 123–133.

18. For an explanation of the differences between medieval and early modern conceptions of sorcery, see Kieckhefer.

19. In 1602, the lawyer Henri Boguet estimated that there were 1,800,000 witches in Europe. He based his estimate on the 1571 confession of an accused witch, who spoke of 30,000 witches active in France alone. Levack, p. 22.

20. Some historians, drawing in part on Jacob Grimm's *Deutsche Mythologie* and Jules Michelet's *La sorcière*, have argued that witches did exist in some fashion. See Margaret Murray, *The Witch Cult in Western Europe*; Montague Summers, *The History of Witchcraft and Demonology*; Julio Caro Baroja, *Las brujas y su mundo*; Carlo Ginzburg, *I benandanti*; Emmanuel le Roy Ladurie, *Les paysans de Languedoc*; and Jeffrey Burton Russell, *Witchcraft in the Middle Ages*. Historians now agree that there existed popular practices of magic and sorcery, but that these practices differed from those attributed to early modern witches, and that elements of devil worship and the witches' Sabbath, of central importance in the witch trials, were absent from them.

21. Jeannine Blackwell has called this process "Zurechtfolterung" (literally, "torturing somebody into something"). Jeannine Blackwell, " 'Die Zunge, der Geistliche und das Weib,' " p. 6. See also Beyer, p. 6; Christina Larner, *Witchcraft and Religion*, pp. 37–38; and letters from those accused of witchcraft in Wilhelm Soldan and Heinrich Heppe, *Geschichte der Hexenprozesse*, 1:472, and in Johann Diefenbach, *Der Hexenwahn vor und nach der Glaubensspaltung in Deutschland*, p. 134.

22. For lists of witch trials during this period, see Hansen, *Quellen*, pp. 596–613, and *Zauberwahn*, pp. 505–508; Soldan and Heppe, 1:465–500; and Annemarie Dross, *Die erste Walpurgisnacht*, pp. 225–263. However, these lists are incomplete and not always sufficiently documented.

23. On his list of witchcraft treatises to 1540, Hansen (*Quellen*, pp. 308–357)

shows no German entry after 1510. This is corroborated by Levack, p. 172, and by Rossel Hope Robbins, *Encyclopedia of Witchcraft and Demonology*, pp. 145–147.

24. E. William Monter, "The Pedestal and the Stake," pp. 129–132.

25. Peter Burke, *Popular Culture in Early Modern Europe*, p. 62.

26. The *Canon episcopi* recorded by Regino of Prüm in 906 was originally designed to discourage popular belief in folk magic. It condemns practitioners of malicious sorcery to no more than banishment from the parish. See Midelfort, *Witch Hunting*, pp. 30–67.

27. See Soldan and Heppe; Hansen, *Quellen*, and *Zauberwahn*; W. E. H. Lecky, *History of the Rise and Influence of the Spirit of Rationalism in Europe*; and Henry Charles Lea, *Materials Toward a History of Witchcraft*. More recent writers continue the argument in slightly modified form, including Hoffman R. Hays, *The Dangerous Sex*; Gordon R. Taylor, *Sex in History*; Richard Wunderer, *Erotik und Hexenwahn*; and Karlheinz Deschner, *Das Kreuz mit der Kirche*.

28. Hansen, *Zauberwahn*; and Nikolaus Paulus, "Die Rolle der Frau in der Geschichte des Hexenwahns," pp. 72–95.

29. Anthropologists who draw on the Romantic tradition of Grimm's *Deutsche Mythologie* and Michelet's *La sorcière* include Ginzburg; Hans Peter Duerr, *Traumzeit*; and Will Erich Peuckert, "Hexen- und Weiberbünde." Feminists — who see witches as heretics, "wise women," female healers, social rebels, and spiritualists — include Dross; Starhawk, *Dreaming the Dark*; Mary Nelson, "Why Witches Were Women"; Ann Campbell, "Labeling and Oppression"; Rosemary Radford Ruether, "Persecution of Witches"; Barbara Ehrenreich and Deidre English, *Witches, Midwives, and Nurses*; and Ines Brenner and Gisela Morgenthal, "Sinnlicher Widerstand während der Ketzer- und Hexenverfolgungen."

30. See Ginzburg.

31. See Carolyn Merchant, *The Death of Nature*; Sigrid Schade, *Schadenzauber und die Magie des Körpers*; and Sylvia Bovenschen, "Die aktuelle Hexe, die historische Hexe und der Hexenmythos."

32. See Schade, who draws on Michel Foucault and Norbert Elias.

33. See Midelfort, *Witch Hunting*; Ivan Illich, *Gender*; D. L. Reissner, "Witchcraft and Statecraft"; Barbara Duden and Pola Fortunati, "Frauen, Staat und Widerstand in den Anfängen des Kapitalismus"; and Gabriele Becker and others, "Zum kulturellen Bild und zur realen Situation der Frau im Mittelalter und in der frühen Neuzeit."

34. Anke Wolf-Graf, *Frauen im Abseits*, p. 376.

35. Wolf-Graf, p. 334; Christopher Middleton, "Sexual Divisions in Feudalism," p. 160.

36. Helen Berger, "Witchcraft and the Domination of Women."

37. Schormann (pp. 76–80, 119) suggests that most alleged witches in Germany came from sectors of the rural poor — the "unpropertied" ("Unbeerbten") and "subpeasants" ("Unterbäuerischen").

38. Becker and others, "Zum kulturellen Bild," pp. 113–117.

39. Levack, p. 132.

40. Wolf-Graf, p. 345.

41. Merry E. Wiesner, "Frail, Weak, and Helpless," pp. 161–169.

42. Berger, pp. 111–113.

43. For a discussion of poverty among alleged witches, see Levack, pp. 134–135; Christina Larner, *Enemies of God*, p. 89; and Ritta Jo Horsley and Richard Horsley, "On the Trail of the 'Witches,'" p. 18. For figures on the age and marital status of alleged witches, see Levack, pp. 129–132; and Monter, "The Pedestal and the Stake," p. 133.

44. See Schormann; Clark Garrett, "Women and Witches"; Carolyn Matalene, "Women as Witches"; Geoffrey Parrinder, "The Witch as Victim"; Hugh V. McLachlan, "Witchcraft and Anti-Feminism"; Keith V. Thomas, *Religion and the Decline of Magic*; Alan Macfarlane, *Witchcraft in Tudor and Stuart England*; Larner, *Enemies of God*, and *Witchcraft and Religion*; Midelfort, *Witch Hunting*, and "Were There Really Witches?"; Monter, *Witchcraft*, and "The Pedestal and the Stake"; and Hartmut Lehmann, "Hexenverfolgungen und Hexenprozesse im Alten Reich zwischen Reformation und Aufklärung."

45. Larner, *Witchcraft and Religion*, p. 46.

46. Larner, *Enemies of God*, p. 95.

47. Larner, *Enemies of God*, p. 97.

48. Quaife, p. 101; Duerr, p. 174; Monter, "The Pedestal and the Stake," p. 134.

49. Theresa de Lauretis, *Technologies of Gender*, p. 5.

50. Joan Wallach Scott, "Deconstructing Equality-Versus-Difference," p. 37.

51. Joan Wallach Scott, *Gender and the Politics of History*, pp. 45–50.

52. Scott, *Gender*, p. 42.

53. Scott, *Gender*, p. 42.

54. Thinking and action that are not oppressive and are oriented toward change are always contextual. Therefore, they cannot be formulated in general. For a discussion of whether there is space for political resistance when appropriating Foucault's theory of discourse within feminist theory, see Biddy Martin, "Feminism, Criticism, and Foucault," p. 12.

55. Merry E. Wiesner, "Spinning Out Capital," p. 229.

56. Wiesner, "Spinning Out Capital," and *Working Women in Renaissance Germany*.

57. Merry E. Wiesner, "Women's Defense of their Public Role."

58. Lyndal Roper, *The Holy Household*.

59. Constance Jordan, *Renaissance Feminism*.

60. Jordan, p. 19; and Margaret L. King, "Book-Lined Cells."

61. Jordan, p. 175.

62. Clara Pirckheimer to Willibald Pirckheimer, February 1525, *Caritas Pirckheimer: Quellensammlung*, 3:202–203.

*Two. The* Malleus maleficarum

1. I follow the translator Montague Summers's practice of referring to the *Malleus maleficarum* by its original Latin title, which I usually shorten to *Malleus*.

2. Joseph Hansen and H. C. Klose present convincing evidence that Kramer was the main author. See Joseph Hansen, *Quellen und Untersuchungen zur Ge-*

*schichte des Hexenwahns*, pp. 404–407; and H. C. Klose, "Die angebliche Mitarbeit des Dominikaners Jakob Sprenger am Hexenhammer nach einem alten Abdinghofer Brief."

3. Hansen, *Quellen*, p. 361.

4. The forgery of the endorsement by the University of Cologne faculty is discussed by Joseph Hansen, "Der *Malleus maleficarum*."

5. Joseph Hansen lists twenty-five editions between 1487 and 1750, Helmut Brackert reports twenty-nine, and Rossel Hope Robbins indicates thirty-five. Hansen, "Der *Malleus maleficarum*," pp. 123–133; Helmut Brackert, " 'Unglückliche, was hast du gehofft?'," p. 131; Rossel Hope Robbins, *Encyclopedia of Witchcraft and Demonology*, p. 337.

6. Wolfgang Behringer concludes that the *Malleus* was usually consulted in witchcraft cases in Bavaria between 1520 and 1574, and that copies were readily available in regional city libraries. Wolfgang Behringer, *Hexenverfolgung in Bayern*, p. 82.

7. Heinrich Kramer's *Nürnberger Hexenhammer*, often confused with the *Malleus maleficarum*, only recently appeared for the first time in print. For more on its early use in Nuremberg, see Hartmut Heinrich Kunstmann, *Zauberwahn und Hexenprozeß in der Reichsstadt Nürnberg*, pp. 11–12.

8. "Quisquis ergo aliquid credit posse fireri, aut aliquam creaturam in melius aut in deterius immutari aut transformari in aliam speciem vel similitudinem, nisi ab ipso creatore, qui omnia fecit per quem omnia facta sunt, procul dubio infidelis est." *Canon episcopi* (906), quoted in Hansen, *Quellen*, p. 39.

9. Heinrich Kramer and Jakob Sprenger, *The* Malleus Maleficarum *of Heinrich Kramer and James Sprenger*, trans. Montague Summers, p. 75, hereafter abbreviated as Summers, p. 75. The Latin original is: "[M]ala quae a modernis maleficis perpetrantur cuncta alia mala, quae Deus vnquam fieri permisit . . . excedunt." The Latin original follows each translation in the note; here it is taken from Heinrich Kramer and Jakob Sprenger, *Malleus maleficarum* (Lyon), 1:77 (Book 1, Question 14), hereafter abbreviated as *Malleus*, 1:77 (1:14). I use the Lyon edition of the *Malleus* for better readability, because the first (Speyer) edition contains common fifteenth-century Latin abbreviations.

10. For a description of how this style of argumentation was used to manipulate evidence, see Sydney Anglo, "Evident Authority and Authoritative Evidence."

11. Joseph Hansen notes that Petrus Mamoris uses the term in his *Flagellum maleficorum* (1462). Johannes Nider also uses it (along with the term "saga") in his *Formicarius* (1437), which Kramer and Sprenger employ extensively as a source.

12. Translated by Sigrid Brauner. "Verum etiam differt ab omni noxia et superstitiosa arte, in hoc quod super omnia genera divinationum ipsa Malificorum haeresis supremum obtinet gradum malitiae, quod etiam nomen a maleficiendo seu male de fide sentiendo sibi usurpat, ut prius tactum est." See also the glossary note: "Maleficae dictae a male de fide sentiendo." *Malleus*, 1:17 (1:2).

13. *Malleus*, 1:210 (3: Introduction).

14. Eleanor Commo McLaughlin, "Equality of Souls, Inequality of Sexes," p. 223.

130 NOTES TO THE *MALLEUS MALEFICARUM*

15. Vern L. Bullough, "Medieval Medical and Scientific Views of Women," p. 497.

16. McLaughlin, p. 217.

17. Jean Bethke Elshtain, *Public Man, Private Woman*, pp. 75–93.

18. Summers, p. 44. "Quod in omnibus viribus, tam animae, quam corporis, cum sint defectuosae, non mirum, si plura maleficia in eos, quos aemulantur, fieri procurant." *Malleus*, 1:42 (1:6).

19. Summers, p. 45. "Et quidem sicut ex primo defectu intelligentiae abnegationem fidei facilius incurrunt: ita ex secundo, scilicet inordinatis affectionibus et passionibus varias vindictas quaerunt, excogitant et infligunt, sive per Maleficas, sive alijs quibuscunque modis." *Malleus*, 1:44 (1:6).

20. Summers, p. 45. "Vnde Theophrastus: Si totam domum ei commiseris ad serviendum, et si aliquid tuo arbitrio reservaveris etiam minimum vel magnam fidem sibi adhiberi non putabit, et iurgia concitabit: nisi cito consulueris, parat venena, aruspices et ariolos consulit . . . ecce maleficia." *Malleus*, 1:44 (1:6).

21. Summers, p. 45. "Unde non mirum tantam multitudinem maleficarum in hoc genere existere." *Malleus*, 1:44 (1:6).

22. Summers, p. 45. "Et revera potissima causa deserviens in augmentum Maleficarum est dolorosum duellum inter maritatas et non maritatas foeminas, et viros." *Malleus*, 1:43 (1:6).

23. Summers, p. 46. "Vnde non mirum, si mundus iam patitur ob malitiam mulierum." *Malleus*, 1:45 (1:6).

24. Summers, p. 46. "Quod aspectus eius pulcher, tactus foetidus, conuersatio mortifera . . . Vnde et earum vox cantui Syrenarum assimilatur, quae dulci melodia transeuntes attrahunt, et tamen occidunt. Occidunt quidem, quia ex marsupio euacuant, vires auferunt, et Deum perdere cogunt." *Malleus*, 1:45 (1:6).

25. Summers, p. 46. "Ut merito cum Catone Vticen dicere possimus: Si absque foemina posset esse mundus, conuersatio nostra non esset absque Diis." *Malleus*, 1:45 (1:6).

26. Summers, p. 47. "Et manus sunt vincula ad detinendum, vbi manum ad malefaciendum creaturae apponunt, tunc diabolo cooperante, hoc efficiunt quod praetendunt." *Malleus*, 1:46 (1:6).

27. Summers, p. 47. "Plura haec deduci possent, sed intelligentibus satis apparet, non mirum quod plures reperiuntur infectae haeresi maleficorum mulieres quam viri." *Malleus*, 1:46 (1:6).

28. The authors make this distinction in *Malleus*, Book 1, Question 16.

29. Summers, p. 47. "In quo vtique cum sic pro nobis nasci et pari voluit, ideo et ipsum priuilegiauit." *Malleus*, 1:46 (1:6).

30. Mary Daly sees this line of argument as typical of androcentric Christian theology. Mary Daly, *Gyn/Ecology*, pp. 178–223.

31. Although Dominicus's *Lectiones* is believed lost, the passage on women is preserved in Antonin of Florence's *Summa theologica* (1477) and reprinted in part in Hjalmar Crohns, "Die *Summa theologica* des Antonin Florenz und die Schätzung des Weibes im *Hexenhammer*," p. 6.

32. *Malleus*, 1:42–45 (1:6).

33. Translated by Sigrid Brauner. "Sunt ne nostro tempore boni viri aliqui decepti per magas vel maleficas tuo iudicio?" Johannes Nider, *Formicarius*, 1:332.

34. Summers, p. 43. "Unde quaecunque vituperationes leguntur, in concupiscentiam carnis interpretari possunt, vt semper mulier pro carnis concupiscentia intelligatur. Iuxta illud: Inveni amariorem morte mulierem, et bona mulier subiecta carnis concupiscentia." *Malleus*, 1:42 (1:6).

35. The Innsbruck interrogation records suggest that allegations of love magic served to explain or justify adultery. See Hartmann Ammann, "Der Innsbrucker Hexenprozeß von 1485."

36. Johann Nider, *Daz sint die X gebot* (1430), cited in Hansen, *Quellen*, p. 439.

37. Michael Dallapiazza, *"Minne, hûsêre und das ehlich leben"*, p. 132.

38. Summers, p. 16. "Ita iam mundi vespere ad Occasum declinate, et malitia hominum excrescente, et charitate refrigecente, superabundat omnis maleficiorum iniquitas." *Malleus*, 1:12 (1:2).

39. Summers, p. 68. "Iam totam Christianitatem depopulare videntur." *Malleus*, 1:70 (1:12).

40. See Will Erich Peuckert, *Die große Wende*, pp. 102–110.

41. *Malleus*, 1:185.

42. Summers, p. 47. "Ideo et illae inter ambitiosas amplius infectae sunt, quae pro explendis suis prauis concupiscentiis amplius inardescunt, ut sunt adulterae, fornicariae, et magnatorum concubinae." *Malleus*, 1:46 (1:6).

43. The theory that the "concubines of the great" corrupt those in authority through witchcraft may be partly inspired by official obstruction of the authors' own efforts to prosecute witches. As papal Inquisitors, Kramer and Sprenger saw themselves as acting on behalf of the pope to preserve God's holy order; therefore, they interpreted any resistance to their efforts as the work of the devil acting through the seductive charms of his female agents, the witches.

44. Midwives are discussed in *Malleus*, Book 1, Question 11.

45. Summers, p. 66. "Nemo fidei catholicae amplius nocet, quam obstetrices." *Malleus*, 1:68 (1:11).

46. For a discussion of the various affirmative and subversive functions of the "world turned upside down" topos, see Natalie Zemon Davis, *Society and Culture in Early Modern France*, pp. 97–151.

47. In the *Malleus*, Book 1, Question 9, and Book 2, Question 1, the authors assert that witches are out to castrate men.

48. Summers, p. 59. "Iterum, sicut supra dictum est de vi generativa, illam impediendo per impositionem alicuius alterius corporis euisdem coloris et apparentiae, ita et aliquod corpus planum figuratum colore carneo interponere possunt inter visum aut tactum oculorum et manuum, et inter ipsum verum corpus patientis, ita quod suo iudicio nihil valeat videre et sentire, nisi corpus planum et nullo membro interruptum." *Malleus*, 1:60 (1:18).

49. McLaughlin, p. 217; Elshtain, pp. 75–93.

50. Summers, p. 121. "Quid denique sentiendum super eas maleficas, quae huiusmodi membra in copioso interdum numero, vt viginti vel triginta membra insimul ad nidum auium vel ad aliquod scrinium includunt, vbi et quasi ad viuen-

tia membra se mouent, ad auenam vel pabulum consumenda, provt a multis visa sunt, et communis fama refert." *Malleus*, 1:130 (1:10).

51. For references to trials in Innsbruck and the Constance area, see *Malleus*, Book 2, Question 1; for trials in Italy held by the Dominican Inquisitor Bernhard of Como, see *Malleus*, Book 1, Question 12, and Book 2, Question 1.

52. The Ravensburg letter is reprinted in Karl Otto Müller, "Heinrich Institoris, der Verfasser des Hexenhammers, und seine Tätigkeit als Hexeninquisitor in Ravensburg im Herbst 1484," p. 400.

53. Hansen, *Quellen*, p. 385.

54. Translated by Sigrid Brauner. "Eo quod in primo aggressu, non iam muliebri, sed virili animo se innoxiam affirmabat." *Malleus*, 1:161 (2:1).

55. For information and documentation on the Innsbruck trials, see Ammann; and Wolfgang Ziegeler, *Möglichkeiten der Kritik am Hexen- und Zauberwesen im ausgehenden Mittelalter*. Although I accept the findings of these authors, I draw my own conclusions on the gender aspect of the trials, because both authors ignore them.

56. Records of the Innsbruck proceedings are reprinted in Ammann, pp. 9–74.

*Three. Martin Luther*

1. Luther refers to Geiler von Kaisersberg as his source in his *Decem praecepta wittenbergensi praedicata populo* (1518) when he questions the ability of witches to fly. See *Decem praecepta*, p. 409.

2. Wilhelm Gottlieb Soldan and Heinrich Heppe, *Geschichte der Hexenprozesse*, 1:432. For more recent assessments, see Ian MacLean, *The Renaissance Notion of Woman*, p. 88; E. William Monter, *Witchcraft in France and Switzerland*, p. 30; Henry Charles Lea, *Materials Toward a History of Witchcraft*, 1:422; and H. C. Erik Midelfort, "Witchcraft and Religion in Sixteenth-Century Germany," p. 270.

3. Nikolaus Paulus, *Hexenwahn und Hexenprozeß*, pp. 20–47.

4. Luther once says that witches have devilish faces: "Tales feminas si inspicias, diabolicas habent facies, vidi aliquas." Luther, *Predigten über das zweite Buch Mose*, p. 551.

5. Luther, *Decem praecepta*, p. 406.

6. Except where otherwise indicated, all Bible translations into English follow the King James version. "O sensati Galatae, quis vos fascinavit, non obedire veritati?" Luther, *In epistolam Pauli ad Galatas commentarius* (1519), p. 505.

7. Luther, *In epistolam Pauli* (1519), p. 590.

8. For example, a Breslau municipal statute in 1350 forbids women from practicing medicine or pharmacology. Hermann Schelenz, *Frauen im Reiche Aesculaps*, p. 51. For a discussion of women in the medical professions in late medieval and early modern German towns, see Gabriele Becker and others, "Zum kulturellen Bild und zur realen Situation der Frau im Mittelalter und in der frühen Neuzeit."

9. *Luther's Works*, ed. Jaroslav Pelikan, 27:369. Except where otherwise indicated, all Luther translations into English are from this edition, hereafter referred to as Pelikan. The Latin original is: "Claret autem tanti Apostoli quoque

autoritate, veneficia illa non esse nihil, sed posse nocere, quod multi non credunt." Luther, *In epistolam Pauli* (1519), p. 590.

10. Translated by Robert H. Brown. "Die Zeuberinnen soltu nicht leben lassen." Luther, *Biblia*, Das ander Buch Mose 22:18. See Luther, *Predigten über das zweite Buch Mose*, p. 549. Luther uses the terms "Zeuberinnen" and "maga" in his translations of Exodus 22:18; both terms were commonly used to describe the modern witch.

11. Luther, *Tischreden*, 4:52. Although the *Table Talks* are sometimes questioned as a source, on the subject of witchcraft they are usually consistent with more verifiable sources. For further arguments made by Luther to justify the death penalty for witchcraft on grounds of harmful sorcery, see his *In epistolam Pauli ad Galatas commentarius* (1535), p. 116; and *Predigten über das zweite Buch Mose*, pp. 551, 601.

12. Translated by Elaine C. Tennant. Luther calls for burning alleged witches at the stake "nicht umb des milchdiebstals, sondern umb der lesterung willen, das sie wider Christum den Teuffel mit seinen Sacramenten und Kirchen sterckt." Luther, *Von den Konciliis und Kirchen*, p. 648.

13. On Luther's changing position on the death penalty for heresy, see Paul Wappler, *Inquisition und Ketzerprozeß in Zwickau zur Reformationszeit*, pp. 85–95.

14. Translated by Robert H. Brown. "Solche Thaten aber geben Zeugniss gnug, daß man sie billig sollte hart bestrafen zum Exempel, damit Andere abgeschreckt würden von solchem teufelischen Fürnehmen." Luther, *Tischreden*, 4:44.

15. Luther, *Tischreden*, 6:no. 6836.

16. Pelikan, 26:192. "Summa, nemo nostrum est, qui non saepius falsis opinionibus fascinetur." Luther, *In epistolam Pauli* (1535), p. 317.

17. Translated by Sigrid Brauner. "Haec idolatria dominatur in omni homine, donec sanetur per gratiam in fide Ihesu Christi." Luther, *Decem praecepta*, p. 399.

18. Luther, *Decem praecepta*, p. 399; and *In epistolam Pauli* (1535), p. 113.

19. Luther calls witchcraft a transgression against the first commandment in all his popular versions of the decalogue, including his catechisms. Luther, *Betbüchlein*, p. 380; *Kleiner Katechismus*, p. 284; *Deutscher Katechismus*, p. 134; and *Eine kurze Erklärung der zehn Gebote*, p. 252.

20. Translated by Robert H. Brown. Luther speaks of Anabaptist and peasant rebel "Prophetin . . . und Pfeffin, . . . welche man bey den Christen heißt Teuffelshuren." Luther, *Von den Konciliis und Kirchen*, p. 648. Much earlier, in his first sermon on Galatians (1519), Luther had similarly warned of rampant witchcraft, only to grow much more optimistic in his second version of this same sermon sixteen years later. See Luther, *In epistolam Pauli* (1519), p. 590; and *In epistolam Pauli* (1535), p. 112.

21. Pelikan, 30:88. The English edition translates "reytzen" as "induce." I have replaced it with the more appropriate term "entice." "[S]o sollen sie sich . . . also halten mit yhrem geperd und wandel, das sie damit die menner zum glawben reytzen." Luther, *Epistel S. Petri gepredigt und ausgelegt*, p. 342.

22. Pelikan, 30:91. "Gemeyntlich ist das der weyber natur, das sie sich fur allem ding schewen und furchten, darumb sie so viel zewberey und aberglawbens

treyben, da eyne die ander leret, das nicht zu zelen ist, was sie fur gauckelwerck haben." Luther, *Epistel S. Petri*, p. 345.

23. Translated by Elaine C. Tennant. "Denn die weyl sie weyss, wie es umb sie stehet, das yhr stand Gott gefelt, was will sie denn furchten?" Luther, *Epistel S. Petri*, p. 345.

24. For Luther's views on Satan's seduction of men and women, see his *Decem praecepta*, p. 410. In Luther's entire work, there are only two passing references to impotence induced by sorcery. See Luther, *Das Evangelium am Tage der heiligen drei Könige*, p. 591; and *Predigt am Sonntag exaudi nachmittags*, p. 560.

25. Luther, *Enarratio in I Cap. Genesis*, pp. 87–90.

26. Heinrich Kramer and Jakob Sprenger, *Malleus*, Book 1, Question 3. See also Rossel Hope Robbins, *Encyclopedia on Witchcraft and Demonology*, pp. 461–468.

27. Luther, *Predigten über das erste Buch Mose*, p. 160.

28. Pelikan, 27:90. "Paulus inter opera carnis enumerat veneficium, quod tamen, ut omnibus constat, non est opus libidinis, sed abusus seu aemulatio idolatriae." Luther, *In epistolam Pauli* (1535), p. 113. I replace "sorcery" in the English edition with the word "witchcraft," because in this context Luther is speaking about modern witchcraft, not sorcery in general.

29. Translated by Sigrid Brauner. "Et quis huius seductilis sexus omnia ludicra, ridicula, falsa, vana et supersticiosa recenseat? Ex prima Heva eis ingenitum est falli et ludibrio haberi." Luther, *Decem praecepta*, p. 407.

30. Luther, *Predigten über das erste Buch Mose*, pp. 131–139.

31. Translated by Sigrid Brauner. "De maga. . . . Quare lex plus feminas quam viros hic nominat, quamquam etiam viri in hoc delinquunt? . . . Ut Eva." Luther, *Predigten über das zweite Buch Mose*, p. 551.

32. Translated by Sigrid Brauner. "Secunda est iuventus et eorum qui coniugio iam sunt astricti, ubi affectus prolis et rerum mulierculas mire seductiles reddit in hoc opere diaboli. . . . [V]el naturalem quaere medicinam, vel deum exora in simplici fide." Luther, *Decem praecepta*, p. 402.

33. Pelikan, 30:91. "Styrbt dyr deyn kind, wirstu kranck, wol dyr, befihls Gott, du bist ynn dem stand der Gott gefelt, was kanstu bessers begeren?" Luther, *Epistel S. Petri*, p. 345.

34. Pelikan, 30:88. "Wilche sich aber das nicht lesst reytzen, da wirt sonst nichts helffen. Denn mit schlagen wirstu nichts ausrichten, das du eyn weyb frum und bendig machst, schlechstu eyn teuffel herauss, so schlechstu yhr zween hyneyn." Luther, *Epistel S. Petri*, pp. 342–343.

35. Luther says that gypsies are sorcerers (*Evangelium am Tage der heiligen drei Könige*, p. 559) and that Jews practice magic (*Decem praecepta*, p. 407). On attitudes towards Jews in the sixteenth century, see Heiko A. Obermann, *Wurzeln des Anti-semitismus*, pp. 56–87.

36. Luther, *Das Evangelium am Tage der heiligen drei Könige*, p. 559.

37. Translated by Sigrid Brauner. "Secunda est iuventus et eorum qui coniugio iam sunt astricti, ubi affectus prolis et rerum mulierculas mire seductiles reddit in hoc opere diaboli. . . . Tercia aetas propria est vetularum aut similia illis operantium ut qui cum daemonibus paciscuntur." Luther, *Decem Praecepta*, pp. 402–406.

38. Kramer and Sprenger discuss the age of witches in *Malleus*, Book 2, Question 1.

39. The figure of the old woman may derive from several sources: the "parcae" (Roman fates); the old woman with the evil eye; and the old women who interpret dreams in medieval lore (see Matthias Lexer, *Mittelhochdeutsches Handwörterbuch*, 3:922–926). For more on the evil wife as an old woman, see Franz Brietzmann, *Die böse Frau in der deutschen Literatur des Mittelalters*, p. 191.

40. Luther, *In epistolam Pauli* (1519), p. 505.

41. Hans-Martin Barth, *Der Teufel und Jesus Christus in der Theologie Martin Luthers*, p. 151.

42. Luther once calls the old hag a "wetterhure," a term he reserves for the witch. See *Das 14. und 15. Kapitel S. Johannis gepredigt und ausgelegt*, p. 683.

43. Luther, *Tischreden*, 6:no. 6908; and 2:no. 1429.

44. Luther, *Das 14. und 15. Kapitel S. Johannis*, pp. 683–684.

45. Desiderius Erasmus, *Colloquia familiaria*, 1:706. See also Clara Hätzlerin, *Liederbuch*, no. 217.

46. Similar ideas were expressed by Albrecht von Eyb in his *Ehebüchlein* (1472). See Michael Dallapiazza, *"Minne, hûsêre und das ehlich leben."*

*Four. Paul Rebhun*

1. For more on Rebhun's background, see Paul F. Casey, *Paul Rebhun.*

2. Matthias Lexer, *Mittelhochdeutsches Handwörterbuch*, 1:330.

3. For more on the shrew ("böses wîp"), see Franz Brietzmann, *Die böse Frau in der deutschen Literatur des Mittelalters.*

4. Barbara G. Walker makes this argument in *The Crone*, p. 139.

5. Silvia Schmitz, *Weltentwurf als Realitätsbewältigung in Johannes Paulis "Schimpf und Ernst."*

6. For examples of and further information on the devil-and-old-woman tale, see Frederic C. Tubach, *Index Exemplorum*, no. 1551, 1552, 1626, 4511, 5361; Antti Amatus Aarne, *The Types of the Folktale*, no. 1353; Stith Thompson, *Motif-Index of Folk-Literature*, no. G303.10.5, K1085; Albert Wesselski, ed., *Märchen des Mittelalters*, no. 5; Johannes Bolte, ed., *Kleinere Schriften von Reinhold Köhler*, 3:12–13; Albert Lecoy de la Marche, ed., *Anecdotes historiques*, no. 245; Juan Manuel, *El libro de los enxiemplos del conde lucanor et de Patronio*, pp. 386–396; Thomas Wright, ed., *A Selection of Latin Stories*, no. 100; Alfons Hilka, "Neue Beiträge zur Erzählungsliteratur des Mittelalters"; and Stanislaus Prato, "Vergleichende Mitteilungen zu Hans Sachs' Fastnachtspiel 'Der Teufel mit dem alten Weib.'"

7. Adelbert von Keller, ed., *Fastnachtspiele des fünfzehnten Jahrhunderts*, 3:no. 57.

8. The figure of the marriage devil is rooted in the Protestant belief that Satan appears in many disguises. A genre of "devil books" appeared in the sixteenth century, depicting Satan in such specialized forms as the "drinking devil" ("Sauffteufel"), "gambling devil" ("Spielteufel"), and "whoring devil" ("Hurenteufel"). The devil books were designed to show their readers how to recognize and deal with every kind of devil. These books became so popular that by the end of the sixteenth century, every fourth German family with at least one literate

member possessed a devil book. See Heinrich Grimm, "Die deutschen 'Teufelsbücher' des 16. Jahrhunderts," p. 1760.

9. Martin Luther, *Biblia*, Vorrhede auffs buch Tobia; and Vorrhede auffs buch Judith.

10. Translated by Elaine C. Tennant. "Das nür ist gsetzt zu guter lehr, / das lass man bleyben ein geticht / Vnd mach ihm niemand draus ein geschicht." Paul Rebhun, *Ein Hochzeit Spiel auff die Hochzeit zu Cana*, p. 93.

11. Casey, p. 107.

12. Translated by Sigrid Brauner. "Du Mann liebe dein Weib / Du Weib gehorche deinem Mann / Das machet Hausfried." Paul Rebhun, *Hochzeitspredigt vom Hausfried*, title page. These lines echo Ephesians 5:22–25: "Wives, submit yourselves unto your own husbands, as unto the Lord . . . Husbands, love your wives, even as Christ also loved the church."

13. Rebhun, *Hausfried*, folio a3r.

14. Martin Luther, *Ein Sermon von dem ehlichen Stand*, p. 168.

15. Translated by Sigrid Brauner. "Denn der gehorsam ist dem weiber Geschlecht [durch den Sündenfall] zur straffe auffgelegt / Und sol seinen fortgang haben / Die Liebe aber ist dem Mann nicht zur straffe auffgelegt / sondern gleich als zur verehrung und belohnung des vorhergehenden gehorsams." Rebhun, *Hausfried*, folio t4v.

16. Rebhun, *Hausfried*, folio dv.

17. Translated by Elaine C. Tennant. "Weil sie sein ordnung so verkern / Wollns besser machen, denn er selb." Rebhun, *Hochzeit zu Cana*, p. 123.

18. Translated by Elaine C. Tennant. "Dann was ich ihr thu blasen ein / Das als verbringt sie wunderfein." Rebhun, *Hochzeit in Cana*, p. 114. The term "einblasen" is reminiscent of Luther's use of the term "blasen" to mean demonic inspiration — the ability of the devil to enter the mind and produce false images that appear real. See Martin Luther, *Das 14. und 15. Kapitel S. Johannis gepredigt und ausgelegt*, p. 684.

19. Translated by Elaine C. Tennant. "Die alzeit streben widern stram / Ihrn willn wolln habn ins Teuffels nahm." Rebhun, *Hochzeit zu Cana*, p. 172.

20. Translated by Elaine C. Tennant. "Verhetz das Weib das sie nicht tregt, / den ghorsam der ihr auffgelegt, / Vnd gib yr auffrürigen mut." Rebhun, *Hochzeit zu Cana*, p. 110.

21. This argument was widely used by the Catholic clergy to encourage prospective nuns to choose the monastic life over marriage; for example, St. Jerome used it in addressing a group of Roman women. Elizabeth Clark and Herbert Richardson, eds., *Women and Religion*, p. 56. By having his witch repeat a traditional Catholic argument against marriage, Rebhun indirectly denounces papistry and monasticism.

22. Translated by Elaine C. Tennant. "Das schwerst wil ich nur zeigen an, / Welchs ist, dass Weib sol ihrem Man / Inn allen dingen ghorsam sein / Vnd lassen ihn sein Herr allein." Rebhun, *Hochzeit zu Cana*, p. 115.

23. Translated by Elaine C. Tennant. Through resistance, says the witch, women will "endlich werden Herrn, / Vnd dürffen thun was sie gelüst / Wo sich sonst eine fürchten müst." Rebhun, *Hochzeit zu Cana*, p. 119.

24. Translated by Sigrid Brauner. "Ich widerfecht nicht Gottes wort / Dann ich auch predigt hab gehort / Da man gesagt, von man vnd weib / Wie sie solln beide sein ein leib / Welchs ich bey mir also vernim / Das auch dem weib so wol gezim / Das regiment als ebn dem man / Vnd das die mann mit gwalt inn han / Darumb es nicht zu leyden sey / Dieweils ihn sein sol beyden frey." Rebhun, *Hochzeit zu Cana*, p. 120.

25. Luther, *Ein Sermon von dem ehlichen Stand*, p. 168. In Ephesians, Paul says that "the husband is the head of the wife, even as Christ is the head of the church: and he is the saviour of the body. . . . So ought men to love their wives as they love their own bodies. . . . For no man ever yet hated his own flesh; but nourisheth and cherisheth it, even as the Lord the church: For we are members of his body, of his flesh, and of his bones." Ephesians 5:23–30.

26. Translated by Sigrid Brauner. "Nun sage myr: Wen ein Mann hynginge und wussche die windel odder thet sonst am kinde eyn verachtlich Werk, unnd yedermann spottet seyn und hielt yhn fur eyn maulaffe und frawen man, so ers doch thett ynn solcher obgesagter meynung [aus ehelicher Liebe] unnd Christlichen glawben, Lieber, sage, wer spottet hie des andern am feynsten? Gott lacht mit allen engeln und creaturn; nicht das er die windel wesscht, sondern das ers ym glawben thut." Martin Luther, *Vom ehelichen Leben*, pp. 296–297.

27. For information on these and other Protestant activist women, see Barbara Becker-Cantarino, "Frauen in den Glaubenskämpfen"; Jane Dempsey Douglass, "Women and the Continental Reformation"; Paul A. Russell, *Lay Theology in the Reformation*, pp. 185–212; and Roland H. Bainton, *Women of the Reformation in Germany and Italy*, pp. 55–79, 97–111.

28. Translated by Elaine C. Tennant. "Es wäre nicht gut für uns arme Ehemänner, dass böse Weiber darinnen lesen." Quoted in Gerta Scharffenorth and Klaus Thraede, *"Freunde in Christus werden . . ."*, p. 242.

29. Translated by Elaine C. Tennant. "Ja ihr vernempt was euch gefelt / Secht aber nicht was weiter helt." Rebhun, *Hochzeit zu Cana*, p. 121. Maria uses the traditional Christian argument against reading Scripture out of context.

30. Waltraud Timmermann, "Theaterspiel als Medium evangelischer Verkündigung," pp. 153–154.

31. Although the use of magic in dealing with household conflicts has yet to be researched, witch trial records suggest that the practice was common. See Wilhelm Gottlieb Soldan and Heinrich Heppe, *Geschichte der Hexenprozesse*, 2:72; and Jeannine Blackwell," 'Die Zunge, der Geistliche und das Weib.' "

32. Lyndal Roper, *The Holy Household*, p. 147.

33. On the limited rights of women in marriage, see Gabriele Becker and others, "Zum kulturellen Bild und zur realen Situation der Frau im Mittelalter und in der frühen Neuzeit," pp. 31–40.

34. "Er wirt des vrsach habn fur sich." Rebhun, *Hochzeit zu Cana*, p. 149. In John 2:5, after Jesus refuses her request for immediate help in providing more wine, Mary tells the servants, "Whatsoever he saith unto you, do it." (Pharaoh tells his servants the same thing in authorizing Joseph to oversee the distribution of food during the famine in Egypt, Genesis 41:55.) Rebhun embellishes the story by stressing Maria's submission to Jesus — Jesus's rudeness is more pro-

nounced than in the Bible, and Maria's assurance that "he must have his reasons" is more explicitly deferential.

35. Translated by Elaine C. Tennant. "Mit Weiber gschefft er ist verstrickt / Das er so langsam her sich schickt / Sein Fraw bevalch ihm was im haus / Das muss er ihr vor richten aus. . . . Mein Fraw die gab mir für ein gschefft / Damit war ich so lang verhefft / Ich must ihr wign ein weil das kindt / Dann wir nicht habn viel haussgesindt." Rebhun, *Hochzeit zu Cana*, pp. 138–139.

36. Luther, *Vom ehelichen Leben*, pp. 295–297.

37. Translated by Elaine C. Tennant. "Ihr habt den namen mit der that," Andreas tells Simon. "Zun Weibern solt ihr sitzen ein / die wolln auch immer Sieman [sic] sein," mocks the bridegroom. Rebhun, *Hochzeit zu Cana*, p. 139.

38. Roper, p. 134.

39. Translated by Elaine C. Tennant. "Mit Weibern ich mich wol vertrag / Vnd lass sie Herrn sein nacht vnd tag." Rebhun, Hochzeit zu Cana, p. 140.

40. Carnival rituals functioned also to criticize authority or protest its abuse. Susan C. Karant-Nunn, *Zwickau in Transition*, p. 183.

41. See Claudia Ulbrich, "Unartige Weiber."

42. Roper cites a 1571 Augsburg ordinance. Roper, p. 134.

43. Translated by Elaine C. Tennant. "Ihr als ein man euch halt der mass / Mannlicher weis inn eurem standt / das ihr behalt die öberhandt." Rebhun, *Hochzeit zu Cana*, p. 165.

44. Translated by Elaine C. Tennant. "Wo man so demütig sich halt / So bringts doch schaden manichfalt / Dann Gottes ordnung wird verkert / Dazu der nechste auch beschwert / Weil solch Exempel stercken thut / Der bösen Weiber ubermut." Rebhun, *Hochzeit zu Cana*, p. 164.

45. Translated by Elaine C. Tennant. Tobias tells the bridegroom that emotional self-control is "besonder . . . mannlich sterck . . . vnd . . . mannes werck." Rebhun, *Hochzeit zu Cana*, p. 167.

46. Luther, *Vom ehelichen Leben*, pp. 296–297.

47. Translated by Elaine C. Tennant. "Das ist bey glaubn ein guter schwanck." Rebhun, *Hochzeit zu Cana*, p. 142.

48. Translated by Elaine C. Tennant. Referring to Shrovetide plays, Rebhun says they "hab der possen viel / Der iederman wol lachen künn / Vnd sey sonst weyter nichts darinn." *Hochzeit zu Cana*, p. 92.

49. Translated by Elaine C. Tennant. "Ihr wist das ich sol haben nun / Zur wirtschaft schöne kleider auch / Wie itzund ist der gemeine brauch / So hab ich weder ditz noch das / Wie ihr dann selber wisset bass." Rebhun, *Hochzeit zu Cana*, p. 103.

50. Translated by Elaine C. Tennant. "Ein perlein band het ich mir gern / Gekaufft, vnd anders was zu ehrn / Der wirtschafft itzt zu tragen töcht." Rebhun, *Hochzeit zu Cana*, p. 103.

51. Translated by Elaine C. Tennant. "Drumb hab ich lang darauff gesorgt / Obs döcht das ich mir kleider borgt / Die ich anlegen möcht zu ehrn / Ich wolt ihr sonst gar nicht begehrn." Rebhun, *Hochzeit zu Cana*, p. 103.

52. Translated by Elaine C. Tennant. "Das dem von Gott gepoten sey / Das er ihm einen gemahel frey / Zu meiden schand und hurerey." Rebhun, *Hochzeit zu*

*Cana*, p. 96. In 1 Corinthians 7:6–9, Paul merely advises people to marry (he speaks "by permission, and not of commandment"), whereas Rebhun claims that God commands marriage.

53. Translated by Robert H. Brown. "Das man kein gelt mehr leihet hin / Es wiss dann einer vor sein gwin." Rebhun, *Hochzeit zu Cana*, p. 106.

54. Translated by Elaine C. Tennant. "Vnd wenn mans auch besicht beim tag / So find es sich fast in der that / Das alls was Gott geordnet hat / Bey vns allhie stets haben muss / Viel anstös, vnd gros hindernus." Rebhun, *Hochzeit zu Cana*, p. 96.

55. Translated by Elaine C. Tennant. "Derselbs [Gott] geordnet hat den standt / Demselben ichs bevehlen thu, / Der wird sein segn noch gebn dazu." Rebhun, *Hochzeit zu Cana*, p. 102.

56. Translated by Elaine C. Tennant. "Gott macht kinder, der wird sie auch wohl erneeren." Luther, *Vom ehelichen Leben*, p. 304.

57. See Barbara Hanawalt, ed., *Women and Work in Preindustrial Europe*; and Merry E. Wiesner, *Working Women in Renaissance Germany*.

*Five. Hans Sachs*

1. Barbara Könneker, *Hans Sachs*, p. 6. See also E. Carlsohn, "Die Bibliothek Hans Sachs."

2. Hans Sachs, "Die zwölff eygenschafft eynes bosshaftigen weybs," p. 377.

3. See Gerald Strauss, *Nuremberg in the Sixteenth Century*, pp. 123–145; and Hans Mottek, *Wirtschaftsgeschichte Deutschlands*, 1:207–212.

4. Rudolf Endres, "Zur Lage der Nürnberger Handwerkerschaft zur Zeit von Hans Sachs," p. 108.

5. Endres, "Zur Lage der Nürnberger Handwerkerschaft," p. 116.

6. Translated by Elaine C. Tennant. "Weyter regirt der geytz gewaltigklich unter den kauffherren und verlegern, die da drucken ire arbeyter und stückwerker. . . . Ist das gut Evangelisch, das die armen also tag und nacht uber und uber arbweyten und sich des hungers mit weyb und kindt kaum erneren mögen?" Sachs, *Ein dialogus des inhalt: ein argument der Römischen wider das christlich heuflein, den geiz betreffend*, pp. 55–56.

7. Rudolf Endres, "Zünfte und Unterschichten als Elemente der Instabilität in den Städten," pp. 152–169.

8. Maria E. Müller, *Der Poet der Moralität*, pp. 250–254.

9. My summary of the role of women in the early modern German artisan household draws on Maria E. Müller, *Der Poet der Moralität*, pp. 243–285; Merry E. Wiesner, "Women's Defense of their Public Role"; and Monika Londner, "Eheauffassung und Darstellung der Frau in der spätmittelalterlichen Märendichtung," pp. 347–360. See also the works mentioned in the next note.

10. Although the split between private and public does not make the artisan's wife a modern housewife, it does mark a beginning tendency in this direction, and many women rebelled against their growing exclusion from the workplace and relegation to the household. See Wiesner, "Women's Defense of their Public Role"; Friederike Höher, "Hexe, Maria und Hausmutter"; Brigitte Rauer, "Hexenwahn — Frauenverfolgung zu Beginn der Neuzeit"; and Barbara Duden and

Pola Fortunati, "Frauen, Staat und Widerstand in den Anfängen des Kapitalismus." On the coincidence between Luther's teachings on marriage and artisan marital values, see Michael Dallapiazza, *"Minne, hûsêre und das ehlich leben"*, pp. 162–164.

11. Norbert Elias, *Über den Prozeß der Zivilisation*, 2:312–336.

12. Translated by Elaine C. Tennant. "Herzlieber Mann, lass faren hin! . . . Ein traum ist nichts dann fantasey." Sachs, *Ein Faßnacht Spil mit vier personen: Der teüffel mit dem alten Weyb*, in *Sämtliche Fastnachtspiele von Hans Sachs*, ed. Edmund Goetze, p. 60. I use this edition instead of *Hans Sachs: Werke* (ed. Adelbert von Keller and Edmund Goetze) whenever the corresponding volume in *Hans Sachs: Werke* was not critically edited by Edmund Goetze. For a discussion of textual problems with *Hans Sachs: Werke*, see Könneker, *Hans Sachs*, p. 14.

13. Translated by Robert H. Brown. "Komb heim, lass uns die Suppen essen." Sachs, *Der teüffel mit dem alten Weyb*, p. 60.

14. See Dallapiazza.

15. For example, see Heinrich Kramer and Jakob Sprenger, *Malleus*, Book 1, Question 7. Kramer and Sprenger base their dream theory in part on Aristotle.

16. Luther, *Das 14. und 15. Kapitel S. Johannis gepredigt und ausgelegt*, p. 684. "Ich hab disem ehvolck dermassen / Wol dreyssig Jar her einblasen lassen / Durch traeum und gsicht, doch in der stillen, / Und sie geraitzt zu widerwillen." Sachs, *Der teüffel mit dem alten Weyb*, p. 61.

17. Translated by Elaine C. Tennant. "Das sie einander schlagen soellen / Noch den tag bey scheinender sonnen." Sachs, *Der teüffel mit dem alten Weyb*, p. 61.

18. Translated by Elaine C. Tennant. "Ey nun, bin ich doch vorhin dein!" Sachs, *Der teüffel mit dem alten Weyb*, p. 62.

19. Translated by Elaine C. Tennant. "Ich darff mit dir ja gar nicht balgen; / Du bist mir vil zu herb und boess." Sachs, *Der teüffel mit dem alten Weyb*, p. 67.

20. "Dann solcher alter Weyber drey / Fiengen im Feld den Teüfel frey." Sachs, *Der teüffel mit dem alten Weyb*, p. 67.

21. Translated by Robert H. Brown. "Nun frew wir uns, dass dise statt / Keinen Jüden mehr in ir hat / . . . / Der [bösen] weib findt man hie keines mehr; / Wann sie sind all jenseit dess bachs, / Da stifftens noch vil ungemachs. / Weit mit in hin! wündschet Hans Sachs." Hans Sachs, *Ein fasnacht Spiel mit fünff Personen: Der Teufel nahm ein alt Weib zu der Eh, die ihn vertrieb*, p. 33.

22. Strauss, pp. 118–123.

23. Heiko A. Oberman, *Wurzeln des Antisemitismus*, pp. 99–105.

24. For example, Kramer and Sprenger assert that witches use the devil's powers of delusion to make men think that they have been castrated. *Malleus*, Book 1, Question 9, and Book 2, Question 1.

25. Kunstmann, p. 62.

26. Translated by Elaine C. Tennant. "So du im glauben Gott erkenst, / So kan dir schaden kein gespenst." Hans Sachs, "Ein wunderlich gesprech von fünff Unhulden," p. 287.

27. Translated by Elaine C. Tennant. "Zu lieb sie [Hexen] nyemand zwingen mügen. / Wer sich die lieb lest ubergan, / Der selb hat im es selb gethan, / Das es laufft wie ain halber narr." Sachs, "Ein wunderlich gesprech," p. 287.

28. In his *Über den Prozeß der Zivilisation*, Elias argues that in early modern Europe an advancing "threshold of shame" (particularly at court and in town) dictated that individuals learn to control such drives as sexuality. "In aristocratic court society," he contends, "sexual life was certainly a good deal more concealed than in medieval society." The same "civilizing" process continued throughout the modern period, so that "measured by the standard of control of the impulses in bourgeois society itself, the concealment and segregation of sexuality in social life, as in consciousness, was relatively slight in this [early modern] phase." Norbert Elias, *The History of Manners*, p. 178.

29. In the introduction to the 1968 edition of his *Über den Prozeß der Zivilisation*, Elias contends that in the civilizing process, an egocentric view of the world emerges from the perspective of the seemingly isolated individual (or "homo clausus"), who perceives reality primarily in terms of himself. See Elias, *The History of Manners*, pp. 254–263.

30. "The devil bends a woman to his will insofar as he persuades her to doubt the faith." Translated by Robert H. Brown. "Der teuffel lest ein weib sich zwingen, / So fern ers inn unglaub müg bringen." Sachs, "Ein wunderlich gesprech," p. 287. The witch who is married to the devil says that her husband "helps me produce bad weather in order to please the speculators." Translated by Robert H. Brown. "Derselbig hilft mir wetter machen, / Das sein die wuchrer mügen lachen." Sachs, "Ein wunderlich gesprech," p. 286.

31. See Sachs's *Der Cortisan mit dem Beckenknecht* (1562) and *Der deuffel mit des alten weibes sel* (1551). For more examples, see Wolf D. Schulz, "Aspekte des Übernatürlichen in den Fastnachtspielen des Hans Sachs" and Anton Zirn, "Stoffe und Motive bei Hans Sachs in seinen Fabeln und Schwänken."

32. Translated by Elaine C. Tennant. "[D]ie alten ehrbern, frommen frawen, / . . . / irn ehmännern sind unterthan." Sachs, *Der Teufel nahm ein alt Weib*, p. 33.

33. Protestant educational manuals carried instructions to keep young women locked away from public view inside the home. See Cornelia Niekus Moore, *The Maiden's Mirror*.

34. Those who contributed to this view include Aristotle, Thomas Aquinas, Johannes Dominicus in his *Lectiones super ecclesiastes* (1380), Johannes Nider in his *Formicarius* (1435), and Kramer and Sprenger in their *Malleus*. See Eleanor Commo McLaughlin, "Equality of Souls, Inequality of Sexes," p. 217; and Jean Bethke Elshtain, *Public Man, Private Woman*, pp. 75–93.

35. Translated by Robert H. Brown. "Mir hat umb sunst nicht traumet heüt, / mein Fraw hab mir mein augn ausskratzt; / Ist auch also auff mich geplatzt. / Wiewols nit ist des traumes schuld. / Wo ist die heütig alt Unhuld, / Das ich sie thet mit Fuessen tretten? / Die hat mit jren falschen räthen / mein frommes weib mir abgericht." Sachs, *Der teüffel mit dem alten Weyb*, p. 68.

36. Translated by Elaine C. Tennant. "Er soll an mir nicht han ein Weyb, / Sonder ein Teüffel, weyl ich leb!" Sachs, *Der teüffel mit dem alten Weyb*, p. 63.

37. Sachs, *Der teüffel mit dem alten Weyb*, p. 66.

38. Hans Sachs, "Die vier natur einer frawen," pp. 144–147. Sachs used as his source a vernacular translation of classical Greek poems published in 1551. Arthur Ludwig Stiefel, "Über die Quellen der Fabeln, Märchen und Schwänke des Hans Sachs," p. 164.

39. Translated by Robert H. Brown. "Ich gühn dir guts und warn dich mit: / Der Eva nemb ich warlich nicht; / Wann sie ist alt, zornig und grentig, / Alt hundt sindt böss zu machen bentig, / Auch vexirt sie die hoffart wol / Und steckt heimlicher list vol. / Schadt, soltu sein erschlagen mit." Sachs, "Von der unglückhafften, verschwatzten Bulschafft," p. 210.

40. Maria E. Müller, *Der Poet der Moralität*, pp. 253–255.

41. Translated by Robert H. Brown. "Ey, ey wer sol trawen eim Mann? . . . Den Schalck er gar wol decken kan." Sachs, *Der teüffel mit dem alten Weyb*, pp. 62–63.

42. Translated by Elaine C. Tennant. "Und thut in [bösen mäulern] kein gelauben geben! / Sondr erfart euch wol und eben, / Ob sey lügen oder war. / Niemandt so ungestüm far / Auff blosse wort so grim und jech, / Auff das im nicht wie uns geschech." Sachs, *Der teüffel mit dem alten Weyb*, p. 69.

43. Translated by Elaine C. Tennant. "Weil aber Gott in dem anfang / Dem man hat geben den vorgang, / Die herrschung und das regiment, / . . . / Auch kaiser Justinianus / Verbotten hat in seinem recht / Die herrschung gantz menschlichem gschlecht, / So kan ich nit brechen zuletz / Götlich und kayserlich gesetz." Sachs, *Comedia oder Kampff-gesprech zwischen Juppiter unnd Juno, ob weiber oder mender zum regimenten tüglicher seyn*, p. 30.

*Six. Burning the Witch to Tame the Shrew*

1. For a discussion of the role of carnival customs and Shrovetide plays in releasing pent-up emotions, see Natalie Zemon Davis, *Society and Culture in Early Modern France*, pp. 97–152.

2. Mentioned at various points in my study, such texts include the woodcut that appeared in the 1533 edition of Johann Pauli's *Schimpf und Ernst* showing evil wives as witches, and a theoretical work on witchcraft by the humanist Theophrastus Paracelsus under the title *De sagis et earum operibus* (1537). For a discussion of the former, see Silvia Schmitz, *Weltentwurf als Realitätsbewältigung in Johannes Paulis "Schimpf und Ernst"*; for more on the latter, see Sigrid Brauner, "Hexenjagd in Gelehrtenköpfen," p. 193.

3. Elias adduces documentary evidence (such as books of manners) from the early modern period to support his contention that what he calls the "civilizing process" is associated with an advancing threshold of socially instilled fears that inhibit the open expression of drives and affects. Norbert Elias, *The History of Manners*, pp. 84–129.

4. Maria E. Müller, "Naturwesen Mann," pp. 58–68.

5. See Sigrid Brauner, "Cannibals, Witches, and Shrews in the 'Civilizing Process.'"

# Bibliography

Aall, L. Weiser. "Hexe." In *Handwörterbuch des Deutschen Aberglaubens*, edited by Bächtold-Stäubli, vol. 3, pp. 1827–1858.

Aarne, Antti Amatus. *The Types of the Folktale: A Classification and Bibliography.* FF Communications, vol. 184. Helsinki: Suomalainen Tiedeakatemia, 1961.

Allen, Richard M. "Rebellion Within the Household: Hans Sachs's Conception of Women and Marriage." *Essays in History* 19 (1975):43–74.

Ammann, Hartmann. "Der Innsbrucker Hexenprozess von 1485." *Zeitschrift des Ferdinandeums für Tirol und Vorarlberg* 34 (1890):1–87.

Anderson, Bonnie S., and Judith P. Zinsser. *A History of their Own: Women in Europe from Prehistory to the Present.* 2 vols. New York: Harper & Row, 1988.

Anglo, Sydney, ed. *The Damned Art: Essays in the Literature of Witchcraft.* London: Routledge & K. Paul, 1977.

Anglo, Sydney. "Evident Authority and Authoritative Evidence." In *The Damned Art*, edited by Anglo, pp. 1–31.

Arnold, Herbert A. "Die Rollen der Courasche: Bemerkungen zur wirtschaftlichen und sozialen Stellung der Frau im siebzehnten Jahrhundert." In *Die Frau von der Reformation zur Romantik*, edited by Becker-Cantarino, pp. 86–110.

Bacon, Thomas I. *Martin Luther and the Drama.* Amsterdamer Publikationen zur Sprache und Literatur, vol. 25. Amsterdam: Rodopi, 1976.

Bächtold-Stäubli, Hans, ed. *Handwörterbuch des deutschen Aberglaubens.* 10 vols. Berlin, Leipzig: de Gruyter, 1927–1942.

Bainton, Roland H. *Here I Stand: A Life of Martin Luther.* New York: Abingdon-Cokesbury Press, 1950.

Bainton, Roland H. *Women of the Reformation in Germany and Italy.* 1971. Reprint. Beacon Paperback, vol. 485. Boston: Beacon, 1974.

Baroja, Julio Caro. *Las brujas y su mundo.* Madrid: Revista de occidente, 1961.

Baroja, Julio Caro. *The World of the Witches.* Translated by Nigel Glendinning. Chicago: University of Chicago Press, 1965.

Barth, Hans-Martin. *Der Teufel und Jesus Christus in der Theologie Martin Luthers.* Forschungen zur Kirchen- und Dogmengeschichte, vol. 19. Göttingen: Vandenhoeck & Ruprecht, 1967.

Baschwitz, Kurt. *Hexen und Hexenprozesse: Die Geschichte eines Massenwahns und seiner Bekämpfung.* Munich: Bertelsmann, 1963.

Baumgarten, Achim R. *Hexenwahn und Hexenverfolgung im Naheraum: Ein Beitrag zur Sozial- und Kulturgeschichte.* Europäische Hochschulschriften, sect. 3 (Geschichte und ihre Hilfswissenschaften), vol. 325. Frankfurt, New York: Lang, 1987.

Beauvoir, Simone de. *Le deuxième sexe.* Paris: Librairie Gallimard, 1949.

Beauvoir, Simone de. *Das andere Geschlecht: Sitte und Sexus der Frau*. Translated by Eva Rechel-Mertens and Fritz Montfort. Reinbek bei Hamburg: Rowohlt, 1968.

Becker, Gabriele, and others. *Aus der Zeit der Verzweiflung: Zur Genese und Aktualität des Hexenbildes*. Frankfurt: Suhrkamp, 1977.

Becker, Gabriele, and others. "Zum kulturellen Bild und zur realen Situation der Frau im Mittelalter und in der frühen Neuzeit." In Becker and others, *Aus der Zeit der Verzweiflung*, pp. 11–128.

Becker-Cantarino, Barbara, ed., *Die Frau von der Reformation zur Romantik: Die Situation der Frau vor dem Hintergrund der Literatur- und Sozialgeschichte*. Modern German Studies, vol. 7. Bonn: Bouvier, 1980.

Becker-Cantarino, Barbara, "Frauen in den Glaubenskämpfen: Öffentliche Briefe, Lieder und Gelegenheitsschriften." In *Deutsche Literatur von Frauen*, edited by Gisela Brinkner-Gabler, vol. 1, pp. 149–172. Munich: Beck, 1988.

Behaim, Michael. *Ein Meistergesang wider Zauberei und Aberglauben*. 1460. Reprint. In *Deutsche National-Litteratur*, edited by Joseph Kürschner, vol. 12.1, pp. 334–338. Berlin: Spemann, 1889.

Behringer, Wolfgang. *Hexenverfolgung in Bayern: Volksmagie, Glaubenseifer und Staatsräson in der frühen Neuzeit*. Munich: Oldenbourg, 1987.

Beifus, Joseph. "Hans Sachs und die Reformation bis zum Tode Luthers." *Mitteilungen des Vereins für Geschichte der Stadt Nürnberg* 19 (1911):1–77.

Bekker, Hugo. "The Lucifer Motif in the German Drama of the Sixteenth Century." *Monatshefte* 51 (1959):237–247.

Benecke, Georg Friedrich, Wilhelm Müller, and Friedrich Zarncke. *Mittelhochdeutsches Wörterbuch*. 3 vols. Leipzig: S. Hirzel, 1854–1866.

Benfield, Ben Barker. "Anne Hutchinson and the Puritan Attitude toward Women." *Feminist Studies* 1 (1972):65–96.

Berger, Helen. "Witchcraft and the Domination of Women: The English Witch Trials Reconsidered." Ph.D. dissertation, New York University, 1983.

Beyer, Christel. *"Hexen-Leut, so zu Würzburg gerichtet": Der Umgang mit Sprache und Wirklichkeit in Inquisitionsprozessen wegen Hexerei*. Europäische Hochschulschriften, sect. 1 (Deutsche Sprache und Literatur), vol. 948. Frankfurt, New York: Lang, 1986.

Beyer, Johanna, Franziska Lamott, and Birgit Meyer, eds. *Frauenhandlexikon: Stichworte zur Selbstbestimmung*. Munich: Beck, 1983.

Beuys, Barbara. *Familienleben in Deutschland: Neue Bilder aus der deutschen Vergangenheit*. Reinbek bei Hamburg: Rowohlt, 1980.

Blackwell, Jeannine. " 'Die Zunge, der Geistliche und das Weib': Überlegungen zur strukturellen Bedeutung der Hexenbekenntnisse von 1500 bis 1700." *Innsbrucker Beiträge zur Kulturwissenschaft* 31 (1986):1–21.

Bloch, Howard, "Medieval Misogyny." *Representations* 20 (1987): 1–25.

Bloch, Howard. *The Scandal of the Fabliaux*. Chicago: University of Chicago Press, 1986.

Bloch, Ruth H. "Untangling the Roots of Modern Sex Roles: A Survey of Four Centuries of Change." *Signs* 14 (1978):237–253.

"Die böse Adelheid." Reprint. *Die deutsche Literatur: Texte und Zeugnisse, 1426–1428*, edited by Helmut de Boor, vol. 1.2. 7 vols. Munich: Beck, 1963.

Bolte, Johannes, ed. *Kleinere Schriften von Reinhold Köhler.* 3 vols. Weimar: Felber, 1898–1900.

Bolte, Johannes, and Georg Polivka. *Anmerkungen zu den Kinder- und Hausmärchen der Brüder Grimm.* 4 vols. 1913–32. Reprint. Hildesheim: Olms, 1963.

Bovenschen, Sylvia. "Die aktuelle Hexe, die historische Hexe und der Hexenmythos. Die Hexe: Subjekt der Naturaneignung und Objekt der Naturbeherrschung." In Becker and others, *Aus der Zeit der Verzweiflung*, pp. 259–311.

Boxer, Marilyn J., and Jean H. Quataert, eds. *Connecting Spheres: Women in the Western World, 1500 to the Present.* New York: Oxford University Press, 1987.

Brackert, Helmut. "Der *Hexenhammer* und die Verfolgung der Hexen in Deutschland." In *Philologie und Geschichtswissenschaft: Demonstrationen literarischer Texte des Mittelalters*, edited by Heinz Rupp, pp. 106–116. Medium Literatur, vol. 5. Heidelberg: Quelle, 1977.

Brackert, Helmut. " 'Unglückliche, was hast du gehofft?': Zu den Hexenbüchern des 15. bis 17. Jahrhunderts." In Becker and others, *Aus der Zeit der Verzweiflung*, pp. 131–187.

Braun, Noel Lacy. "The Renaissance Passion of Melancholy: The Paradox of its Cultivation and Resistance." Ph.D. dissertation, Stanford University, 1965.

Brauner, Sigrid. "Cannibals, Witches, and Shrews in the 'Civilizing Process.' " In *"Neue Welt"/"Dritte Welt": Interkulturelle Beziehungen Deutschlands zu Lateinamerika und der Karibik*, edited by Sigrid Bauschinger and Susan Cocalis, pp. 1–27. Tübingen: Francke, 1994.

Brauner, Sigrid. "The Demonization of the Shrew: Witchcraft and Gender Relations in Shrovetide Plays by Hans Sachs." In *Writing on the Line: Transgression in Early Modern German Literature*, edited by Lynne Tatlock, pp. 131–146. Amsterdam: Rodopi, 1991. [Also in *Daphnis* 20.1 (1991): 131–145.]

Brauner, Sigrid. "Gender and Its Subversion: Reflections on Literary Ideals of Marriage." In *The Graph of Sex and the German Text: Gendered Culture in Early Modern Germany 1500–1700*, edited by Lynne Tatlock and Christiane Bohnert, pp. 179–200. Amsterdam: Rodopi, 1994.

Brauner, Sigrid. "Hexenjagd in Gelehrtenköpfen." *Women in German Yearbook* 4 (1988):187–217.

Brauner, Sigrid. "Martin Luther on Witchcraft: A True Reformer?" In *The Politics of Gender in Early Modern Europe*, edited by Jean R. Brink and others, pp. 29–42. Sixteenth-Century Essays and Studies, vol. 12. Kirksville, MO: Sixteenth-Century Journal Publishers, 1989.

Brenner, Ines, and Gisela Morgenthal. "Sinnlicher Widerstand während der Ketzer und Hexenverfolgungen: Materialien und Interpretationen." In Becker and others, *Aus der Zeit der Verzweiflung*, pp. 188–240.

Bridenthal, Renate, and Claudia Koonz. *Becoming Visible: Women in European History.* 1977. 2nd revised edition. Boston: Houghton Mifflin, 1987.

Brietzmann, Franz. *Die böse Frau in der deutschen Literatur des Mittelalters.* Palaestra, vol. 42. Berlin: Mayer & Müller, 1912.

Brückner, Wolfgang, Peter Blickle, and Dieter Breuer, eds. *Literatur und Volk im 17. Jahrhundert: Probleme populärer Kultur in Deutschland.* 2 vols. Wolfenbütteler Arbeiten zur Barockforschung, vol. 13–14. Wiesbaden: Harrassowitz, 1985.

Brückner, Wolfgang, ed. *Volkserzählung und Reformation: Ein Handbuch zur Tradierung und Funktion von Erzählstoffen und Erzählliteratur im Protestantismus.* Berlin: Erich Schmidt, 1974.

Brunner, Horst, Gerhard Hirschmann, and Fritz Schnelbögl, eds. *Hans Sachs und Nürnberg: Bedingungen und Probleme reichsstädtischer Literatur.* Nürnberger Forschungen, vol. 19. Nuremberg: Verein für Geschichte, 1976.

Bücher, Karl. *Die Frauenfrage im Mittelalter.* 1882. Reprint. Tübingen: H. Laup, 1910.

Bullough, Vern L. "Medieval Medical and Scientific Views of Women." In *Marriage in the Middle Ages,* edited by John Leyerle, pp. 485–501. Viator, vol. 4. Berkeley: University of California Press, 1973.

Burke, Peter. *Popular Culture in Early Modern Europe.* New York: Harper & Row, 1978.

Camerlynck, Elaine. "Féminité et sorcellerie chez les théoriciens de la démonologie a la fin du Moyen Age: Étude du *Malleus maleficarum.*" *Renaissance and Reformation* 7 (1983):13–25.

Campbell, Mary Ann. "Labeling and Oppression: Witchcraft in Medieval Europe." *Mid-American Review of Sociology* 3 (1979):55–82.

*Canon Episcopi.* 906. Reprint. Leutenbauer, *Hexerei und Zaubereidelikt,* p. 177.

Carlsohn, E. "Die Bibliothek Hans Sachs." In *Der Volksdichter Hans Sachs,* edited by Weller, no page number.

Casey, Paul F. *Paul Rebhun: A Biographical Study.* Stuttgart: Steiner, 1986.

Catholy, Eckehard. *Fastnachtspiel.* Sammlung Metzler, vol. 56. Stuttgart: Metzler, 1966.

Clark, Elizabeth, and Herbert Richardson, eds. *Women and Religion: A Feminist Sourcebook of Christian Thought.* Harper Forum Books RD, vol. 178. New York: Harper & Row, 1977.

Clark, Stuart. "Inversion, Misrule and the Meaning of Witchcraft." *Past and Present* 87 (1980):98–127.

Cohn, Norman. *Europe's Inner Demons: An Enquiry Inspired by the Great Witch-Hunt.* London: Heinemann, 1975.

Couliano, Joan P. *Eros and Magic in the Renaissance.* Translated by Margaret Cook. Chicago: University of Chicago Press, 1987.

Cramer, Thomas, and Erika Kartschoke. *Hans Sachs: Studien zur frühbürgerlichen Literatur im 16. Jahrhundert.* Beiträge zur älteren deutschen Literaturgeschichte, vol. 3. Frankfurt, Bern, Las Vegas: Lang, 1978.

Crohns, Hjalmar. "Die *Summa theologica* des Antonin Florenz und die Schätzung des Weibes im *Hexenhammer.*" *Acta Societatis Scientiarum Fennicae* 32 (1906):1–23.

Croissant, Werner. "Die Berücksichtigung geburts- und berufsständischer und soziologischer Unterschiede im deutschen Hexenprozeß." Ph.D. dissertation, University of Mainz, 1953.

Dallapiazza, Michael. *"Minne, hûsêre und das ehlich leben"*: *Zur Konstitution bürgerlicher Lebensmuster in spätmittelalterlichen und frühhumanistischen Didaktiken.* Europäische Hochschulschriften, sect. 1 (Deutsche Sprache und Literatur), vol. 455. Frankfurt: Lang, 1981.

Daly, Mary. *Gyn/Ecology: The Metaethics of Radical Feminism.* Boston: Beacon, 1978.

Davies, Kathleen. "Continuity and Change in Literary Advice on Marriage." In *Marriage and Society: Studies in the Social History of Marriage*, edited by R. B. Outhwaite, pp. 58–80. 2nd edition. New York: St. Martins Press, 1982.

Davis, Natalie Zemon. *Society and Culture in Early Modern France: Eight Essays.* Palo Alto: Stanford University Press, 1975.

de Bruyn, Lucy. *Woman and the Devil in Sixteenth-Century Literature.* Tisbury: Compton Press, 1979.

de Lauretis, Theresa. *Technologies of Gender: Essays on Theory, Film and Fiction.* Bloomington: Indiana University Press, 1987.

Degn, Christian, Hartmut Lehmann, and Dagmar Unverhau, eds. *Hexenprozesse: Deutsche und skandinavische Beiträge.* Studien zur Volkskunde und Kulturgeschichte Schleswig-Holsteins, vol. 12. Neumünster: K. Wachholtz Verlag, 1983.

Deschner, Karlheinz. *Das Kreuz mit der Kirche: Eine Sexualgeschichte des Christentums.* Düsseldorf, Vienna: Econ-Verlag, 1974.

Diefenbach, Johann. *Der Hexenwahn vor und nach der Glaubensspaltung in Deutschland.* Mainz: F. Kirchheim, 1886.

Diefenbach, Johann. *Der Zauberglaube des 16. Jahrhunderts nach den Katechismen Dr. Martin Luthers und des Petrus Canisius.* Mainz: F. Kirchheim, 1900.

Dölger, Franz Josef. " 'Teufels Großmutter': Magna mater deum und magna mater daemonum." *Antike und Christentum* 3 (1932):153–176.

Douglas, Jane. "Luther and Women." *Luther Jahrbuch* 52 (1985):294–295.

Douglas, Mary, ed. *Witchcraft Confessions and Accusations.* A.S.A. Monographs, vol. 9. London, New York: Tavistock Publications, 1970.

Douglass, Jane Dempsey. "Women and the Continental Reformation." In *Religion and Sexism*, edited by Ruether, pp. 292–318.

Dross, Annemarie. *Die erste Walpurgisnacht: Hexenverfolgung in Deutschland.* Frankfurt: Roter Stern, 1978.

Duden, Barbara, and Pola Fortunati, "Frauen, Staat und Widerstand in den Anfängen des Kapitalismus." In *Frauen als bezahlte und unbezahlte Arbeitskräfte: Beiträge zur Berliner Sommeruniversität für Frauen, 1977*, edited by Dokumentationsgruppe der Sommeruniversität. Berlin: Frauenbuchvertrieb, 1978.

Dülmen, Richard von, ed. *Hexenwelten: Magie und Imagination vom 16.–20. Jahrhundert.* Frankfurt: Fischer, 1987.

Duerr, Hans Peter. *Traumzeit: Über die Grenze zwischen Wildnis und Zivilisation.* Frankfurt: Syndikat, 1978.

Dworkin, Andrea. *Woman-Hating.* New York: Dutton, 1974.

Easlea, Brian. *Witch Hunting, Magic and the New Philosophy: An Introduction to Debates of the Scientific Revolution, 1450–1750.* Sussex: Harvester Press, 1980.

Ehrenreich, Barbara, and Deidre English. *Witches, Midwives, and Nurses: A History of Woman Healers.* New York: Feminist Press, 1973.

Elias, Norbert. *Über den Prozeß der Zivilisation: Soziogenetische und psychogenetische Untersuchungen.* 2 vols. 1939. Reprint. Frankfurt: Suhrkamp, 1978.

Elias, Norbert. *The Civilizing Process.* 2 vols. Vol. 1, *The History of Manners,* trans. by Edmund Jephcott. New York: Pantheon Books, 1978.

Elshtain, Jean Bethke. *Public Man, Private Woman: Women in Social and Political Thought.* Princeton: Princeton University Press, 1981.

Endres, Rudolf. "Zünfte und Unterschichten als Elemente der Instabilität in den Städten." In *Revolte und Revolution in Europa: Referate und Protokolle des Internationalen Symposiums zur Erinnerung an den Bauernkrieg 1525,* edited by Peter Blickle, pp. 151–170. Munich: Oldenbourg, 1975.

Endres, Rudolf. "Zur Lage der Nürnberger Handwerkerschaft zur Zeit von Hans Sachs." *Jahrbuch für Fränkische Landesforschung* 37 (1977):107–123.

Engelsing, Rolf. *Analphabetentum und Lektüre: Zur Sozialgeschichte des Lesens in Deutschland zwischen feudaler und industrieller Gesellschaft.* Stuttgart: Metzler, 1973.

Engelsing, Rolf. *Der Bürger als Leser: Lesergeschichte in Deutschland, 1500–1800.* Stuttgart: Metzler, 1974.

Erasmus, Desiderius. *Colloquia familiaria.* 1523. Reprint. Desiderius Erasmus, *Opera omnia,* vol. 1. Leiden: P. Vander Aa, 1703.

Estes, Leland L. "The Medical Origins of the European Witch Craze: A Hypothesis." *Journal of Social History* 17 (1983):271–284.

Evans-Pritchard, E. E. *Witchcraft, Oracles and Magic among the Azande.* Oxford: Clarendon, 1937.

Fabian, Ernst. "Hexenprozesse in Zwickau und Umgegend." *Mitteilungen des Altertumsvereins für Zwickau und Umgegend* 4 (1894):122–131.

Ferguson, Margaret W., Maureen Quilligan, and Nancy J. Vickers, eds. *Rewriting the Renaissance: The Discourses of Sexual Difference in Early Modern Europe.* Chicago: University of Chicago Press, 1986.

Fischer-Homberger, Esther. *Krankheit Frau und andere Arbeiten zur Medizingeschichte der Frau.* Bern, Stuttgart, Vienna: Huber, 1979.

Franck, Johannes. "Geschichte des Wortes Hexe." In *Quellen und Untersuchungen,* edited by Hansen, pp. 614–670.

Franken, Irene, and Ina Hoerner. *Hexen: Die Verfolgung von Frauen in Köln.* Cologne: K. Henoth-Kreis, 1987.

Frenkel, F. E. "Sex-Crime and its Socio-historical Background." *Journal of the History of Ideas* 25 (1964):331–352.

Garrett, Clark. "Women and Witches: Patterns of Analysis." *Signs* 3 (1977): 461–470.

Gehlen, Rolf, and Bernd Wolf, eds. *Der gläserne Zaun: Aufsätze zu Hans Peter Duerrs "Traumzeit".* Frankfurt: Syndikat, 1983.

Ginzburg, Carlo. *I benandanti: Stregoneria e culti agrari tra cinquecento e seicento.* Torino: Einaudi, 1966.

Ginzburg, Carlo. *The Night Battles: Witchcraft and Agrarian Cults in the Sixteenth and Seventeenth Centuries.* Translated by John Tedeschi and Anne Tedeschi. 2nd edition. New York: Penguin Books, 1985.

Gloger, Bruno and Walter Zöllner. *Teufelsglaube und Hexenwahn.* Leipzig: Koehler & Amelang, 1983.

Götze, Alfred. "Teufels Großmutter." *Zeitschrift für Deutsche Wortforschung* 7 (1905–1906):28–35.

Götze, Alfred, and Hans Volz. *Frühneuhochdeutsches Glossar.* 1912. Reprint. Berlin: De Gruyter, 1967.

Goody, Jack. *The Development of the Family and Marriage in Europe.* Cambridge: Cambridge University Press, 1983.

Greenblatt, Stephen. "Fiction and Friction." In *Shakespearean Negotiations: The Circulation of Social Energy in Renaissance England,* edited by Stephen Greenblatt, pp. 66–94. Berkeley: University of California Press, 1988.

Griffin, Susan. *Woman and Nature: The Roaring inside Her.* New York: Harper & Row, 1978.

Grimm, Heinrich. "Die deutschen 'Teufelsbücher' des 16. Jahrhunderts: Ihre Rolle im Buchwesen und ihre Bedeutung." *Börsenblatt für den deutschen Buchhandel.* 15.100a (1959):1733–1790.

Grimm, Jacob. *Deutsche Mythologie.* Göttingen: Dieterich, 1835.

Grimm, Jacob, and Wilhelm Grimm. *Deutsches Wörterbuch.* 33 volumes. 1877. Revised edition. Munich: Deutscher Taschenbuch Verlag, 1985.

Grundmann, Herbert. *Religiöse Bewegungen im Mittelalter: Untersuchungen über die geschichtlichen Zusammenhänge zwischen der Ketzerei, den Bettelorden und der religiösen Frauenbewegung im 12. und 13. Jahrhundert und über die geschichtlichen Grundlagen der deutschen Mystik.* Hildesheim: Olms, 1961.

Hätzlerin, Clara. *Das Liederbuch der Clara Hätzlerin,* edited by Carl Haltaus. 1840. Reprint. Berlin: de Gruyter, 1966.

Hallissy, Margaret. *Venomous Woman: Fear of the Female in Literature.* Contributions in Women's Studies, vol. 87. New York: Greenwood Press, 1987.

Hammes, Manfred. *Hexenwahn und Hexenprozesse.* Frankfurt: Fischer, 1977.

Hanawalt, Barbara, ed. *Women and Work in Preindustrial Europe.* Bloomington: Indiana University Press, 1986.

Hansen, Joseph. "Der *Malleus maleficarum,* seine Druckausgaben und die gefälschte Kölner Approbation vom Jahre 1487." *Westdeutsche Zeitschrift für Geschichte und Kunst* 17 (1898):119–169.

Hansen, Josef, ed. *Quellen und Untersuchungen zur Geschichte des Hexenwahns und der Hexenverfolgung im Mittelalter.* 1901. Reprint. Hildesheim: Olms, 1963.

Hansen, Josef. *Zauberwahn, Inquisition und Hexenprozeß im Mittelalter und die Entstehung der großen Hexenverfolgung.* 1900. Reprint. Historische Bibliothek, vol. 12. Aalen: Scientia Verlag, 1964.

Harksen, Sybille. *Die Frau im Mittelalter.* Leipzig: Edition Leipzig, 1974.

Hartfelder, Karl. "Der Aberglaube Philipp Melanchthons." *Historisches Taschenbuch* 6 (1889):233–269.

Hausschild, Thomas, Heidi Staschen, and Regina Troschke. *Hexen: Katalog zur Ausstellung.* Hamburg: Hochschule für Bildende Künste, 1979.

Hays, Hoffman R. *The Dangerous Sex: The Myth of Feminine Evil.* New York: Putnam, 1964.

Heinemann, Evelyn. *Hexen und Hexenglauben: Eine historisch-sozialpsychologische Studie über den europäischen Hexenwahn des 16. und 17. Jahrhunderts.* Campus Forschung, vol. 478. Frankfurt, New York: Campus, 1986.

Heinsohn, Gunnar, and Otto Steiger. *Die Vernichtung der weisen Frauen: Beiträge zur Theorie und Geschichte von Bevölkerung und Kindheit.* Herbstein: März Verlag, 1985.

Helm, Karl. "Von dem üblen Weibe." *Beiträge zur Geschichte der deutschen Sprache* 34 (1908–1909):292–306.

Henningsen, Gustav, and John Tedeschi, eds. *The Inquisition in Early Modern Europe: Studies on Sources and Methods.* DeKalb: Northern Illinois University Press, 1986.

*Hie hebt an ain guot Vasnachtspiel.* 1494. Reprint. *Fastnachtspiele des 15. Jahrhunderts,* edited by Adelbert von Keller, vol. 2, pp. 498–511. Bibliothek des Stuttgarter Litterarischen Vereins, vol. 29. Leipzig: Stuttgarter Litterarischer Verein, n.d. (1853–1858).

Hildegard von Bingen. *Wisse die Wege: Scivias.* 1141–1151. Translated and edited by Maura Böckeler. Salzburg: Müller, 1954.

Hilka, Alfons. "Neue Beiträge zur Erzählungsliteratur des Mittelalters." *Neunzigster Jahres-Bericht der Schlesischen Gesellschaft für Vaterländische Cultur* 1 (1912):1–24.

Hodge, Johanna. "Hexen und die Entstehung der modernen Rationalitat." *Beiträge zur feministischen Theorie und Praxis* 5 (1981):77–83.

Höher, Friederike. "Hexe, Maria und Hausmutter: Zur Geschichte der Weiblichkeit im Spätmittelalter." In *Frauen in der Geschichte: Fachwissenschaftliche und fachdidaktische Beiträge zur Geschichte der Weiblichkeit vom frühen Mittelalter bis zur Gegenwart,* edited by Annette Kuhn and Jörn Rüsen, vol. 3, pp. 13–63. Düsseldorf: Schwann, 1984.

Hoffmeister, Gerhart. "Engel, Teufel oder Opfer: Zur Auffassung der Frau in der sentimentalen Erzählung zwischen Renaissance und Aufklärung." *Monatshefte* 69 (1977):150–58.

Honegger, Claudia, ed. *Die Hexen der Neuzeit: Studien zur Sozialgeschichte eines kulturellen Deutungsmusters.* Frankfurt: Suhrkamp, 1978.

Honegger, Claudia. "Hexe." *Frauenhandlexikon,* edited by Beyer and others, pp. 130–133.

Horsley, Richard A. "Who Were the Witches? The Social Roles of the Accused in the European Witch Trials." *Journal of Interdisciplinary History* 9 (1979): 689–715.

Horsley, Ritta Jo, and Richard A. Horsley. "On the Trail of the 'Witches': Wise Women, Midwives and the European Witch Hunts." *Women in German Yearbook* 3 (1986):1–29.

Illich, Ivan. *Gender.* New York: Pantheon, 1982.

Innocent VIII. *Summis desiderantes affectibus.* 1484. Reprint. *Quellen und Untersuchungen,* edited by Hansen, pp. 24–27.

Jöcher, Christian Gottlieb. *Allgemeines Gelehrtenlexikon.* 4 vols. Leipzig: n.p., 1750–1751.

Jordan, Constance. *Renaissance Feminism: Literary Texts and Political Models.* Ithaca: Cornell University Press, 1990.

Karant-Nunn, Susan C. "Continuity and Change: Some Effects of the Reformation on the Women of Zwickau." *Sixteenth-Century Journal* 13 (1982):17–42.

Karant-Nunn, Susan C. *Zwickau in Transition, 1500–1547: The Reformation as an Agent of Change.* Columbus: Ohio State University Press, 1987.

Karlsen, Carol F. *The Devil in the Shape of a Woman: Witchcraft in Colonial New England.* New York: Norton, 1987.

Kartschoke, Erika, and Christiane Reins. "Nächstenliebe—Gattenliebe—Eigenliebe: Bürgerlicher Alltag in den Fastnachtspielen des Hans Sachs." In *Hans Sachs,* edited by Cramer and Kartschoke, pp. 105–139.

Kawerau, Waldemar. "Lob und Schimpf des Ehestandes in der Literatur des sechzehnten Jahrhunderts." *Preußisches Jahrbuch* 69 (1892):760–781.

Kieckhefer, Richard. *European Witch Trials: Their Foundations in Popular and Learned Culture, 1300–1500.* Berkeley: University of California Press, 1976.

King, Margaret L. "Book-Lined Cells: Women and Humanism." In *Beyond their Sex: Women and Humanism,* edited by Patricia N. Labalme, pp. 66–90. New York: New York University Press, 1980.

Kingdon, Robert M., ed. *Transition and Revolution: Problems and Issues of European Renaissance and Reformation History.* Minneapolis: Burgess, 1974.

Klaits, Joseph. *Servants of Satan: The Age of the Witch Hunts.* Bloomington: Indiana University Press, 1985.

Klose, H. C. "Die angebliche Mitarbeit des Dominikaners Jakob Sprenger am Hexenhammer nach einem alten Abdinghofer Brief." In *Paderbornensis Ecclesia: Beiträge zur Geschichte des Erzbistums Paderborn,* edited by Paul-Werner Scheele, pp. 197–205. Munich, Paderborn, Vienna: Schöningh, 1972.

Könneker, Barbara. *Die deutsche Literatur der Reformationszeit: Kommentar zu einer Epoche.* Munich: Winkler, 1975.

Könneker, Barbara. "Die Ehemoral in den Fastnachtspielen von Hans Sachs: Zum Funktionswandel des Nürnberger Fastnachtspiels im 16. Jahrhundert." In *Hans Sachs und Nürnberg,* edited by Brunner and others, pp. 219–244.

Könneker, Barbara. *Hans Sachs.* Sammlung Metzler, vol. 94. Stuttgart: Metzler, 1971.

Koppitz, Hans Joachim. "Zur Verbreitung unterhaltsamer und belehrender deutscher Literatur durch den Buchhandel in der zweiten Hälfte des 16. Jahrhunderts." *Jahrbuch für Internationale Germanistik* 7 (1975):5–27.

Koszyk, Kurt. *Vorläufer der Massenpresse: Ökonomie und Publizistik zwischen Reformation und Französischer Revolution.* Munich: Goldmann, 1972.

Kramarae, Cheris, and Paula A. Treichler, eds. *A Feminist Dictionary.* London, Boston: Pandora Press, 1985.

Kramer, Heinrich [Henricus Institoris]. *Nürnberger Hexenhammer.* 1491. Reprint. Edited by Günter Jerouschek. Hildesheim: Olms, 1989.

Kramer, Heinrich, and Jakob Sprenger [Henricus Institoris and Jacobus Sprenger]. *Malleus maleficarum.* Speyer: Drach, 1487.

Kramer, Heinrich, and Jakob Sprenger [Henricus Institoris and Jacobus Sprenger]. *Malleus maleficarum.* 1487. Reprint. *Malleus maleficarum et earum haeresim framea conterens, ex variis auctoribus compilatus,* vol. 1, pp. 1–304. Lyon: Bourgeat, 1669. Reprint. Brussels: Culture et Civilisation, 1969.

Kramer, Heinrich, and Jakob Sprenger [Henricus Institoris and Jacobus Sprenger]. *The Malleus Maleficarum of Heinrich Kramer and James Sprenger.* Translated by Montague Summers. 1928. Reprint. New York: Dover, 1971.

Kramer, Karl S. "Schaden- und Gegenzauber im Alltagsleben des 16. bis 18. Jahrhunderts nach archivalischen Quellen aus Holstein." In *Hexenprozesse,* edited by Degn and others, pp. 222–231.

Kriminalmuseum Rothenburg ob der Tauber. *Strafjustiz in alter Zeit.* Schriftenreihe des mittelalterlichen Kriminalmuseums Rothenburg ob der Tauber, vol. 3. Rothenburg: Mittelalterliches Kriminalmuseum, 1980.

Kunstmann, Hartmut Heinrich. *Zauberwahn und Hexenprozeß in der Reichsstadt Nürnberg.* Nuremberg: Stadtarchiv, 1970.

Kunze, Michael. *Die Straße ins Feuer: Vom Leben und Sterben in der Zeit des Hexenwahns.* Munich: Kindler, 1982.

Längin, Georg. *Religion und Hexenprozeß.* Leipzig: n.p., 1888.

Larner, Christine. *Enemies of God: The Witch-Hunt in Scotland.* Baltimore: Johns Hopkins University Press, 1981.

Larner, Christine. *Witchcraft and Religion: The Politics of Popular Belief.* New York: Blackwell, 1984.

Le Roy Ladurie, Emmanuel. *Les paysans de Languedoc.* 2 vols. Paris: Mouton, 1966.

Lea, Henry Charles. *Materials toward a History of Witchcraft.* 3 vols. 1939. Reprint. New York: Yoseloff, 1957.

Lecky, W. E. H. *History of the Rise and Influence of the Spirit of Rationalism in Europe.* 2 vols. N.p., 1865.

Lecoy de la Marche, Albert, ed. *Anecdotes historiques: légendes et apologues d'Étienne de Bourbon.* Paris: Librairie Renouard, 1877.

Lehmann, Edvard. "Teufels Großmutter." *Archiv für Religionswissenschaft* 8 (1904):411–430.

Lehmann, Hartmut. "Hexenverfolgungen und Hexenprozesse im Alten Reich zwischen Reformation und Aufklärung." *Jahrbuch des Instituts für Deutsche Geschichte* 7 (1978):13–70.

Leutenbauer, Siegfried. *Hexerei und Zaubereidelikt in der Literatur von 1450 bis 1550: Mit Hinweisen auf die Praxis im Herzogtum Bayern.* Münchner Universitätsschriften (Juristische Fakultät), Abhandlungen zur rechtswissenschaftlichen Grundlagenforschung, vol. 3. Berlin: J. Schweitzer, 1972.

Levack, Brian P. *The Witch-Hunt in Early Modern Europe.* London: Longman, 1987.

Lexer, Mathias. *Mittelhochdeutsches Handwörterbuch.* 3 vols. Leipzig: S. Hirzel, 1870–78.

Londner, Monika. "Eheauffassung und Darstellung der Frau in der spätmittelalterlichen Märendichtung: Eine Untersuchung auf der Grundlage rechtlich-sozialer und theologischer Voraussetzungen." Ph.D. dissertation, University of Berlin, 1973.

Luther, Martin. *D. Martin Luthers Werke: Kritische Gesamtausgabe*, 90 vols. in 4 sects. Weimar: H. Böhlau, 1883–1977. (This edition is referred to below as WA.)

Luther, Martin. *Luther's Works*. Edited by Jaroslav Pelikan. 55 vols. St. Louis, MO: Concordia Press, 1955–1986.

Luther, Martin. *Betbüchlein*. 1522. Reprint. WA, sect. 1, vol. 10.2, pp. 331–502.

Luther, Martin. *Biblia/das ist/die gantze heilige Schrifft Deudsch*. 1534. Reprint. 2 vols. Leipzig: Reclam, 1983.

Luther, Martin. *Decem praecepta Wittenbergensi praedicata populo*. 1518. Reprint. WA, sect. 1, vol. 1, pp. 394–522.

Luther, Martin. *Deutscher [Großer] Katechismus*. 1529. Reprint. WA, sect. 1, 30.1, pp. 125–238.

Luther, Martin. *Enarratio in I Cap. Genesis*. 1535. Reprint. WA, sect. 1, 42, pp. 3–56.

Luther, Martin. *Epistel S. Petri gepredigt und ausgelegt*. 1522. Reprint. WA, sect. 1, vol. 12, pp. 259–399.

Luther, Martin. *Das Evangelium am Tage der heiligen drei Könige*. 1522. Reprint. WA, sect. 1, vol. 10.1.a, pp. 519–555.

Luther, Martin. *In epistolam Pauli ad Galatas commentarius*. 1519. Reprint. WA, sect. 1, vol. 2, pp. 436–619.

Luther, Martin. *In epistolam Pauli ad Galatas commentarius*. 1535. Reprint. WA, sect. 1, vol. 40.1, pp. 33–688; 4.2, pp. 1–184.

Luther, Martin. *Kleiner Katechismus*. 1529. Reprint. WA, sect. 1, vol. 30.1, pp. 239–475.

Luther, Martin. *Eine kurze Erklärung der zehn Gebote*. 1518. Reprint. WA, sect. 1, vol. 1, p. 247.

Luther, Martin. *Predigt am 2. Sonntag nach Epiphania*. 1533. Reprint. WA, sect. 1, vol. 37, pp. 9–12.

Luther, Martin. *Predigt am Sonntag exaudi nachmittags*. 1524. Reprint. WA, sect. 1, vol. 15, pp. 558–562.

Luther, Martin. *Eine Predigt vom Ehestand*. 1525. Reprint. WA, sect. 1, vol. 17, pp. 12–29.

Luther, Martin. *Predigten über das erste Buch Mose*. 1523–1524. Reprint. WA, sect. 1, vol. 14, pp. 92–489.

Luther, Martin. *Predigten über das zweite Buch Mose*. 1526. Reprint. WA, sect. 1, vol. 16, pp. 549–651.

Luther, Martin. *Ein Sermon von dem ehlichen Stand*. 1519. Reprint. WA, sect. 1, vol. 2, pp. 166–171.

Luther, Martin. *Tischreden*. 1536–1540. Reprint. WA, sect. 2. 6 vols.

Luther, Martin. *Das 14. und 15. Kapitel S. Johannis gepredigt und ausgelegt*. 1537. Reprint. WA, sect. 1, vol. 45, pp. 465–734.

Luther, Martin. *Vom ehelichen Leben*. 1522. Reprint. WA, sect. 1, vol. 10.2, pp. 267–304.

Luther, Martin. *Von den Konziliis und Kirchen*. 1539. Reprint. WA, sect. 1, vol. 50, pp. 488–654.

Luther, Martin. *Vorlesungen über 1 Mose*. 1535–1545. Reprint. WA, sect. 1, vol. 42.

Luther, Martin. *Wochenpredigten über Matthias 5–7*. 1530–1532. Reprint. WA, sect. 1, vol. 32, pp. 299–556.

Macfarlane, Alan. *Witchcraft in Tudor and Stuart England: A Regional and Comparative Study*. London: Routledge & K. Paul, 1970.

MacLean, Ian. *The Renaissance Notion of Woman: A Study in the Fortunes of Scholasticism and Medical Science in European Intellectual Life*. Cambridge, New York: Cambridge University Press, 1980.

Mann-Gillet, Myrtle. "Woman in German Literature before and after the Reformation." *Journal of English and Germanic Philology* 17 (1918):346–375.

Manuel, Juan. *El libro de los enxiemplos del conde Lucanor et de Patronio*. Edited by Hermann Knust and Adolf Birch-Hirschfeld. Leipzig: Seele, 1900.

Martin, Biddy. "Feminism, Criticism, and Foucault," *New German Critique* 27 (1982):3–30.

Marwick, Max, ed. *Witchcraft and Sorcery: Selected Readings*. 2nd edition. New York: Penguin, 1982.

Maschke, Erich. *Die Familie in der deutschen Stadt des späten Mittelalters*. Heidelberg: Winter, 1980.

Matalene, Carolyn. "Women as Witches." *International Journal of Women's Studies* 1 (1978):573–587.

McLachlan, Hugh V. "Witchcraft and Anti-Feminism." *Scottish Journal of Sociology* 4 (1980):228–238.

McLaughlin, Eleanor Commo. "Equality of Souls, Inequality of Sexes." In *Religion and Sexism*, edited by Ruether, pp. 213–266.

Melanchthon, Philipp. *Kirchenordnung:/Wie es mit Christlicher Lere,/reichung der Sacrament Ordination der Diener des Evangelij, ordentlichen Ceremonien, in den Kirchen, Visitation, Consistorio und Schulen/Im Herzogthum zu Mecklenburg etc. gehalten wird*. 1552. Reprint. Philipp Melanchthon, *Opera quae supersunt omnia*, edited by Karl Gottlieb Bretschneider and Heinrich Ernst Bindseil, vol. 23, pp. 22–111. Halle: Schwetschke & Sohn, 1855.

Merchant, Carolyn. *The Death of Nature: Women, Ecology, and the Scientific Revolution*. San Francisco: Harper & Row, 1981.

Michael, Wolfgang Friedrich. *Das deutsche Drama der Reformationszeit*. Bern: Lang, 1984.

Michelet, Jules. *La sorcière*. Paris: n.p., 1862.

Middleton, Christopher. "Sexual Divisions in Feudalism." *New Left Review* 113–114 (1979):147–168.

Midelfort, H. C. Erik. "Heartland of the Witchcraze: Central and Northern Europe." *History Today*, February 1981, pp. 27–31.

Midelfort, H. C. Erik. "Were There Really Witches?" In *Transition and Revolution*, edited by Kingdon, pp. 189–205.

Midelfort, H. C. Erik. *Witch Hunting in Southwestern Germany, 1582–1684*. Stanford: Stanford University Press, 1972.

Midelfort, H. C. Erik. "Witchcraft and Religion in Sixteenth-Century Germany: The Formation and Consequences of Orthodoxy." *Archiv für Reformationsgeschichte* 62 (1971):266–278.

Midelfort, H. C. Erik. "Witchcraft, Magic and the Occult." In *Reformation Eu-*

rope: *A Guide to Research*, edited by Steven Ozment, pp. 183–209. St. Louis, MO: Center for Reformation Research, 1982.

Mies, Maria. *Patriarchy and Accumulation on a World Scale*. London: Zed Books, 1985.

Monter, E. William. "The Historiography of European Witchcraft: Progress and Prospects." *Journal of Interdisciplinary History* 2 (1972):435–451.

Monter, E. William. "Patterns of Witchcraft in the Jura." *Journal of Social History* 5 (1971):1–25.

Monter, E. William. "The Pedestal and the Stake: Courtly Love and Witchcraft." In *Becoming Visible*, edited by Bridenthal and Koonz, pp. 119–136.

Monter, E. William. "Protestant Wives, Catholic Saints, and the Devil's Handmaid: Women in the Age of Reformation." In *Becoming Visible*, edited by Bridenthal and Koonz, pp. 203–221.

Monter, E. William. *Witchcraft in France and Switzerland: The Borderlands during the Reformation*. Ithaca: Cornell University Press, 1976.

Moore, Cornelia Niekus. *The Maiden's Mirror: Reading Material for German Girls in the Sixteenth and Seventeenth Centuries*. Wolfenbütteler Forschungen, vol. 36. Wiesbaden: Harrassowitz, 1987.

Mottek, Hans. *Wirtschaftsgeschichte Deutschlands: Ein Grundriß*. 2 vols. Berlin: VEB, 1971.

Müller, Karl Otto. "Heinrich Institoris, der Verfasser des Hexenhammers, und seine Tätigkeit als Hexeninquisitor in Ravensburg im Herbst 1484." *Württembergische Vierteljahreshefte für Landesgeschichte* 5 (1910):397–417.

Müller, Maria E. "Naturwesen Mann: Zur Dialektik von Herrschaft und Knechtschaft in Ehelehren der frühen Neuzeit." In *Wandel der Geschlechterbeziehungen zu Beginn der Neuzeit*, edited by Heide Wunder and Christina Vanja, pp. 43–68. Frankfurt: Suhrkamp, 1991.

Müller, Maria E. *Der Poet der Moralität: Untersuchungen zu Hans Sachs*. Bern: Lang, 1985.

Murner, Thomas. *Narrenbeschwörung*. 1512. Reprint. Deutsche National-Litteratur, edited by Joseph Kürschner, vol. 17.1, pp. 59–306. Berlin: Spemann, n.d. (1882–1899).

Murray, Margaret. *The Witch-Cult in Western Europe: A Study in Anthropology*. Oxford: Clarendon, 1921.

Nelson, Mary. "Why Witches Were Women." In *Women: A Feminist Perspective*, edited by Jo Freeman, pp. 335–351. Palo Alto: Mayfield, 1975.

Newall, Venetia, ed. *The Witch Figure: Folklore Essays by a Group of Scholars in England Honouring the 75th Birthday of Katharine M. Briggs*. London: Routledge & K. Paul, 1973.

Nider, Johannes. *Daz sint die X gebot, die VII sacrament und vil kostlicher predigen uss den evangelien und episteln*. 1430. Reprint. *Quellen und Untersuchungen*, edited by Hansen, pp. 437–444.

Nider, Johannes. *Formicarius*. 1435. Reprint. *Malleus maleficarum et earum haeresim framea conterens, ex variis auctoribus compilatus*, vol. 1, pp. 305–354. Lyon: Bourgeat, 1669. Reprint. Brussels: Culture et Civilisation, 1969.

Nider, Johannes. *Preceptorium divinae legis*. Nuremberg: Anton Sorg, 1475.

Niewöhner, Heinrich. "Das böse Weib und die Teufel." *Zeitschrift für deutsches Altertum* 83 (1951–1952):142–156.

Noonan, John Thomas. *Contraception: A History of its Treatment by the Catholic Theologians and Canonists.* Cambridge: Belknap Press, 1965.

Oberman, Heiko A. *Werden und Wertung der Reformation.* Tübingen: Mohr, 1977.

Oberman, Heiko A. *Wurzeln des Antisemitismus: Christenangst und Judenplage im Zeitalter von Humanismus und Reformation.* Berlin: Severin & Siedler, 1981.

Okin, Susan M. *Women in Western Political Thought.* Princeton: Princeton University Press, 1979.

Osborn, Max. *Die Teufelliteratur des 16. Jahrhunderts.* Berlin: Mayer & Müller, 1893.

Osborne, Martha Lee, ed. *Woman in Western Thought.* New York: Random House, 1979.

Ozment, Steven. "The Family in Reformation Germany: The Bearing and Rearing of Children." *Family History* 8 (1983):159–177.

Ozment, Steven. *When Fathers Ruled: Family Life in Reformation Europe.* Cambridge: Harvard University Press, 1983.

Parrinder, Geoffrey. "The Witch as Victim." In *The Witch Figure*, edited by Newall, pp. 125–139.

Pauli, Johannes. *Schimpff und Ernst.* 1533. Reprint. Edited by Hermann Österley. Stuttgart: Litterischer Verein, 1866.

Paulus, Nikolaus. *Hexenwahn und Hexenprozeß, vornehmlich im 16. Jahrhundert.* Freiburg: Herder, 1910.

Paulus, Nikolaus. "Die Rolle der Frau in der Geschichte des Hexenwahns." *Historisches Jahrbuch im Auftrage der Görresgesellschaft* 29 (1908):72–95.

Peuckert, Will Erich. *Die große Wende.* Hamburg: Claassen & Goverts, 1948.

Peuckert, Will Erich. "Hexen und Weiberbünde." *Kairos: Zeitschrift für Religionswissenschaft und Theologie* 2 (1960):101–105.

Pfeiffer, Gerhard. *Nürnberg: Geschichte einer europäischen Stadt.* Munich: Beck, 1971.

Pirckheimer, Caritas. *Caritas Pirckheimer: Quellensammlung.* 3 vols. Landshut: Caritas Pirckheimer-Forschung, 1966.

Prato, Stanislaus. "Vergleichende Mitteilungen zu Hans Sachs' Fastnachtspiel 'Der Teufel mit dem alten Weib.'" *Zeitschrift des Vereins für Volkskunde* 9 (1899):311–321.

Quaife, G. R. *Godly Zeal and Furious Rage: The Witch in Early Modern Europe.* New York: St. Martin's, 1987.

Quaife, G. R. *Wanton Wenches and Wayward Wives: Peasants and Illicit Sex in Early Seventeenth-Century England.* New Brunswick: Rutgers University Press, 1979.

Rabb, Theodore K., and Jerrold E. Seigel. *Action and Conviction in Early Modern Europe: Essays in Memory of E. H. Harbison.* Princeton: Princeton University Press, 1969.

Rauer, Brigitte. "Hexenwahn — Frauenverfolgung zu Beginn der Neuzeit: Ein Beitrag zur Frauengeschichte im Unterricht." In *Frauen in der Geschichte:*

*Fachwissenschaftliche und fachdidaktische Studien zur Geschichte der Frauen,* edited by Annette Kuhn and Jörg Rüsen, vol. 2, pp. 97–125. Düsseldorf: Schwann, 1983.

Rebhun, Paul. *Hochzeitspredigt vom Hausfried: Was für Ursachen den christlichen Eheleuten zu bedencken, den lieben Haussfrieden in der Ehe zu erhalten.* 1546. Reprint. Nuremberg: Gerlatz, 1568.

Rebhun, Paul. *Ein Hochzeit Spiel auff die Hochzeit zu Cana.* 1538. Reprint. Paul Rebhuns Dramen, edited by Hermann Palm, pp. 89–174. Darmstadt: Wissenschaftliche Buchgesellschaft, 1969.

Reissner, D. L. "Witchcraft and Statecraft: A Materialist Analysis of the European Witch Persecution." *Women and Revolution* 7 (1974):9–14.

Riezler, Sigmund. *Geschichte der Hexenprozesse in Bayern: Im Lichte der allgemeinen Entwicklung dargestellt.* Stuttgart: Cotta, 1896.

Robbins, Rossel Hope. *Encyclopedia of Witchcraft and Demonology.* 1959. Reprint. New York: Bonanza, 1987.

Robbins, Rossel Hope. *Witchcraft: An Introduction to the Literature of Witchcraft.* Millwood, NY: KTO Press, 1978.

Rörich, Lutz. *Erzählungen des späten Mittelalters und ihr Weiterleben in Literatur und Volksdichtung bis zur Gegenwart.* 2 vols. Bern: Francke, 1962–1967.

Rogers, Katherine M. *The Troublesome Helpmate: A History of Misogyny in Literature.* Seattle: University of Washington Press, 1966.

Roper, Hugh Trevor. *The European Witch-Craze of the Sixteenth and Seventeenth Centuries.* San Francisco: Harper & Row, 1967.

Roper, Lyndal. *The Holy Household: Women and Morals in Reformation Augsburg.* Oxford: Oxford University Press, 1989.

Rose, Mary Beth, ed. *Women in the Middle Ages and the Renaissance: Literary and Historical Perspectives.* Syracuse: Syracuse University Press, 1986.

Ruether, Rosemary Radford. "Persecution of Witches: A Case of Sexism and Ageism?" *Christianity and Crisis* 34 (1975):291–295.

Ruether, Rosemary Radford, ed. *Religion and Sexism: Images of Woman in the Jewish and Christian Traditions.* New York: Simon & Schuster, 1974.

Russell, Jeffrey Burton. *Witchcraft in the Middle Ages.* Ithaca: Cornell University Press, 1972.

Russell, Paul A. *Lay Theology in the Reformation: Popular Pamphleteers in Southwest Germany, 1521–1525.* Cambridge, New York: Cambridge University Press, 1986.

Sachs, Hans. *Hans Sachs: Sämtliche Fabeln und Schwänke.* Edited by Edmund Goetze and Karl Drescher. 6 vols. Neudrucke Deutscher Literaturwerke des 16. Jahrhunderts, vols. 110–117, 126–134, 164–169, 193–199, 207–211, 231–235. Halle: Niemeyer, 1893–1913. (This edition is referred to below as *Fabeln.*)

Sachs, Hans. *Sämtliche Fastnachtspiele von Hans Sachs.* Edited by Edmund Goetze. 7 vols. Neudrucke Deutscher Literaturwerke des 16. Jahrhunderts, vols. 26–27, 31–32, 39–40, 42–43, 51–52, 60–61, 63–64. Halle: Niemeyer, 1880–1886. (This edition is referred to below as *Fastnachtspiele.*)

Sachs, Hans. *Hans Sachs: Werke.* Edited by Adelbert von Keller and Edmund

Goetze. 26 vols. Bibliothek des Stuttgarter Litterarischen Vereins, vols. 102–106, 110, 115, 121, 125, 131, 136, 140, 149, 159, 173, 179, 181, 188, 191, 193, 195, 201, 220, 225, 250. Leipzig: n.p., 1870–1908. (This edition is referred to below as *Werke*.)

Sachs, Hans. *Comedia oder Kampff-gesprech zwischen Juppiter unnd Juno, ob weiber oder mender zum regimenten tüglicher seyn*. 1534. Reprint. *Werke*, vol. 4, pp. 3–30.

Sachs, Hans. "Der dewffel mit dem alten weib." 1545. Reprint. *Fabeln*, vol. 4, pp. 47–49.

Sachs, Hans. *Ein dialogus des inhalt: ein argument der Römischen wider das christlich heuflein, den geiz betreffend*. 1524. Reprint. *Werke*, vol. 22, pp. 51–68.

Sachs, Hans. *Ein Faßnacht Spil mit vier personen: Der teüffel mit dem alten Weyb*. 1545. Reprint. *Fastnachtspiele*, vol. 2, pp. 59–69.

Sachs, Hans. *Ein fasnacht Spiel mit fünff Personen: Der Teufel nahm ein alt Weib zu der Eh, die ihn vertrieb*. 1557. Reprint. *Werke*, vol. 21, pp. 17–34.

Sachs, Hans. "Gesprech der alten hexen mit dem dewffel." 1553. Reprint. *Fabeln*, vol. 6, pp. 42–44.

Sachs, Hans. "Der kampf mit dem poesen weib." 1541. Reprint. *Fabeln*, vol. 3, pp. 284–286.

Sachs, Hans. "Die vier natur einer frawen." 1562. Reprint. *Werke*, vol. 21, pp. 144–147.

Sachs, Hans. "Von der unglückhafften, verschwatzten Bulschafft." 1552. Reprint. *Werke*, vol. 14, pp. 188–219.

Sachs, Hans. "Ein wunderlich gesprech von fünff Unhulden." 1531. Reprint. *Werke*, vol. 5, pp. 285–288.

Sachs, Hans. "Die zwölff eygenschafft eynes bosshaftigen weybs." 1530. Reprint. *Werke*, vol. 4, pp. 376–385.

Scarre, Geoffrey. *Witchcraft and Magic in Sixteenth- and Seventeenth-Century Europe*. Atlantic Highlands, NJ: Humanities Press International, 1987.

Schade, Richard E. *Studies in Early German Comedy: 1500–1650*. Studies in German Literature, Linguistics, and Culture, vol. 24. Columbia, SC: Camden House, 1988.

Schade, Sigrid. *Schadenzauber und die Magie des Körpers: Hexenbilder der frühen Neuzeit*. Worms: Wernersche Verlagsanstalt, 1983.

Scharffenorth, Gerta, and Klaus Thraede. *"Freunde in Christus werden . . .": Die Beziehung von Mann und Frau als Frage an Theologie und Kirche*. Kennzeichen, vol. 1. Gelnhausen, Berlin: Burckhardthaus, 1977.

Schelenz, Hermann. *Frauen im Reiche Aesculaps: Ein Versuch zur Geschichte der Frau in der Medizin und Pharmazie*. Leipzig: Ernst Günthers Verlag, 1900.

Schmitz, Silvia. *Weltentwurf als Realitätsbewältigung in Johannes Paulis "Schimpf und Ernst": Vorgeführt am Beispiel der lasterhaften Frau*. Göppinger Arbeiten zur Germanistik, vol. 346. Göppingen: Kümmerle, 1982.

Schormann, Gerhard. *Hexenprozesse in Deutschland*. Kleine Vandenhoeck-Reihe, vol. 1470. Göttingen: Vandenhoeck & Ruprecht, 1981.

Schützeichel, Rudolf. *Althochdeutsches Wörterbuch*. Tübingen: Niemeyer, 1969.

Schützin, Katharina. *Entschuldigung*. Strasbourg: n.p., 1524.

Schulz, Wolf D. "Aspekte des Übernatürlichen in den Fastnachtspielen des Hans Sachs." Ph.D. dissertation, University of Washington, 1965.

Scott, Joan Wallach. "Deconstructing Equality-Versus-Difference," *Feminist Studies* 14 (1988):33–50.

Scott, Joan Wallach. *Gender and the Politics of History.* New York: Columbia University Press, 1988.

Soldan, Wilhelm Gottlieb, and Heinrich Heppe. *Geschichte der Hexenprozesse.* 2 vols. Stuttgart: J. G. Cotta, 1880.

Staber, J. "Die Predigten des Tegernseer Priors Augustin Holzapfler als Quelle für das spätmittelalterliche Volksleben Altbayerns." *Bayerisches Jahrbuch für Volkskunde* (1960):123–135.

Starhawk. *Dreaming the Dark: Magic, Sex and Politics.* Boston: Beacon, 1982.

Stauffen, Argula von. *Wie Eyn Christliche fraw des Adels/in Beiern durch jren jn Gotlicher Schrifft/wollgegründeten Sendtbryeffe/die Hoheschul zu Ingolstadt/ umb das sie eynen Evangelischen Jüngling zu widersprechung des wort gottes/ betrangt habe/straffet.* Strasbourg: Martin Flach, 1523.

Stiefel, Arthur Ludwig. "Über die Quellen der Fabeln, Märchen und Schwänke des Hans Sachs." In *Hans Sachs-Forschungen: Festschrift zur 400. Geburtsfeier des Dichters,* edited by Arthur Ludwig Stiefel, pp. 33–192. Nuremberg: Kommission der J. P. Raw'schen Buchhandlung, 1894.

Strauss, Gerald. *Nuremberg in the Sixteenth Century: City Politics and Life between the Middle Ages and Modern Times.* Bloomington: Indiana University Press, 1966.

Strong, James. *The Exhaustive Concordance of the Bible.* Nashville, TN: Abingdon, 1894.

Summers, Montague. *The Geography of Witchcraft.* New York: University Books, 1958.

Summers, Montague. *The History of Witchcraft and Demonology.* New York: Knopf, 1926.

Tappolet, Walter. *Das Marienlob der Reformatoren Martin Luther, Johannes Calvin, Huldrych Zwingli, Heinrich Bullinger.* Tübingen: Katzmann Verlag, 1962.

Tauber, Walter. *Der Wortschatz des Hans Sachs.* 2 vols. Studia Linguistica Germanica, vols. 19–20. Berlin, New York: de Gruyter, 1983.

Taylor, Gordon R. *Sex in History.* London: Thames, 1959.

Thomas, Keith V. *Religion and the Decline of Magic: Studies in Popular Beliefs in Sixteenth- and Seventeenth-Century England.* London: Weidenfeld, 1971.

Thompson, Stith. *Motif-Index of Folk-Literature: A Classification of Narrative Elements in Folktales, Ballads, Myths, Fables, Medieval Romances, Exempla, Fabliaux, Jest-Books, and Local Legends.* 6 vols. Bloomington: Indiana University Press, 1955–1958.

Timmermann, Waltraud. "Theaterspiel als Medium evangelischer Verkündigung: Zur Aussage und Funktion der Dramen Paul Rebhuns." *Archiv für Kulturgeschichte* 66 (1984):117–58.

Tubach, Frederic C. *Index Exemplorum: A Handbook of Medieval Religious Tales.* 1969. FF Communications, vol. 204. Reprint. Helsinki: Suomalainen Tiedeakatemia, 1981.

Ulbrich, Claudia. "Unartige Weiber." In *Arbeit, Frömmigkeit und Eigensinn*, edited by Richard van Dülmen, pp. 13–42. Frankfurt: Fischer, 1990.

Unverhau, Dagmar. "'Meisterinnen' und deren 'Kunstfruwen' in Schleswig und in Angeln um die Mitte des 16. Jahrhunderts: Von magischen Frauengemeinschaften und Hexensekten." *Jahrbuch des Heimatvereins Schleswigsche Geest* (1984):60–80.

Walker, Barbara G. *The Crone: Woman of Age, Wisdom, and Power.* San Francisco: Harper, 1985.

Walker, Barbara G. *The Woman's Encyclopedia of Myths and Secrets.* San Francisco: Harper & Row, 1983.

Wappler, Paul. *Inquisition und Ketzerprozeß in Zwickau zur Reformationszeit: Dargestellt im Zusammenhang mit der Entwicklung der Ansichten Luthers und Melanchthons zur Glaubens- und Gewissensfreiheit.* Leipzig: Heinsius, 1908.

Warner, Maria. *Alone of All her Sex: The Myth and the Cult of the Virgin Mary.* New York: Wallaby, 1978.

Wehrenpfennig, Maria. "Die Stellung der deutschen Frau um 1450 bis Luthers Einfluß um 1520." Ph.D. dissertation, University of Vienna, 1939.

Wehrli, Max. *Geschiche der deutschen Literatur vom Mittelalter bis zum Ende des 16. Jahrhunderts.* Vol 1. Geschichte der deutschen Literatur von den Anfängen bis zur Gegenwart. Stuttgart: Reclam, 1980.

Weller, Emil. *Der Volksdichter Hans Sachs und seine Dichtungen: Eine Bibliographie.* 1868. Reprint. Wiesbaden: Sändig, 1966.

Wesselski, Albert, ed. *Märchen des Mittelalters.* Berlin: Stubenrauch, 1925.

Widdowson, John. "The Witch as a Frightening and Threatening Figure." In *The Witch Figure*, edited by Newall, pp. 200–221.

Wiesner, Merry E. "Beyond Women and the Family: Towards a Gender Analysis of the Reformation." *Sixteenth-Century Journal* 18 (1987):311–321.

Wiesner, Merry E. "Frail, Weak, and Helpless: Women's Legal Position in Theory and Reality. In *Regnum, Religio et Ratio: Essays Presented to Robert M. Kingdon*, edited by Jerome Friedman, pp. 161–169. Sixteenth-Century Essays and Studies, vol. 8. Kirksville, MO: Sixteenth-Century Journal Publishers, 1987.

Wiesner, Merry E. "Spinning out Capital." In *Becoming Visible*, edited by Bridenthal and Koonz, pp. 221–249.

Wiesner, Merry E. "Women's Defense of their Public Role." In *Women in the Middle Ages and Renaissance*, edited by Rose, pp. 1–27.

Wiesner, Merry E. *Working Women in Renaissance Germany.* New Brunswick, NJ: Rutgers University Press, 1986.

Wiltenburg, Joy. *Disorderly Women and Female Power in the Street Literature of Early Modern England and Germany.* Charlottesville: University of Virginia Press, 1992.

Wittman, Alfred. "Die Gestalt der Hexe in der deutschen Sage." Ph.D. dissertation, University of Heidelberg, 1933.

Wolf-Graf, Anke. *Frauenarbeit im Abseits: Frauenbewegung und weibliches Arbeitsvermögen.* Munich: Frauenoffensive, 1981.

Wright, Thomas. *A Selection of Latin Stories.* London: Percy Society, 1842.

Wunder, Heide. "Hexenprozesse im Herzogtum Preußen während des 16. Jahrhunderts." In *Hexenprozesse*, edited by Degn and others, pp. 179–203.

Wunderer, Richard. *Erotik und Hexenwahn: Eine Studie zur Entstehung des Hexenwahns in der vorchristlichen Zeit bis zu den Pogromen unserer Vergangenheit.* Stuttgart: Weltspiegel, 1963.

Young, Alan R. "Elizabeth Lowys: Witch and Social Victim." *History Today* 22 (1972):833–842.

Zambelli, Paola. "Scholastiker und Humanisten Agrippa und Trithemius zur Hexerei: Die natürliche Magie und die Entstehung kritischen Denkens." *Archiv für Kulturgeschichte* 67 (1985):41–79.

Ziegeler, Wolfgang. *Möglichkeiten der Kritik am Hexen- und Zauberwesen im ausgehenden Mittelalter: Zeitgenössische Stimmen und ihre soziale Zugehörigkeit.* Kollektive Einstellungen und sozialer Wandel im Mittelalter, vol. 2. Cologne, Vienna: Böhlau, 1973.

Zirn, Anton. "Stoffe und Motive bei Hans Sachs in seinen Fabeln und Schwänken." Ph.D. dissertation, University of Würzburg, 1924.

# Index